Beat Spirit

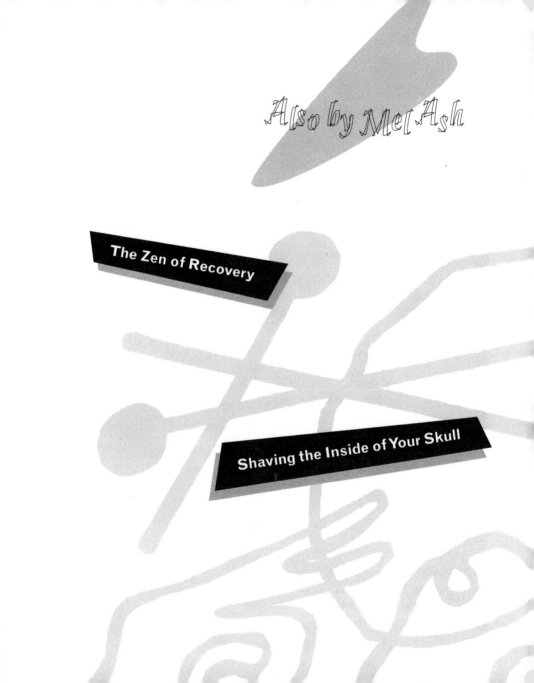

Also by Mel Ash

The Zen of Recovery

Shaving the Inside of Your Skull

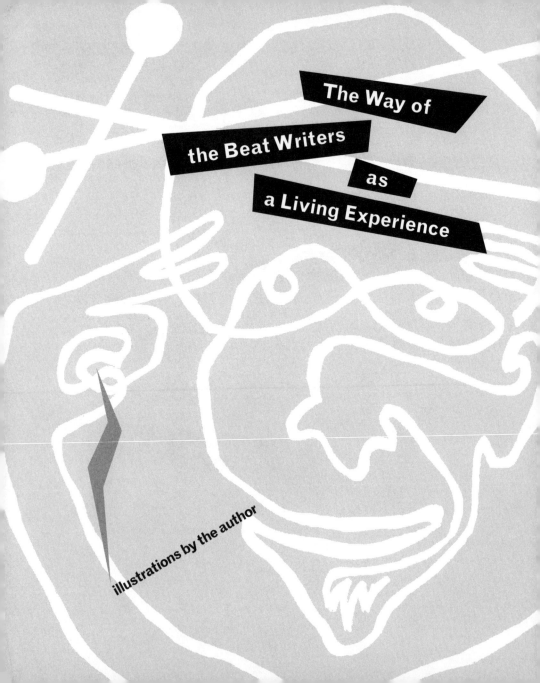

The Way of
the Beat Writers
as
a Living Experience

illustrations by the author

Beat Spirit

An Interactive Workbook

Mel Ash

Jeremy P. Tarcher/Putnam
• a member of •
Penguin Putnam Inc.
• new york •

Cover illustrations © 1997 by Mel Ash

Cover design by Judith Stagnitto Abbate

Book design by Susan Shankin

Jeremy P. Tarcher/Putnam
a member of
Penguin Putnam Inc.
200 Madison Avenue
New York, NY 10016
http://www.putnam.com

Library of Congress Cataloging-in-Publication Data

Ash, Mel.
Beat spirit : the way of the beat writers as a living experience : an
interactive workbook / Mel Ash ; illustrations by the author.
p. cm.
Includes bibliographical references.
ISBN 0-87477-880-8
1. American literature—20th century—Problems, exercises, etc.
2. American literature—20th century—History and criticism.
3. Beat generation—Problems, exercises, etc. I. Title.
PS228.B6A9   1997
810.9'0054—dc21   97-14662 CIP
Printed in the United States of America

1 3 5 7 9 10 8 6 4 2

This book is printed on acid-free
paper. ∞

Acknowledgments

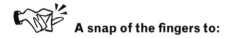 **A snap of the fingers to:**

Big Daddy-O publisher, mentor and stealth editor Jeremy Tarcher; Main Man editor and keeper of the hip flame Alan Rinzler; David Groff, Cool Cat, associate editor and friend, who always pulls it all together; Irene Prokop; Joel Fotinos; Susan Shankin, for her flipped-out cover; David Koral, angelheaded copyeditor; Claire Vaccaro; Judith Stagnitto Abbate; Ken Siman; Barbara Lowenstein; comrade Alison Myers; and Ray Haaker, renowned Beat collector and scholar, who shared much enthusiasm for this project and subject.

 **And a beat on the bongos to:**

Rev. Tom Ahlburn and the First Unitarian Church of Providence, Aren and Ethan Ash, Bob Jazz, Maynard Silva, Norma Goldberg, Ann Charters, Hannah, Kay, Joe and Jana, Emily Seah, Joe Plett, V. Majestic, dread Cthulhu, who lies dreaming in sunken R'yleh, the memory of Allen Ginsberg, and Scott Rundlett, urban archaeologist.

Beat Spirit

is for
Sarah Owens-Ash,
with whom I have at long last found what we are all looking for
and believe we'll never find;

and my mom and dad, with much love, surprise and joy:
Yes, I'm still a beatnik.
No, I'm not going to grow up.
What do you mean? This *is* my real job!

and also Ann Patrick,
who has heard my footsteps and typing
and howls on both her skull and ceiling for many years.

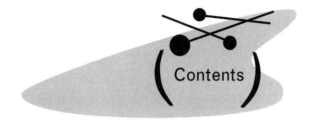

Contents

Be in love
with yr life

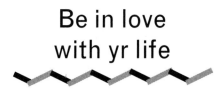

Jack Kerouac

finally found out that I wasn't alone as a young teenager in the mid-sixties when I discovered books by Jack Kerouac, Gary Snyder, Allen Ginsberg, Lew Welch, Lawrence Ferlinghetti, Diane DiPrima, Michael McClure, Gregory Corso and William S. Burroughs and their cronies.

I hadn't been too aware of all this beatnik stuff, not even the stereotypes that the media used to wave like Halloween cutouts in front of the nation in an attempt to keep the trick-and-treating sixties at bay. But when I was about fourteen I found a tiny book on Buddhism by Kerouac and devoured it. I lived not far from a college so I easily found more of this stuff and went in the directions that it led. Buddhism was implicit in most of the writing or at least in the necessity for revolt.

I felt like somebody was telling me the truth for the first time in a language that I could understand. It was a lot like the stuff I'd already been reading by Thoreau, Emerson and Whitman, that trinity of New England's "sensitive" youth.

I couldn't understand the general condemnations of the Beats by parents and media as "immoral" or "subversive." Never had I encountered anything so strongly imbued with real morality and integrity. I guess their only crime was in saying that the emperor had no clothes. The emperor and his propaganda ministers were not amused. They still aren't.

I'd hide these books and read them at study hall, leaning against a big oak tree outside the school. A couple of other kids were into it, too, I found out, and we'd swap books and have those long, heated, serious conversations that adolescents have when solving the world's problems in an afternoon. Of course, I proudly wore a black turtleneck sweater constantly now, stereotype or not.

Remember, these are the days just before the hippies gained any sort of national attention, at least in our little town. The sixties, as we remember them, had only just begun. I no longer felt alone. Someone out there thought like I did. Maybe they'd felt as weird and isolated as I had been, as well. It seemed so. How else could they possibly know this stuff?

The "greasers," those last survivors of the fifties, usually exiled to the Gulag of Shop Class to learn how to do body work and make wooden bowls on lathes, would throw stones at us nascent beatniks and hippies and threaten to slice us up with their switchblades. I doubt they even knew what a switchblade was in our small farm town, but it sounded good to them, I guess. Too many James Dean and Marlon Brando movies, maybe.

My best friend and I were walking under a stairwell one day when one of them spit on our heads as we passed beneath them. My friend raised his head to look up at them. While they waited for our outrage, my friend smiled, opened his mouth and let the spittle drip from his forehead into his mouth. They all gasped and took off. They never bothered us again.

By the time I was a senior, the "greasers" and the hippies/beats (usually relegated to the art room) had recognized our common marginalization and made a sort of peace, united as we were against our common enemies, the administration and, of course, the principal. As a result of the spitting episode, the greasers had realized we were as weird, and perhaps as dangerous, as they were. A strange sort of respect followed.

Without the writings and teachings of the Beats we had been reading, we might have fought the greasers for spitting on us and caused a bloody four-year war to erupt instead of the eventual brotherhood and smiles that ensued. Instead, we fought back with the spontaneity, humor and absurdity that filled the books of our Beat mentors.

All of this is to say that some of the men who fathered me and taught me courage, honesty, respect for life and liberty and the importance of joy were for the most part homosexuals, drug addicts, alcoholics, anarchists, Buddhists and commies, not a popular mix, then or now.

Beat Spirit is a more "mature" effort to do those same things: to fight back against cynicism, despair and unthinking conformity. It's my way of sharing what has been, for me, a lifelong experience of learning; my way of honoring the tradition that has made my own life larger; my way of passing on the "tribal" wisdom of the Beat elders to those of us still young enough, at heart or in age, to push back the boundaries of limitation to discover what it truly means to be fully human.

O my Big Daddy-O's!

This is a letter home
from a son you never knew,
from a son you raised
on words alone,
words sent home in lieu of child support.

For a forsaken and lonely child
lost in America those years,
it was definitely better
to be Beat
than beaten.

I'd build a house
on their subversive foundations any day.
In fact,
I'd build a whole nation.

What is the Beat spirit? What makes the Beat lifestyle and approach so perennially fascinating, generation after generation? Just when the cultural pundits pronounce "Beat" safely dead, the spirit of impolite inquiry and adventure returns among the barely living to hold up a mirror of recrimination and possibilities.

Are there other ways of doing things? Are we all that we can be? Does life have to be so boring, so predictable, so . . . robotic? Is there some way of freeing ourselves without becoming slaves of the way itself, without conversion, brainwashing or selling ourselves short? Is transformation possible?

Why not?

These are the perennial questions that motivate what we call the Beat spirit, a gnawing, nagging feeling that we've been missing out on something; that something has been lost or distorted. These questions plant the seeds of an incipient rebellion, a revolt against conformity, blandness and spiritual limits that begins with the question "Why?" and is hastened by its logical answer, "Why not?"

Why not indeed? Why not take a risk, push life to the limits and see if life doesn't respond with wonder, magic and fulfillment? We've been told otherwise, but the Beat spirit would tell us that we've been lied to and used, limited and cut short in our growth to who we really are.

There has been a Beat spirit as long as there have been people, a rebellious, nonconformist and fiercely independent path traditionally taken by artists, writers and musicians, the very people who create what is new in culture, who create and innovate what the rest of us consume, who bravely (and sometimes recklessly) discover new frontiers of the spirit.

"Oh, Just Grow Up!"

Often called a "Bohemian" lifestyle, the Beat way is often derided as adolescent and immature. Real people "grow up," become "realists" and settle for the best that life can offer. In other words, they give up, cave in and surrender, and the world is that much poorer in spirit, and the possibility of changing the order of things lessens with the defection of another soul to the ranks of the drones and sheep.

The spirit of nonconformity and rebellion is, this book will hold, not a temporary phase of humans that they pass through on the road to "responsible" adulthood, but rather the natural spiritual state of potentially divine beings. It is the path to self-knowledge and spiritual enlightenment. The Beat or Bohemian spirit can be identified in most of history's prophets, revolutionaries and inventors, people for whom "settling" wasn't enough and who dreamed reality into being. Are we so very different from them? Can we become creators rather than consumers, spiritual warriors rather than cultural captors?

Drug-Crazed Beatniks
and Hipster Saints

The term *Bohemian* traditionally meant a person who experimented with loose and liberal lifestyles, sexually, chemically and even spiritually. Images of starving artists in Parisian garrets come to mind as do those of finger-snapping beatniks in smoky Greenwich Village jazz joints, or perhaps spaced-out nude hippies meditating on a farm or a group of pierced and leather-clad mohawked punks glaring from the street corner. While the Bohemian spirit is, to be honest, a part of all these superficial stereotypes, it remains something more and something deeper and more primeval.

Representing a perpetual alternative to the way most people live, hemmed in by codified and rigid social behaviors, and stringent limitations on psyche and soul, the Beat spirit is a rude and insistent wake-up call to what is most alive in each of us. In a world where we are told there is only one way of doing things, the Beat spirit is valuable for providing a loud nay-saying to what passes for common sense and "grown-up behavior."

The Bohemian spirit of this century exploded onto the national consciousness with the so-called Beat writers of the fifties. Their spiritual and cultural descendants, the hippies, formed a human tidal wave in the sixties that flooded the world with many of the ideas the Beats had pioneered, such as Buddhism, sexual liberation and psychedelic awareness.

The punk movement of the late seventies and early eighties, while itself a reaction to the perceived mushy-headed hippie idealism, eagerly embraced the Beat forefathers, particularly William S. Burroughs. And now, at the end of the bloodiest century in history, the Beat spirit remains strong and robustly contemporary.

A Contemporary **Solution**

Far from a dated and quaint literary movement of mid-century, the Beats have been shown to be prophetic and widely influential in affecting the course of the culture and inspiring whole new spiritual cultures. Interest in the Beats is today at an all-time high with books, CDs, films and performances flooding the mainstream market. Most of the original Beats are still living and contributing their work in a completely modern and cutting-edge fashion, refusing to become captives and cartoons of their own histories.

Today's so-called neo-Beats represent a sizable portion of the population, from teenagers to GenXers; even and especially to jaded Boomer yuppies who've realized they have one last chance to reclaim the promise of their youth, that they've, in some ways, sold themselves short to what Allen Ginsberg referred to as Moloch—the greedy, destructive spirit of a mercantile life. In their midlife reawakening, perhaps they realize it's not too late to avoid turning into mimicries of their own parents.

A deep dissatisfaction, cynicism, distrust and even paranoia infect the culture, and the Beat spirit is increasingly seen as a viable alternative to the deadening ways in which we think and live.

The old ways of viewing the Beat spirit persist. On the one hand are the self-appointed cultural warriors who declare Beat a dead historical phenomenon, one that is subversive, immoral and adolescent. On the other hand are those who see Beat as unbearably "cool," chic and hip, as a pose to adopt in gaining status or acceptance.

The Beat spirit to be discussed in this book is neither. It is neither wild-eyed nihilistic hairy beatniks trying to get your kids hooked on "dope," nor is it angst-ridden poets in black turtlenecks declaiming their sensitive poetry over expensive espresso. It is something very far indeed from stereotypes and cultural cartoons.

We will be examining the lives, methods and thoughts of real flesh-and-blood men and women who bravely sought a better and different way to *be*. That's all. No more. Very simple. We are essentially no different than they are, and the things they discovered can help us in our personal quests to become fully human.

Gestures of Faith

The Beat spirit represents a solid and definable tradition outside of mainstream, approved culture. It is, in its own way, an essentially religious and spiritual movement that seeks to liberate human potential, transforming it into something gentler, kinder and more exciting. Lacking churches, membership rolls and ministerial leaders, the Beat spirit is democracy at its finest and most gloriously chaotic, a spiritual movement composed of people attracted to the ideas rather than compelled or converted, a movement continually evolving in response to its "members" and the culture they move in. The spiritual values of the Beats are to be found in real life, in real activities and in real actions rather than in automatic and defensive gestures of faith.

The biggest gesture of faith is perhaps to take risks, expand limits and see what happens. To simply stay alive is in itself a gesture of faith, that the world does indeed have meaning for us, and that the best is yet to be. This is a Beat gesture and the one gesture that we must make not only with our spirits, but with our bodies and minds as well.

Who This Book Is For

Beat Spirit is for anyone interested in Beat issues, experts and neophytes alike. For those of you newly curious about Beat culture, you'll gain a deep and working knowledge of what all the fuss was/is about, as well as gaining some guidance on what and where to turn to next as you continue on your Beat path.

For those of you with a lifelong acquaintance and practice of Beat issues, the exercises will provide a three-dimensional aspect to what previously might have been only a vicarious experience, and perhaps even renew the excitement you felt when you first began your Beat journey.

If you are reading this book, you obviously have some interest in the Beats, alternative ways of thinking and being, or are simply disenchanted with "what is," and are fishing around for a "way out" to what "might be." This book makes some assumptions about you from the start and we continue from those premises; namely that you think that the way things are now basically suck, and that you've been taken like a mark at a carnival game. You know there's a better way, or at least a more interesting one. You're my ideal reader, and together we'll explore what it means to be Beat in a very experiential fashion.

What This Book Is

Beat Spirit is the first and, so far as I know, only workbook to exclusively feature actual exercises and things to do inspired by the Beat spirit. There are countless histories, memoirs and critiques of the Beat movement, but until now no actual manual, as it were, on how to participate in the living spirit.

What is Beat? Everybody wants to know these days. The only way to really find out is by *doing it*. This book is your door to that experience, making Beat a living, breathing contemporary experience, instead of a literary and historical parlor game, or something that happened to other people. This is going to happen to you! I deliver it to you still very much alive and kicking.

The point of this book is that we not become passive armchair bohemians or mere consumers of countercultural commodities. That way lies the path of selling out and surrender. To truly understand the Beat spirit, you must *be* Beat, in the same way that one cannot know what, say, an orange tastes like from reading about it. This book is your orange. Take a bite. Get sticky.

This Is a Manual

This book is an exhaustive operating manual that you *must* participate in. Without your presence, it remains a dead lump of paper and ink. You are the spirit that will animate and direct it. Passive consumption is anathema to the Beat spirit. Active participation is the ideal.

The book is divided into sections based primarily on author, personality or subgroup. Through your reading and doing of the exercises, you will gain an immediate and very real sense of what that person or aspect of Beat is all about. In essence, you will be recapitulating or living some part of their experience through your involvement with the exercises. You'll gain far more than just facts or a shallow intellectual understanding. Hopefully, as you read and involve yourself, you'll experience an actual personal transformation for the better.

This Is **Not** a **Normal** "Book"

This is a hands-, hearts- and heads-on book. You've been warned. This book is dangerous in that it will change, outrage, provoke and prod you to real action and authentic thought. This is your brain. This is your brain on Beat Spirit. Any questions?

It is, in fact, not really a book at all, in any traditional sense, but in actuality, a collection of several Beat genies ready to come forth from their magic lamp, ready to challenge your assumptions about nearly everything and, perhaps, even grant some of your wishes.

What This **Book** Is **Not**

Beat Spirit is *not* a history of the Beats. It is not a fact-filled and exhaustive time line of the movement, and it is not the authoritative and last word on the subject. Many, many excellent scholarly and popular histories and memoirs of the Beats already exist, and it is not the intent of this book to duplicate material better done elsewhere by better writers than me. *Beat Spirit* is limited in scope and highly focused in intent, presenting exercises in the form of a workbook. Undoubtedly, the end result and accumulation of work will leave you with a deep working knowledge of the Beats.

This Book **Is** My **Take**

The exercises I've derived, the information I present and the conclusions and interpretations I sometimes draw are mine and mine alone. *Beat Spirit* represents an intersection of my personality and experience with those of the Beats and their texts. It's my *take* on the movement and only mine. What and who I've included or left out was an extremely arbitrary decision, based solely upon what interests or attracts me personally. *Beat Spirit* is a labor of love and a tribute to those who inspired me.

Others will surely disagree or honestly find fault with the scope or content. I can only say that in meeting these Beats in this book, you meet me as well. For the time being, I will be your guide, your filter and your interpreter in this sometimes alien land. Keep that in mind as you grow in your own knowledge of the Beat spirit. Feel free to disagree, argue with me or even dismiss my intent. Or to applaud, enthuse or approve. Above all, respond! Be moved!

This Is a Book of Permissions

Nothing more and nothing less. Create your own experience in response to the Beat material, as I have done throughout my life. In the words of William S. Burroughs, "Nothing is true. Everything is permitted."

In the spirit of Whitman's *Leaves of Grass,* of which he said whoever touches the book, touches a man, I hope that in some way my enthusiasm and gratitude for the Beats will come across and infect you with a thirst for real freedom, a hunger for complete fulfillment, a rage at the forces that diminish us and a vow to make a difference.

Be cool.

Mel **Ash**
Providence, R.I., **1997**

How to Use Beat Spirit

If *Beat Spirit* is your course or workbook, then consider what follows to be the rest of the course requirements, all suggested of course.

1) Your Beat Journal

Along with getting one or more of the suggested books at the end of this chapter, I would recommend that you get a blank book in which to do many of the exercises and artwork you will be asked to do in the course of *Beat Spirit*. Use it *only* for your Beat work and keep it together with the other books.

Throughout *Beat Spirit*, I'll be reminding you (ad nauseam, sometimes) to *use* your Beat Journal. The blank spaces following many of the exercises have been purposely kept to a minimum for two reasons: first, to give you more Beat for your buck, and second, to encourage you to get a Journal and *use* it. The point of this entire book, and of your participation in it, is to create your own vision of life and how to live it, not to copy mine or those of the Beats. *Beat Spirit* is an *unfinished* book, just waiting for the right co-author and sequel: you and your Journal.

You can divide it up like this book, by author or by subject (some of which I suggest in the course of the book) such as "Sex," "Artwork," "Photos" and so on. Or even better, start with *no* plan in mind and let your Journal grow itself organically. Don't treat the Journal as sacred, don't be afraid to make mistakes, cross out, take it out for a coffee, or even rip out pages. In a very real way, the Journal will become emblematic of your life as you explore the Beat spirit.

When you're finished with *Beat Spirit,* you should also have your *own* Beat book, your Journal, to pull off the shelf from time to time. Don't cut corners on this. You've already bought *this* book, so treat yourself to a blank book that will beckon to and invite you. As your first exercise, you could design a cool cover for it, with fabric, collaged pictures or just a big scrawled *Beat Journal* by (author's name: yours).

2) Method

As mentioned earlier, you can do this work straight through or skip around, finding what interests you. In the Beat spirit, I refuse to prescribe any surefire method for working this book. The best I can offer, however, is the suggestion that you complete whole chapters before moving on to another. Try to gain the complete picture and experience I've designed for you in order to reap maximum benefit from the activities.

Each section starts with a short introduction to the subject, after which we move right into the Beat experience. The exercises and activities are all divided into two parts, the first of which is a mini-essay on the topic, followed by the exercise itself. You'll know when you've hit the interactive part when you see this:

The snapping fingers, a stereotype of Beat approval in place of applause, and a symbol of action, will become your familiar guide as you explore the Beat spirit. Snap your fingers right now, congratulating yourself in advance for some very cool things you're about to do.

Doing the workbook with other people will increase the benefits and heighten the adventure and sense of personal discovery. Most of the Beats emphasized group action and mutual influence and disclosure, and I hope you will include others in your new experiments in consciousness.

Try to do at least one exercise daily. Some of them you'll want to make into habits. Make using the Journal your first habit.

3) **Additional** Readings

Following this chapter you'll find a suggested reading list. I strongly encourage you to read one or more of the books suggested along with this workbook. These histories and anthologies are invaluable for their presentations of the actual Beat documents, as well as for their critiques and organization.

There is no substitute for the real thing and this can be found in these suggested auxiliary readings. When doing one of the activities, it'll be easy to turn to one of these works to read the actual prose or poem. *Beat Spirit* is like the workbook you got along with your other, more formal schoolbooks. You can write in this book, even erase or cross out.

At the end of each section is found a separate reading, listening and viewing list for each personality if you wish to pursue studying that particular individual. The lists are by no means all-inclusive, but selected by me and are what I regard as the most accessible and valuable work.

4) **Attitude**

While many of the exercises call for writing or art activity, this is most emphatically *not* a workbook for writers or artists. In fact, those with little or no previous exposure to the arts will probably reap the most benefit, bringing a fresh mind and untrained hand to the material. It's just that writing and art are valuable, free, time-tested and always available methods for personal growth.

Please don't be intimidated by the writing and art. As Jack Kerouac says, "Secret wild typewritten pages for your own joy." You don't have to show this stuff to anyone, so feel free to write as uninhibitedly as possible. In fact, this is the only MUST in the entire book:

The Beat Commandment

YOU MUST BE AS FEARLESS, OPEN AND HONEST AS POSSIBLE WHEN DOING THE WORK.

Attitudes helpful when exploring the Beat spirit: honesty, joyous anticipation, fearlessness, eagerness, sometimes fear and outrage, openness to personal change, risk taking, disdain for convention, thirst for adventure, delight in the new and shocking—if you don't have these attitudes now, I guarantee you'll have most of them by the end of the book!

The Raw Materials of Spirituality

How do we actually transform and become free? By some sort of Beat osmosis? By merely reading about change? No, we will transform ourselves by looking very deeply in some unusual ways at a huge variety of issues that make up the totality of who we are and affect who we might become.

In the context of the Beat spirit, all these things qualify as components of spirituality, no matter what lies you've been told to the contrary. Spirituality is not something *out there,* "holy," or removed from our everyday activity. If we are spiritual beings by nature, then it follows that *anything* we do is spiritual. Some of the things we'll be working with as our raw spiritual materials are:

Sex of all varieties and orientations, ethnicity, personal names, religion, media influence, corporate politics, clothing, art, music, food, aliens, computers, nudity, meditation, parents, smells, animals, death, suicide, friendships, comic books, tools, biology, insanity, Zen, sports, ecology, making a living, magic, erotica, dirty words, publishing, telepathy, television, pirates, murder, alcoholism, authority, drugs, breathing, paganism, Kabbalah, karma, graffiti, synchronicity, criminal behaviors, and even housecleaning!

The Goals of the Book

If you use the materials, do the auxiliary readings, keep the mental attitudes and utilize your raw spiritual materials as outlined above, you will gain a thorough understanding of Beat spiritual and artistic approaches to life, but that is really beside the point. The point is *you,* and you will inevitably become, like the Beats themselves,

1) less conforming to meaningless codes and strictures
2) less tolerant of intolerance
3) less reliant on exterior forms of approval and reinforcement
4) less anxiety ridden and fear filled
5) more prone to risk taking
6) more open to different and even strange experiences
7) more creative in seeking ways to become who you really are
8) more emotionally spontaneous and responsive
9) more sensually aware and sexually daring
10) more spiritually fulfilled and liberated.

All of these, numbers 1 through 10, when added together in Beat math, add up to 11): a much more interesting and authentic person, both to yourself and others.

12) is your first exercise: please write in the personal goal you have for your work in this book, the reason you even opened it in the first place. Refer back to it when you've finished the book. How'd you do?: _____

Suggested Readings
and Other Media

I'd recommend obtaining at least one of the following anthologies to read in conjunction with *Beat Spirit,* if you at present have no other Beat literature. Even if you do, they are still valuable reference works:

The Portable Beat Reader, edited by Ann Charters. New York: Penguin, 1992. Original and representative texts compiled by the foremost chronicler of the Beats, with excellent commentaries and historical overviews. Indispensable.

Big Sky Mind, edited by Carole Tonkinson. New York: Riverhead, 1995. Anthology of original Beat writings on Buddhism and other spiritual topics, good selection of the women Beats.

The Beat Book: Poems and Fiction of the Beat Generation, edited by Anne Waldman. Boston: Shambhala, 1996. Anthology of Beat writings and commentary.

For straightforward histories of the historical movement itself, either one of the following books is excellent:

The Beat Generation by Bruce Cook. New York: Quill, 1994. The classic story of the movement, along with excellent follow-up of the sixties, now reissued and updated.

Birth of the Beat Generation: Visionaries, Rebels, and Hipsters, 1944–1960, by Steven Watson. New York: Pantheon, 1995. A recent entry, fun layout with quotes, pix, charts and maps.

(Individual biographies of the writers themselves also serve as excellent histories of the Beats. See individual lists for suggestions.)

Additional Readings

Aquarius Revisited, by Peter O. Whitmer with Bruce Van Wyngarden. New York: Macmillan, 1987. Interviews and essays on Burroughs, Ginsberg, Leary, Robbins and others.

Bohemia: Where Art, Angst, Love, and Strong Coffee Meet, by Herbert Gold. New York: Touchstone, 1993. A wry, latter-day look at the counterculture spawned by the Beats.

Go, by John Clellon Holmes. New York: Thunder's Mouth, 1988. The first book published about the Beat generation, by a friend of Kerouac and the other early Beats. Captures the ambiance of the generation.

Growing Up Absurd, by Paul Goodman. New York: Vintage, 1960. Important psychologically oriented early overview of the society the Beats rebelled against; contains references to the Beats.

How the Swans Came to the Lake: A Narrative History of Buddhism in America, by Rick Fields. Boston: Shambhala, 1986. Contains the best treatment of the influence of Buddhism and Beat on each other.

The Making of a Counter Culture: Reflections on the Technocratic Society and Its Youthful Opposition, by Theodore Roszak. Garden City, N.Y.: Doubleday, 1969. Details the formidable influence of the Beats on the hippies; a seminal and still valuable work.

Naked Angels: The Lives and Literature of the Beat Generation, by John Tytell. New York: Grove, 1986. Classic literary and psychological analysis of the three Beat granddaddies: Burroughs, Ginsberg and Kerouac.

Women of the Beat Generation: The Writers, Artists, and Muses at the Heart of the Revolution, edited by Brenda Knight. Berkeley: Conari, 1996. An important corrective to the often male-dominated Beat movement, superb and indispensable anthology of writing and herstory. (Also see list of women's memoirs following this section).

Women's **Memoirs**

The Beat movement was primarily male dominated, and despite the sometimes misogynist attitudes of the Beats themselves, contributed much to the erosion of gender stereotypes and sexism. The few women who participated are the subjects of later sections in *Beat Spirit,* but the following books also provide a different take on the era and its ideas.

How I Became Hettie Jones, by Hettie Jones. New York: Penguin, 1990. Memories of New York's Village scene in the fifties.

Minor Characters, by Joyce Johnson. Boston: Houghton Mifflin, 1983. Memoir of the scene by former Kerouac girlfriend, now a novelist herself.

Off the Road, by Carolyn Cassady. New York: William Morrow, 1990. Subtitled *My Years with Cassady, Kerouac, and Ginsberg* by the woman at the center of it all.

On **Availability**

The books listed in this and other places in *Beat Spirit* are generally all in print and easily available at most bookstores and libraries. The editions and dates I list are from my own collection and, in some cases, do not reflect current ordering information.

For those books that are out of print, try the library or search the shelves of used bookshops. Despite the popularity of Beat literature, you can still find a lot of good buys and real treasures out there. But be careful! Beat collecting is highly addictive. One guy I know even took a second, part-time job to finance his "hobby."

Essential CD **Sets** for **the** Serious **Student**

On **Listening**

There is no substitution for hearing authors read their own works. When you read their books or poems after hearing them live or recorded, the experience is fuller and the texts come completely alive.

The Beat movement is probably the first of its kind to be so thoroughly and exhaustively documented. The writers proved themselves adept at utilizing all media, in addition to publishing, to spread the Beat gospel, becoming photographers, artists and musicians as well. The audio recordings of the Beats assume nearly the same stature as their writings in presenting the flesh-and-blood immediacy that they demanded from their readers.

Suggested recordings follow each individual chapter as well.

Howls Raps & Roars, 4 CDs, Fantasy Records, compiled by Ann Charters. Contains archival readings and music by most of the principals, excellent notes and booklet.

The Beat Generation, 3 CDs, Rhino Records. Audio time capsule with readings, music, news and interviews of the Beat fifties. Great fun.

The Beat Experience, CD ROM, Voyager. Images and words from the era for your computer.

Individual reading, listening and viewing lists (labeled "-ographies") follow each chapter.

The **Beat** Background

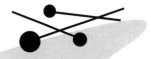

*T*he generation that came of age during and after the Second World War was unlike any that had come before. The unthinkable genocide of the Holocaust, the possibility of planetary annihilation from atomic weapons, and the new order of homogenized conformist fifties culture gave rise to questions about the lives people led on a scale and depth previously unthinkable, except to isolated and prophetic thinkers such as Margaret Fuller, Walt Whitman and Henry Miller.

If the old ways were spiritually bankrupt, then new ones must need be sought. This complete disgust and rejection of the status quo found its earliest postwar expression in New York City, where the founding Beat authors, William S. Burroughs, Allen Ginsberg and Jack Kerouac, met for the first time in 1945. Ginsberg and Kerouac, students at Columbia, became close friends with Burroughs, a few years older, and explored ideas and activities concerning sexuality, spirituality and politics.

The three men, well read and conversant in the history and literature of resistance, became the nucleus and ground zero for a cultural revolution that has yet to be played out. The issues they explored and the questions and alternatives they sent into the world still fuel the cultural wars and mark a dividing line between the old world of the past and the approaching one of the future. From their innocent start were launched lifestyles and spiritual techniques that to this day continue to inspire and empower people to do things their own way and to reclaim their own experience from the dominant paradigm.

"Subvert the Dominant Paradigm."

Thus said Beat writer and publisher Lawrence Ferlinghetti. What does this mean? And how is it to be accomplished? And what is to take its place?

The dominant paradigm Ferlinghetti refers to is the dominant culture we've been referring to all along, the so-called mainstream, the great middle-of-the-road area where a form of mass hypnosis and unquestioned commercial and political propaganda passes for consciousness. The dominant paradigm is what marginalizes other ways of being and thinking; it is what oppresses the human spirit, represses our mammalian natures and suppresses our godlike potentials. It is the great leveler where fear of sticking out from the crowd like an errant nail is to risk being hammered down.

To subvert or change this dominant paradigm is to take action, not just use words. Real changes in the way we do things, the way we believe, make love, worship and spend or not spend money. These acts can all become subversive and liberating in nature by the way we choose to use them.

Three Ways to Beat Nirvana: The Three Ts

There exist three classic phases or steps in resisting and subverting the dominant paradigm, both interior and exterior, and becoming who you really are. These steps can be retraced through nearly all the Beat documents and if you look closely enough, in your own life as well. Look for these themes throughout the book as you become conversant in Beat values.

A) **Transgression**

is obviously what the Beats called for with their willful breaking of societal taboos, laws and interior personal limitations and boundaries. To transgress initially fills one with fear and guilt, but also a tingling sense of exhilaration and incipient freedom.

Without transgressing our limits and stretching the boundaries of what is considered possible and permissible, we'll never, ever know what could be waiting on the other side. Transgression is the first step in any process of self-transformation.

B) **Transformation**

is what occurs when one has become comfortable with transgression, with risk taking, self-exposure and the shedding of old, limiting beliefs. When transgression becomes a habit, just as your old reticence and slavery were habits pounded into you by the dominant paradigm, you become transformed, perhaps subtly and imperceptibly at first, but transformed nonetheless, becoming a new being aware of frightening possibilities. Transformation of self is possible, despite the prevailing cynicism and lowering of expectations. It is inevitable once one begins transgressing. Your first assignment: transgress and refuse cynicism. Believe that change is possible and even probable.

The process of transformation is an ongoing one, not cumulating in any grand final state. It becomes self-directed though acts of transgression and ultimately leads to the goal recognized by most philosophies and religions:

C) **Transcendence**

was always the goal of the Beat spirit. Allen Ginsberg has said that the project was to "widen the area of consciousness." The Beat emphasis on religious, spiritual and psychological experimentation all had as a goal the idea of transcending limited, suffering, controlled ego and inhabiting a larger form of being, a form we are destined for.

Call it God, Buddha Mind, Brahman, the Force or simply a universal process, the goal is this:

1) Transcend the dominant pardigm by subverting it with transgression. Doing this, you subvert your own control systems and programming.

2) Transcend the limits of yourself and what you believe.

3) Transcend, transcend, transcend. Unlike other traditions, the Beat spirit represents an open and even anarchistic ideal of what the transcendent transformation will be or look like. It's different for each of us and incumbent upon each to reach it.

Six Elements **of** the **Beat** Spirit

1) The word "Beat" itself was taken from a friend of the original Beats, Herbert Huncke, a hustler, small-time thief and junkie who hung around Times Square (and later author of *Guilty of Everything*), who used the word in the street sense of being totally beat, as in beaten down, dead tired, an apt description for the generation that had just gone through the world war, the Depression, the Holocaust and the atomic bomb. The Beats themselves came of age during this momentous era and their world vision was inexorably shaped by the common experience that had left them beaten and horrified, fearful, even, of what the future might hold.

Kerouac applied the word to himself and his group of friends in post-war New York. Later on, he revised his meaning of the word, claiming it meant beatific or saintly. It is this latter meaning that we will pursue throughout this book, the idea that we are divine creatures that can be transformed through our own sudden recognition and fearless actions.

2) Action always informed the Beat literary experiments. Unlike former literary movements that traded only in ideas, the Beats were more reporters than fiction writers, drawing on their own experiences along the edge of the paradigm. They were themselves the laboratories from which they issued the results of their spiritual experiments.

Kerouac's *On the Road,* Burroughs's *Naked Lunch* and Ginsberg's *Howl,* the three original Beat texts, all derive from the experiences of their writers. Kerouac's marathon road trips, Burroughs's exploration of the depths of addiction and Ginsberg's relentless self-confession became much more important as spiritual revelations in and of themselves than the books they subsequently wrote.

In many ways, the books are actual extensions of the men themselves, and in reading them, we ourselves are moved to seek our own experiences. Throughout this book, you will be asked to take some very real-life risks and actions, gambling that the payoff will be worth it. Personal transformation and spiritual fulfillment come about only through commitment to a course of fearless action. Sterile words and pretty poetry never changed a thing if they weren't grounded in actual experience and demonstrable results. Action first. Words later. Change yourself in the Beat tradition. Then report the results.

3) Reclaim the dignity of your own experience was one of Kerouac's maxims and could easily stand as a motto for the entire Beat experience. Rather than living other people's lives vicariously through media, or feeling inferior because you don't measure up to others or their standards, the Beats insisted upon one's own direct experience as the only compass for one's journey, the only barometer for one's spiritual weather.

4) Spontaneity of action, thought and emotion was one of the most prized of the Beat values. Coming of age in a repressed, conformist, commodified and mannered society, they sought to reclaim natural human reactions and to shed the inbred and artificial shame or embarrassment that follows displays of spontaneity. Throughout *Beat Spirit,* this value will be emphasized over and over.

5) The collage aesthetic permeates a lot of the Beat spirit, not only in art and literature but in spirituality as well. By collage, I mean the juxtaposition and recombination of disparate ideas or objects to form new ones, even new paradigms. Kerouac, for example, was able to "collage" his Catholic beliefs with his Buddhist ones. The Beat spirit insists that we not limit ourselves to one path, but feel free to cut up and repaste together our own versions of spiritual and aesthetic reality.

6) Spirituality is implicit and immanent in absolutely everything we do. It is not to be found in churches or temples, books or statues but rather, in fellow Beat traveler Robert Anton Wilson's words, "right where you are sitting now."

This means, in very real terms, that the way you make love is a spiritual statement, the way you react to others emotionally is a spiritual experience. Even the ways in which we dress for work or prepare breakfast for our children can be indicative of our spiritual development. In the Beat spirit, there is no division between this world and that one. Throughout this book, you will be doing activities that the dominant paradigm wouldn't remotely consider spiritual or enlightening or redemptive. All the more reason for doing them.

Ancestors

The **Way** of Spiritual **Transmission**

(*"A new, undying order, dynasty, from age to age transmitted."*
Walt Whitman)

*T*he Beat spirit's antecedents reach far back into time and history. Individuals who resisted the brainwashing of their times abound. Movements similar to the Beats, such as the Romantics, Surrealists and Transcendentalists, who all envisioned "something more" from life, preceded the modern Beat experiment.

The uncompromising political anarchism of Thomas Paine, propagandist for the American Revolution, the visionary and prophetic religious poetry and art of William Blake, the astounding poetry and life of Rimbaud, the "decadent" musings of Baudelaire, the postmodern consciousness pioneered by Gertrude Stein, Greenwich Village Bohemians of the teens and twenties such as John Reed and Mabel Dodge, ancient Zen masters and Delta blues musicians—all these have been claimed as ancestors by various of the Beats.

History is written by the victors in ways that present only one "reality," only one version of what happened. Some cultural and spiritual heroes are held up while others are put down, omitted or simply obliterated in Orwellian fashion from the pages of common history.

There exists an alternative history of consciousness, one that can be found and pieced together with the aid of clues gleaned from readings.

Inevitably, one personality or oppositional culture will point you toward another until you have arrived at an entirely different portrait of history, and draw as well some very radical ideas about the future that could come into being, as opposed to the one being forced upon us by "historical and economic imperatives."

I've chosen just a few of the more significant Beat ancestors for us to take a look at before we move on to the Beats themselves. Knowing a bit about where we've been will serve as a useful guide for where we're going.

Whitman's Prophecy

Walt Whitman, now a respected American poet and prophet (they're always safer dead), was savagely criticized and marginalized in his own time as a Bohemian-type person of loose morals and wild, undisciplined writing, charges we still hear bandied about today.

Whitman is one of the primary Beat ancestors, a man who eagerly embraced Eastern mysticism, refuted gender roles, and advocated a wide-open political vision, all earmarks of Beat ethics. With his long white hair and beard, and often explicit celebration of same-sex love, Whitman seems a nineteenth-century Allen Ginsberg, for whom he was, of course, an important role model and inspiration. Whitman for one century, Ginsberg for the next.

Whitman witnessed the very beginnings of modern culture under the guise of capitalism and industrialism. Even in his time, he mourned the passing of the older, more humane values and the tarnishing of the revolutionary American dream. Usually optimistic to a cosmic degree, he became increasingly pessimistic about the chances of the great American experiment, not unlike Mark Twain, whose faith in human nature, never that strong, vanished into bitterness at the end of his life, calling the species the "Damned Human Race."

Whitman foresaw two roads for American culture, one lit by spirituality, art, literature, simplicity, loving comradeship, robust health, and the other, he said, consisting of "solely materialistic bearings" that must be firmly countered with the elimination of repressive Puritan ideals.

The other road consists, he said, of solely materialistic "values that must be strongly countered by spiritualization." Without this spiritual component, Whitman believed the culture to be headed for a destiny of "the fabled damned." The materialistic forces at work in Whitman's time were all too obvious to him, as were the nation's imperialistic tendencies to impose its values worldwide—in this case, its commercial values.

In *Democratic Vistas,* he calls for brave and true individuals, in small or large bands separated by miles or centuries, conscience conserving, to become accomplished in the arts, and the spirit to defend and maintain the true American dream and ensure that the nation take the right road, much like the knights of old.

In this prophecy, as well, was Whitman proven correct. The Beats and their heirs of the twentieth century stand in an unbroken line of descent from the "Gentle Gray Bard" of New York, standing watch and calling alarm, providing a corrective culture of resistance to the headlong rush to the modern religion of "progress."

The Transparent Eyeball

Other ancestors of the Beat spirit who were creative in their opposition to the smug pretensions and dogma of their day were the Transcendentalists, centered in Concord, Massachusetts, with whom Whitman was well acquainted and even on visiting terms.

Foremost amongst these thinkers (and doers) was Ralph Waldo Emerson, who is best known for his essays, particularly "Self-Reliance," a virtual handbook for nineteenth-century Beat philosophy, in which we find the oft-quoted "Nothing is at last sacred but the integrity of one's own mind."

Emerson had resigned from the Unitarian ministry as his ideas advanced along Transcendentalist lines, moving him ever further from even the liberal Unitarian faith of the time. As his thought enlarged, he absorbed Eastern ideas, most notably Hindu ones, as a result of his readings of the first translations of the Upanishads.

Ridiculed in his time for his image of himself as a gigantic meditative "transparent eyeball" that saw and observed all without critical comment, Emerson prefigured the Beat/Buddhist alliance of a hundred years later and laid important groundwork for this very American tradition of questioning the unquestionable and shaking up "polite society."

Woman in the Nineteenth Century

Primarily a male-dominated group, as was the original Beat nucleus later, the Transcendentalists gave the world one of its first modern female rebels, Margaret Fuller, who wrote *Woman in the Nineteenth Century*, one of the first feminist tracts. Fiercely independent in a heavily patriarchic society and gifted with an intellect apparently unequaled even among the Transcendentalists, Fuller refused to merely live the life of ideas, but lived the life of reality as well, a sign of the Beat spirit's insistence on direct experience.

Editor of the Transcendentalist paper *The Dial,* she eventually went to Italy, where she participated in that country's revolution. Fleeing the military reaction, she boarded a ship to America with her Italian lover and baby, only to go down with the ship as it sank within sight of New York City. It is said that Thoreau combed the beach for days looking for her remains.

A Life with Principles

The third most important member of the Transcendentalist group was Henry David Thoreau. (The Beat triumvirate of Burroughs, Kerouac and Ginsberg comes immediately to mind as we consider the similarity between the groups.) Author of the world-famous *Walden,* Thoreau was the consummate nonconformist, considered by even his friends to be bordering on the eccentric. A natural recluse and ascetic, Thoreau went so far as to spend a night in jail rather than pay a tax to support the Mexican War.

When asked by Emerson why he was in there, Thoreau asked him instead why he, Emerson, wasn't in jail. His "Essay on Civil Disobedience," which grew out of his experience in jail, has gone on to have revolutionary impact around the world, deeply influencing Gandhi, Martin Luther King Jr. and the antiwar protests of the late sixties.

Probably the most "Beat" of his time, eschewing formalities, disdaining "proper" appearance, dismissing money-based economy, avoiding most forms of "respectable" work and fascinated with nature, poetry and Eastern mysticism, Thoreau, like other early American Beats such as Whitman, is now treasured as a national icon.

Again, safer dead and in libraries than walking around causing trouble. Thoreau, the original dropout, represented an oppositional culture of one, showing the power of what one person can do; that cynicism need not triumph and that one person can make a real difference.

The Cosmological Eye

An important link between the Transcendentalists and the Beats was author Henry Miller, best known for his frank literary treatment of sex. Another oppositional culture consisting of one, Miller belonged to no group or movement and worked in relative intellectual isolation most of his life. An expatriate in France and stricken with dire poverty, Miller didn't publish his first books until he was well into his forties. His books, *Tropic of Cancer* and others, were immediately banned as "pornographic" and guaranteed Miller a nearly permanent outsider status in American letters and culture.

Miller, like his heroes Thoreau and Whitman, of whom he has written perceptive essays and critiques, was largely self-educated and in perpetual revolt to the soulless society he saw around him, a culture based, he believed, on crass utilitarianism, which said that there was no place in the world for a dreamer. He called America (and one of his books) *The Air-Conditioned Nightmare,* and constantly decried the shallow hypocrisy of the country he attempted to love.

Miller fully lived out the ideas in his books, embracing a life of robust sexuality and experimentation with then exotic ideas such as Taoism, astrology and even UFOs. Despite his nearly lifelong poverty, Miller enjoyed both the sensual and spiritual delights of this world, seeing, like the Beats, no difference

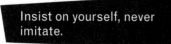

Insist on yourself, never imitate.

between them. Miller went on to author many books concerning spiritual issues such as *The Cosmological Eye* and *The Colossus of Maroussi.*

Living in Big Sur, California, in his later years, he met many of the original Beats who took him as their spiritual and literary godfather. The locale of Big Sur itself of course became an almost human personality and a center for Beat-inspired activity throughout the sixties, with the establishment of Esalen Institute, where many of the Beats and their fellow travelers taught the new countercultural wisdom of human potential and transformation, inspiring a series of shock waves that are still rippling through the culture and creating the future that is already here.

Other contemporaries of Miller, such as the poets Kenneth Rexroth and Kenneth Patchen, also exercised a strong and acknowledged influence on the Beat movement with their contributions of anarchist philosophy and surrealist imagery.

Now that we have some sense of the foundations laid by the Beat forebears, we can begin to explore the Beat spirit with an examination of the original three men who set loose the spirit of nonconformity, joyous risk taking and alternative visions upon the world. We begin in New York City, where William S. Burroughs became the mentor and teacher to two other unknown young men, Allen Ginsberg and Jack Kerouac.

Genesis: **East** Coast

he beginning of our workbook begins also at the beginning of the historic Beat movement: in mid-forties New York City, where William S. Burroughs had taken up residence. Born in St. Louis in 1914 to a wealthy WASP family, he later attended prep school at Los Alamos, ominously later the site of the first atomic bomb test.

A graduate of Harvard and a onetime medical student in Vienna before the Nazis assumed power, Burroughs had already made a career of exploring the soft white underbelly of the American soul, engaging in petty crime and becoming addicted to heroin. At the time of his residence in New York, he had yet to realize his true calling as cultural visionary and postmodern writer, but had made the acquaintance of Allen Ginsberg, a Jewish New Jersey native, who at nineteen years of age was a student at Columbia wrestling with his sexuality, career choices and the madness of his mother, as well as his own doubts about where he would fit in.

Jack Kerouac, born in 1922 in Lowell, Massachusetts, to a family of French-Canadian ancestry, also was at Columbia, on a football scholarship and about to drop out. Both he and his friend Ginsberg began a student-mentor relationship with the older Burroughs, who was extremely erudite on cultural and psychological matters and possessed of a dry and sardonic wit.

Kerouac had always wanted to be a writer and encouraged his new friends in the mutual endeavor. Ginsberg's father, Louis, was a poet of some renown and Allen himself had literary aspirations, as well as a drive to effect some sort of social change, as evidenced by his college desire to become a labor leader.

As the novel ideas and circle of exotic friends expanded, so did the feeling that something new and different was afoot. Experiments with drugs, Asian religion, and sexuality, virtually unknown at the time, came to embody the early Beat spirit of transgression as a means of transformation and transcendence.

Kerouac, borrowing a term from the street slang of associate Herbert Huncke, called the group emblematic of a "Beat" generation. Out of this mundane and chance meeting of three young men eventually came three works that would change the consciousness of a nation: *On the Road* by Kerouac, *Howl* by Ginsberg, and *Naked Lunch* by Burroughs. These three books, derived directly from their own experiences, remain the essential Beat literature. Ginsberg, a tireless promoter of his friends, was influential in getting both Kerouac and Burroughs into print.

> Others can measure their visions by what we see.

With the publication of these books in the late fifties and early sixties, the Beat movement surfaced from the underground and began its inexorable influence on contemporary spirituality and culture. More space is dedicated to these three individuals than anyone else in *Beat Spirit,* and with good reason: they remain the founding fathers, the Beat Trinity, if you will, of the Beat spirit, and nobody wanting to understand contemporary culture and alternative forms of spirituality can afford to be ignorant of their impact.

Jack Kerouac barely survived his fame, and succumbed to alcoholism, dying in 1969 in Florida. He left one daughter, Jan, also a writer, who herself died of alcohol-related illnesses in 1996. Allen Ginsberg, who died of cancer at the age of seventy in 1997, had remained as active as ever right up to the end, releasing new collections of work, networking with young writers and countercultural workers, giving readings nationally and even appearing in his own music video on MTV.

William S. Burroughs, well into his eighties, has only gained stature and credibility the older he gets, remaining on the cutting edge of postmodern (and pre-apocalyptic) thought, spinning off new and radical ideas like sparks off a grindstone, influencing everyone from cyberpunk authors and gay liberationists to feminist performance artists and film directors. Assuming iconic power at the end of the century, his voice and face have become nearly ubiquitous in Gap and Nike ads, on record and in film. Burroughs, born at the optimistic beginning of the century, foreshadows, in his writing, the ominous onset of the next.

> Woe unto those who spit on the Beat Generation, the wind'll blow it back.

William S. Burroughs

The **Way** of **Spiritual** Decontrol

(*"We're here to go."*)

hat is it about William Burroughs that has made him, of all the Beats, such a contemporary cultural force? His books, while widely discussed, attacked and praised, are, at best, difficult and disjointed to most readers, and the large body of his work lies unread, unlike that of Kerouac or Ginsberg.

And yet Burroughs emerges as the most prophetic of them all. The ideas that animate his work, widely considered bizarre and even repulsive at the time of their initial writing, are now commonplace on the front pages of our papers: cloning and bioengineering, gay sexuality, and exploration of the body as the ultimate frontier. His use of drug addiction as a metaphor for our addictions to words, materialism and ideologies has also gained wide acceptance and usage.

These issues, submerged during most of his career, now engage our attention on an intensely personal level as the millennium approaches and the borders between science fiction and "reality" become indistinct and fuzzy. It is indeed this shadowy borderland which Burroughs explores, the terrifying terrain that he knows best.

The oldest of the Beats, at times behaving like an old-fashioned gentleman from another century, Burroughs nevertheless has become the most modern, postmodern and even apocalyptic in appeal. The widespread paranoia that now seeps through society was and is a mainstay of his work, with its emphasis on sinister conspiracies and control of human behavior. Even the popular phenomena of alien abduction and extraterrestrial intercession in earthly affairs remain an ongoing theme in his work.

Decades before the advent of deconstruction theory, which examines the hidden structures of word and text, and nearly half a century before MTV, the psychology of advertising and the recognition of a new symbolic, man-made environment of words and graphic images, Burroughs was sounding the alarm, regarding words and images as viruses that infect each and every one of us.

His ideas, often challenging, and always confrontational, have not only reflected the cultural and technological revolution around us, but in many subtle ways, through his influence on other generations, shaped the modern consciousness itself. His philosophical, artistic and intellectual children are legion.

In looking at Burroughs, we look at ourselves. In looking at his past, we also preview our future. What we see may be disquieting, but like any good mirror, Burroughs is incapable of lies or flattery. He explained the title of his novel *Naked Lunch* as being that moment suddenly frozen in time when you see exactly what's on the end of your fork.

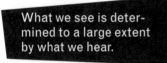

What we see is determined to a large extent by what we hear.

In the mirror of Burroughs, it's often ourselves we see dangling from the fork of consciousness. Whether we choose to continue dining or not is our decision. Burroughs just provides the menu.

1 / Cut It Up

One of William S. Burroughs's most well known (some might say notorious) achievements was in his use of what he termed "cut-ups."

Suggested originally by his collaborator, the artist Brion Gysin, and having roots in the Dada experiments of Tristan Tzara, cut-ups are simply what they imply: one literally cuts up texts and rearranges them. It was Gysin and Burroughs's discovery that by cutting up a page of text and realigning it back together at a different point, new and often astounding sentences or images were formed. Burroughs used this technique in the construction (or deconstruction) of his early sixties novels *The Ticket That Exploded, The Soft Machine* and others.

The novels as a result have little in the way of recognizable plot. This was Burroughs's intention all along in using cut-ups. Believing that consciousness, as we know it, is a fiction having only the appearance of linear continuity, Burroughs sought to disrupt the flow of expectation and jar the reader into some sort of realization.

He says that, in fact, all our awareness is based on cut-ups. An example he gives is walking down the street. If you were to later write down what you saw, you would be amazed. What normally seems continuous and flowing is in fact a series of fragmented images juxtaposed against one another, seemingly at random: the flash of a chrome bumper, a bit of music, a letter on a sign, a passing odor of food. It is the brain that imposes "order" on these phenomena and presents them to us as a linear experience, almost in a cinematic form.

Burroughs's deep conviction is that, ultimately, language is a method of control and that, basically, words are lies. That is, they are not the thing they stand for—this thing you are reading is *not* a book. Book is the mental shorthand for it. All too often, we mentally replace the real experience with its abstract symbol, no longer really perceiving reality, and easily subject it to the sway of word control, be it as innocuous as "I love you" or as pernicious as war propaganda. In his cut-ups, Burroughs sought to subvert this process; deconstruction of language as an act of spiritual rebellion. The tongue is the enemy of the spirit, says the Sufi poet Rumi.

> You can cut the truth out of any written or spoken words.

A side effect of the cut-ups, already mentioned, is the seemingly random appearance of new meanings and messages, not consciously intended by the writer. Burroughs saw these newly revealed "messages" quite seriously and took them to heart, that these new sentences or fragments were actually the true meaning of the text, only lying in wait for our scissors to reveal them.

There are a couple of ways of going about doing your own cut-ups. First try it with a newspaper, using a cut-up technique Burroughs calls the fold-in. Simply fold the right side of the paper over to the left side as in the illustration.

Now read the resulting column, alert for any new combinations or images. Sometimes it works and sometimes it doesn't. A single striking image or "message" is worth the bother. Record any striking passages you create in the spaces on the lines below or in your Journal. By arranging these fold-in results you will have created your own "news story" as well as demonstrating to yourself the hallucinatory power of the word. They can be arranged however you like, but for this first exercise write them in the order they appear, separated by dashes until you've filled the empty lines. So what are you really being told in the newspaper? Newspaper fold-ins:

_____

_____

_____

_____

To create your own cut-ups, use your own writing. In the form below, write an autobiography. Keep it simple and non-literary. It really doesn't matter what you write. What we need here is some raw text to cut up. You could start by writing "I was born in Omaha, my parents were German, blah blah, had three sisters . . ." Whatever: you get the idea. Write this until the form is filled. (If you don't want to cut up this very excellent book, then duplicate the form in your Beat Journal, on a separate sheet of paper or photocopy it.)

As you write, be sure to end and begin words before and after the vertical lines (that's where we'll do the cutting).

Normal autobiography

(to be used for cut-up)

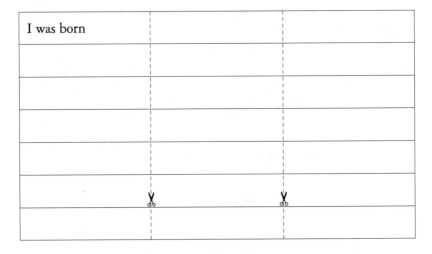

I was born		

Now take a pair of scissors and cut the two vertical lines. What you'll have left is three strips of text. Experiment with them, pushing them up and down beside each other. Exchange the left-to-right order at times. In the form below or in your Journal, write your new cut-up biography as it appears through your experiments. Simply write down striking, odd or even meaningless phrases and fragments, separated by dashes. You don't have to fill the entire form. Just record the ones that appear in the order in which they appear. Forget linear continuity, plot or sequence. You can rearrange them later as a "poem" or "story" if you like.

Any surprises? Often the cut-up text reveals unintentional and surreal humor. Even a newly constructed phrase of two words is often worth the effort.

Have fun with this one and remember to apply it in real life when confronted with language that you find controlling or demeaning. It's just words. Your scissors are your best weapon in dehypnotizing yourself from their often spiritually deadening effects. By doing this exercise, you become aware that symbols are merely that and become less easily manipulated by them, returning to real, unmediated experience.

Cut-up autobiography

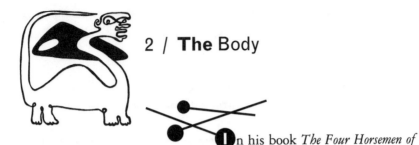

2 / **The** Body

n his book *The Four Horsemen of the Apocalypse,* Burroughs states that the human body is an artifact. What does he mean by this? By way of analogy, he gives examples of things such as airplanes and guns, demonstrating how they've evolved more efficiently through the years. On the other hand, Burroughs asserts, human beings remain in a state of arrested development, increasingly unfit for survival.

It is one of Burroughs's basic theses that "we are here to go." Go where? Why, into space, he asserts. Whether propelled by spaceships into the galaxy or by astral bodies into higher consciousness is a moot question. For Burroughs, the fact remains: we are here to leave the planet for higher states of being and are woefully unevolved for the task. Space he regards as more than a definition (or lack) of volume. It is a state of being, transcending limited awareness. He worries that even now we are entering space with the same old cultural baggage, with no new paradigms of being. After all, what did the first American astronauts do on the moon? They played golf. What became the primary use of the LSD experience? Party!

He believes us to be as doomed as countless other extinct experiments by Nature unless we *consciously* self-direct our evolution. In his writings, he points out the shortcomings of the human artifact and makes suggestions for its modification and improvement, suggestions which I will not repeat so as to give you immense freedom when doing the following exercise, which is this:

On the following chart are two outlines of human bodies, or artifacts. The future of the human species now lies in your hands. Please pencil in what you regard as flaws and evolutionary dead ends. These attributes can be emotional and spiritual as well as physical, the heart obviously standing in for a wide range of metaphors. You needn't do both if you don't want, as the artifacts are very similar, unless you examine gender flaws. Perhaps the contemporary phenomena of piercing, tattooing and even cosmetic surgery represent this unconscious yearning of the species for actual physical transformation; a choice made consciously for one's own individual human artifact.

Now that we've identified the basic flaws in the artifacts, let's do some redesign work. On the same outlines, pencil in your suggested modifications. Draw them in graphically if they are of that drastic a nature (third eyes, wings, gills, extra arms . . .).

> It is necessary to travel. It is not necessary to live.

(The inside joke about the outlines I chose is this: they are taken from the metal plate NASA sent aboard the space probe *Pioneer*. Along with other information about earth, these pictures are supposed to represent the human form to any "aliens" who find *Pioneer* adrift in the galactic void. There you have it: my graphics of the human artifact are from another artifact, one designed, it is said, to last a billion years! If Burroughs is correct in his gloomy assessment of our future, then all that will remain of us as a sentient species will be these pictures that follow.)

If you want, I'd recommend redrawing these figures in your Beat Journal. Trace them, if you're not feeling particularly artistic. Remember: as well as experiencing the Beats, you're creating your *own* cool book of experiences, compiling your own reports just as the Beats did.

By this book's end, you'll have created your own book! Personal creation, as opposed to idle consumption, is perhaps the foremost Beat ethic, and by keeping your Beat Journal up to date, you'll be doing the really important work, which is simply that: doing! From time to time in this book, I'll be reminding you of your obligation to your *own* creation. We'll do this *together,* just like the Beats.

Having completed this exercise, what personal modifications can you make in your own life to begin to ensure your evolutionary fitness (within reason and however you define it), such as quitting smoking, cosmetic surgery, a new hairstyle, or even a commemorative tattoo? List them here and resolve to implement them.

1) _____

2) _____

3) _____

3 / **Becoming** Invisible

Burroughs is often called "El Hombre Invisible," or the Invisible Man. This nickname was given him by residents in Tangier, where he lived in the fifties, writing *Naked Lunch.* They noted that in his ubiquitous suit, fedora and midwestern physiognomy, he blended in and never called attention to himself. This trait was invaluable to Burroughs in his role as self-appointed clinical observer of the human species, but Burroughs himself reveals that there was much more at work in his "invisibility" than mere appearance.

The technique of invisibility is simple, he says, calling it the "Walk Exercise." Next time you walk down a city street, make a point of noticing people before they notice you. If you see them first and mentally register it, you render yourself somehow nearly nondescript and unmemorable in their consciousness. He gives no clue, scientific or mystical, why this happens, but states for the record that it does indeed occur.

He claims that if someone were to interview the other people on the street after you had passed, utilizing this technique, they wouldn't remember having seen you, or only in the most vague sense.

Try this exercise out next time you're walking. It might make you invisible, a positive trait if you're a spy or wanted for a crime; a more beneficial attribute if you're, like Burroughs, in the business of observing the easily controlled herd called "humanity." Aside from the invisibility factor, you will notice yourself becoming wonderfully alert and keenly present, taking in details not previously noticed. You will soon come to the realization that if you did not formerly notice it, the world around you has, in many ways, been invisible to you, in much the same way that the people believe you to be invisible. This exercise works both ways! Now disappear from this book and go try it out. Afterward, you might want to record your results in your Beat Journal. Not with invisible ink, though.

4 / **World** Beat

usic was enormously influential on all the Beat writers, particularly on Kerouac, who took spiritual clues from the free-form spontaneity of fifties jazz. This particular influence will be addressed more fully when we examine the literary jazz stylings of Kerouac. Ginsberg explored music from India and other cultures as well, believing that poetry and prose are merely written transcriptions of basically musical forms. This is one of the easiest, most enjoyable, passive (and expensive) exercises in this book.

Burroughs was introduced to Moroccan music when living in Tangier by Brion Gysin, particularly the Master Musicians of Jajouka. These musicians have handed down their musical tradition for generations and specialize in what Burroughs calls "the pipes of Pan." It is a music so ancient and primordial that it struck Burroughs at once as the sonic equivalent of what he was attempting in his experiments with words.

It was a music straight from pre-Christian, pre-scientific times, reflecting a sort of controlled chaos, the sound of the original energy.
Burroughs has called them a "four-thousand-
year-old rock band" and introduced their music to the Rolling Stones in the sixties. A CD
of the Master Musicians of Jajouka was finally

Let the music pene-
trate you and move
you.

released in 1992 with liner notes by both Burroughs and Gysin.

Just as many of the Beat exercises in this book are attempts to wake
oneself up from the relentless assault of consumer culture and the allure of the "new," so too is this exercise in music. What often passes for
"new" music in our stores and on our airwaves is simply a repackaging
job. Music and language, at their very best and most effective, challenge and change the listener or reader, providing opportunities for
free association, awakenings of dormant impulses and the liberation of
true nature.

Your exercise is this: stop consuming (for a while, anyway) product disguised as "art." Go out and buy a tape or CD of ancient music such as
the Master Musicians, Indian classical, Javanese Gamelan, Chinese Han,
Japanese shakuhachi, Yiddish klezmer or whatever strikes your fancy.

Buy it unheard. Bring it home and *really* listen to it. It's so old it
sounds new, avant-garde and radical! It's so handmade and genuine
that it feels slightly subversive to the culture of manufactured desire. If
you really get into it, read up on the cultural tradition behind the music. Let the cultural messages of the music suggest new ways of being.

Listen to it until it sounds "normal" and it's the first thing you un-
consciously reach for, instead of the newest Billboard hit. Listen to the
sound of your own body, ancient yet completely modern, as it wells up

through the speakers. Want to know what Beat really means? Just listen and move!

Keep a "record" of the next few pieces of music you consume. Review them in your Journal:

1) _____

2) _____

3) _____

5 / **Word** Virus **Vaccine**

One of the dominant and recurring themes in Burroughs's works is the idea that "language is a virus"; that the word is both alien and akin to infection.

In several of his books, he postulates that language or the ability to abstract thought into symbols was an actual virus that came to this planet from outer space. The result of this "virus" was a mutation in the human species. The mutation consists primarily of an "addiction" to words rather than what they represent.

In Burroughs's worldview, our addiction to words becomes the means of our control, both by terrestrial political, religious and economic forces and even by extraterrestrial forces with more insidious purposes in mind. Those who control both the supply and meaning of words can control those addicted to them.

Control is a word that recurs often in his books. His preoccupation with forms of control and the means for their subversion form the context for a clear understanding of Burroughs's worldview. One of the first steps toward widespread decontrol and liberation of the human animal takes place personally, pushing the limits of what we've been told is possible and permissible.

Much like the technique of cut-ups, deconstructing and rearranging of words in a single sentence or thought can start the process of decontrol. Many of us, controlled as we are by the sense of the sacred surrounding the "word," have a certain amount of resistance to these sorts of exercises. Being able to dispassionately examine even our resistance is in itself a valuable exercise in revealing how truly controlled we are by abstract things.

Just as in the cut-ups, the rearrangement of words often subverts their original message and even reveals new, ominous and startling new meanings perhaps more important than the original.

To begin the process of inoculating yourself against the power of words, start by writing a single sentence consisting of no more than six or seven words. Here's an example to get you going:

"Idle hands are the devil's playground."

To attack the control messages in this sentence, simply rearrange the order of words until other possibilities reveal themselves:

Hands idle are the devil's playground
playground hands are the devil's idle
devil's hands are the idle playground
are the playground devil's hands idle
are devil's hands playground idle . . .

and so on until you've reached the end of your semantic rope. Try this with both a common, accepted cliché and then with a phrase personally important to you, one to which you are addicted, perhaps a catchphrase you use a lot to justify things, such as, "This can't be for real?":

Can't this be for real? So you see, it's not so much what you say, but the *order* in which you say it.

Write your phrase here (or better, in your Beat Journal!), followed by some new recombinations:

Original phrase:

Cut-up phrases:

1)

2)

3)

4)

6 \ **The** Reality **Studio**

n his early books, Burroughs speaks of something he calls the "Reality Studio." It is from this mythical (maybe) place that the show we call reality is projected, run, edited, spliced and controlled.

As in much of Burroughs's work, the reality studio is never really defined or fleshed out, but functions as a metaphor much like the addiction syndrome. It is, in fact, intimately connected to his other ideas about control, addiction and viruses.

STORM THE REALITY STUDIO! is a command Burroughs gives us in his writing. Assault those places where Control is concentrated and reclaim the right to write your own script, realizing that this is YOUR movie.

In the reality studio is the film; that's right: THE FILM, the original archetypical film that defines reality and forces us to be scripted and predictable characters. When the film begins to wear out, fray or disintegrate, what we perceive as "reality" does the same thing. Whatever is happening in the reality studio HAPPENS.

Our task: Storm and take over the reality studios in our own lives. Can you identify the location of your reality studio? Who is directing your film? Who is calling the shots? Is it an ideology? A religion?

To begin the assault on your scripted reality, *name* the film of your life that is being projected all around you. Choose a name of an already existing movie (or TV show), one that closely matches (in title) the feel of your life. In addition to the title, also write a short, *TV Guide*–type synopsis, succinct and pithy enough to pitch as a film idea to a producer, two or three sentences. It can be the actual script or one that you make up.

> There is no real thing—Maya—Maya—It's all show business.

The name of my film would be: *E.T.* Synopsis: Alien boy mistakenly left on earth. His attempts to fit in and make sense of earth culture and hopefully return to his home planet. Humor and pathos. Running time: eighty-plus years (hopefully).

Your film title and synopsis (here or in your Beat Journal): _____

To storm the reality studio (or take back control of the film of your life) write a different ending for the movie you feel you're in. For example: The alien boy in my movie discovers that everyone else on the planet is an alien as well, except that they've forgotten their original identities. His job, he realizes, is to wake them up to the fact. He feels much less "alienated" and much, much happier. Perhaps you feel you're in *Rebel Without a Cause.* If you were James Dean, how would you *really* like the movie to end? Choose a film that you identify with the most.

If you believe your movie has a bad ending, change it. By changing it mentally, you can probably change it in real life as well. Nothing is preordained unless you allow yourself to be a mere actor in a film run by others. Write your own scripts.

7 / **Watersheds**

While living in Mexico, Burroughs killed his wife during a "William Tell" routine, in which he placed a glass on top of her head. The bullet hit her in the forehead, killing her instantly. This shooting determined most of his subsequent life and he himself has said that much of his writing was a way to exorcise the dark force inside him that caused this to happen, accidentally or not.

The incident was the great watershed and dividing line for Burroughs. We all have such divides in our lives that affect us the way body English does a billiard ball, putting a new spin on our karma and fate. While not as dramatic for most of us, we can, if perceptive enough, identify *one* incident that marked us for life. It needn't be an awful thing, either.

For example, when I was sixteen I was a passenger in a bad car accident and required hospitalization for a couple of weeks. Because of the incident, I was welcomed into the home of a family different from the one I'd been living with at the time (I was not living at my parents' home during high school). Their family and ethnic culture were radically different from what I was accustomed to, and the two years I lived with them changed my psyche forever. Because of the experience, I feel myself part of their culture (old New England Yankee/WASP) as well as my others. All because of a car accident on a dark country road.

What *one* actual incident or, most accurately, accident, self- or other-imposed, in your life changed you forever? If you do this in your Beat Journal, you could even do a little sketch, or glue in a photo or picture that reminds you of the incident. My picture would be of a car wreck and perhaps the *Mayflower*.

8 / **Pirate** Utopias

One of Burroughs's most consistent themes is that of small "utopias" based on consensus consciousness and similarity of interests. He holds up the "pirate utopias" of the seventeenth century as the model for potential communities that could oppose mass imposition of behavior and thought; in short, these small self-chosen communities are the antidote to Control and are the very embodiment of anarchistic philosophy at its best and most enlightened.

These communities were usually founded on islands in the Caribbean and opposed the powers, regal and commercial, that ruled. In *Ghost of Chance,* Burroughs uses the concept of a pirate utopia as the impetus for his story. As society's edges start to fray under the sheer size of its numbers and its voracious and insistent need for homogenization of people for easy "handling," "pirate utopias" seem an increasingly attractive idea; increasingly realistic alternatives to what passes for consumer-control culture.

The hippie communes of the sixties were a naive attempt at such intentional communities but foundered when most of their members and promoters traded their tie-dyes for wingtips, their vans for BMWs and their ideals for deals.

Dissent could shatter the hallowed mold.

What Burroughs is talking about here is not merely cultural fad or fashion but rather a life-and-death commitment to freedom in its most absolute and experiential form. What is significant about the "pirate utopias" is that they were formed by people distinctly outside the law, in fact usually in active and criminal conscious violation of it. This aspect in itself ensures a depth of commitment not found in contemporary experiments in alternative community.

The element of purposeful and defiant transgression in the utopias is what makes them so fascinating and at the same time frighteningly exhilarating.

Imagine yourself about to embark upon the founding of a "pirate utopia." What laws would you joyfully and defiantly break as the basis for the community? Most often, it is what we oppose rather than what we support that reveals our true agenda. What sort of people do you fancy having around you in this experiment? What would be the name of your new utopia?

If it is at all possible, in any degree, no matter how slight, begin immediately to form such a utopia with even one other person. In so doing, you hasten the day when the structure of Control and friendly fascism collapses and humans become truly free, tasting the forbidden fruits and at long last gaining true sustenance.

My pirate utopia would be in violation of the following laws (list at least three):

_____

_____

The ideal location for the utopia (Africa, South America . . .): _____

_____

Our chief threat and enemy would be: _____

Three people I would most like to join
me in forming a pirate utopia: _____

Our main activity would consist of: _____

_____

9 / **Live** Forever

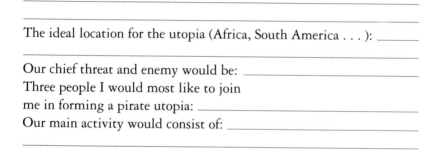

In the final installment of his *Cities of the Red Night* trilogy, *The Western Lands,* Burroughs delves deeply into the subject of death and the immortality of souls. Fear not. His treatment of this popular subject is not like those that line the pop psychology and spirituality shelves, confirming what you already wish to believe.

Burroughs takes as his model the soul and immortality theories of the ancient Egyptians. Death, he says, is a biological necessity, like dreams. Facing death, he claims, for that time, you become immortal. How can this be? Perhaps the near or imminent experience of death lifts one above time and life like a surfer poised on a frozen wave, able to transcend one's small ego and glimpse the shores of eternity. This is close to what many veterans report from combat experiences.

The immortality that one attains is present in the split-second recognition of one's mortality. It is said that the Buddha's "enlightenment" lasted one-millionth of a second and yet in that time, he attained complete knowledge, transcending time and space, realizing them to be inventions of the mind. Peak experiences, such as near-death, seem to have this spiritually energizing effect, dissolving the limits of time and body.

Burroughs wonders if there isn't a technique to face death, gaining the immortality experience with physical danger? Burroughs often refers to earth as a death camp; a terminal penal colony. The question then is escape: from Control, from the planet, and ultimately from death.

Desperation is the raw material of drastic change.
Only those who can leave behind everything they have
ever believed in can hope to **escape.**

In other words, decontrol, erase the recordings, jettison all your conditioning and free your soul.

How would you attempt to survive physical death and attain immortality? He calls the place of immortality "the Western Lands" and says that we are kept in bondage to our mortal selves by fear. To reach the Western Lands one must relinquish fear and confront death.

Would you like to live forever? Please remember a close encounter you've had with death:

Would you like to reach the Western Lands? Please list your ultimate fear about death: annihilation, judgment, what?

Would you like to leave behind other baggage besides the hulk of your body when you escape this penal colony? Please list something you deeply believe in that must be left behind in order to complete the process:

10 / **Dreams**

One of Burroughs's most recent books is *My Education.* While it doesn't refer to his prep school or time at Harvard, it does record many of his dreams, apparently the most important education he's received. Like most of the Beat writers, Burroughs places a lot of stress on the importance of dreams. Dreams, most of them believe, hold the key of liberation from Control, from conditioning and slavery to the cultural and spiritual norm.

Says Burroughs: "If you intend to destroy an individual or a culture, destroy their dreams. This is happening now on a global scale."

What we are being subjected to is a program of extermination. What better place to start than with a people's dreams, replacing them with word and image viruses gleaned from propaganda saturation in the media, workplace and home?

Our once-rich imaginations are being replaced with impoverished sitcom approaches to life, our treasure stores of dream images being cheapened by the images of advertising and the icons of popular culture. Have you ever dreamed about a product, a media personality or something you saw on a sign? Most of us have, and these intrusions are what we have to resist.

> You need your dreams, they are a biologic necessity and your lifeline to space, that is, to the state of a God.

To resist this colonization, this imperialization of consciousness, one must reclaim the right and necessity of one's own dreams, cut loose from Control's manipulations.

What? You have your own dreams and thoughts, ones not sanctioned by TV or force-fed you by corporate culture? Dreams that take place beyond the constraints of artificial "values," logos and slogans and have no discernible commercial value? Dreams that might even transgress, trespass and transcend normal values?

Write them down as Burroughs did in *My Education,* no matter how shocking, bizarre or "immoral." Writing them down creates your own form of word virus, ones that will reinfect and inoculate you against the widespread plague of monotonous sameness and fearful conformity.

Keep your Beat Journal beside your bed and record your dreams as soon as you wake, as they linger all too briefly. Doing this, you will begin to reclaim your right to be a real human being and start to leave the reservation.

Start tomorrow morning by writing your dreams in your Journal or at least a synopsis of one here. Do it every time you remember a dream.

11 / **Shit** List

Burroughs has a name for those one can trust and those one can't. He says that there are basically two types of people: the Shits and the Johnsons.

A Shit is someone who has to be right, is incapable of minding his own business because he has no business to mind. They are professional minders of other people's business, he says.

The other type is a Johnson; a person who minds his own business, who doesn't call the law when they smell pot, leaves gays alone and doesn't turn people in. A Johnson will help out when needed. A Johnson will save someone from drowning, stop an animal from being abused or stop a fight. A Johnson figures these are everybody's business.

Burroughs says that current politics and police thinking tell us that nobody has the *right* to mind their own business anymore. We're becoming a nation of righteous snoops, finks and informers. Burroughs refers to his division of Shits and Johnsons as old-fashioned, a throwback. So just who is really espousing old-time American family values here; notorious old Bill or the modern and virtuous self-appointed morality squads?

Our exercise is fairly obvious. Whom do you regard as Shits and whom do you prize as Johnsons? List two people personally known to you in each category. Then list two national figures. You might want to make a longer list in your Journal, updating it occasionally. I'll bet this is the first "self-help" book you've bought that has its own shit list, huh?

Shit List

1) _____
2) _____
3) _____
4) _____

Stay away from these people at all cost.

Johnson List

1) _____
2) _____
3) _____
4) _____

Associate with these people at every opportunity, perhaps forming a pirate utopia free of Shits.

12 / **Sex** Crimes

Men ejaculating as they are hung; women wearing steel dildos; homosexual rape; sex with loathsome alien creatures and lustful centipedal rapists; repetitive scenes of public masturbation; castration; cannibalism . . . OK, I think we've just lost the Shits who might have stayed with us till now, spying on this book.

If there's one thing Shits can't handle, it's sex. Nothing gets them going hotter more than sex outside of lights off and under the sheets between man and wife for procreation only. The list that opened this section is taken from various Burroughs books and is really just the tip of the Burroughsian iceberg regarding the sexual palette of his writing.

We are controlled through sexual manipulation and toxic shame. What is forbidden, like drugs, is most often illegal. What is forbidden is usually not only a tool for our control by others, but also a tool for our own self-liberation.

Until very recently, it was even illegal to write and publish about sexually explicit acts. Burroughs's book *Naked Lunch* along with Henry Miller's *Tropic of Cancer* and Allen Ginsberg's *Howl* were among the first books to legally contest and defeat Control's censorship and criminalization of thought and art.

Transgression of legal and social limits is one of the hallmarks of the Beat spirit. Sexual fantasies are often transgressive, self-liberatory and taboo-breaking in nature.

Please write out your sexual fantasy in your Beat Journal or below. Maybe dedicate a section of your Journal to sexual fantasy writing. Illustrate it even. Be sure it has absolutely *no* redeeming social value. If it appeals to your prurient interest and turns you on, all the better! After you've written your fantasy, let someone read it. Burroughs let us into his most secret world. How about you?

_____

_____

_____

Writing out sexual fantasy is another way of storming the reality studio, of reclaiming our entire beings from the artificial structures of shame and guilt. Through writing them out, we can see the entire mosaic of our personalities. By acknowledging your fantasies, you will have knocked down another wall between who you appear to be and who you really are. Our bodies stop being prisons of flesh and cages of bone, instead becoming launching pads for flights of liberation.

Continue your fantasy writing if you find it to be a powerful tool of transformation for you, using the flashlight of fantasy to search out the dark, cluttered corners of your soul and psyche. There are treasures there.

13 \ Cats

And now for something really different! After all this talk about Control, hanging, Johnsons and Shits, we turn to the "sunnier" side of Bill Burroughs, one that many find uncharacteristic upon a superficial reading of his work. Despite all the seeming brutality, cynicism and outright shock value, Burroughs is essentially a tender and often sentimental person, one who often insists that his values represent older and better perspectives.

Nowhere else is this more apparent than in his unabashed love for cats. A longtime cat lover, Burroughs himself owns and cares for many cats, lavishing much attention on them and noting their individual personalities.

In *The Cat Inside,* he writes of cats as ancient spirits, familiars and beings that have been sorely treated by humankind. He calls them "psychic companions" and says that cats can even take on the attitudes of people in his life who have died, such as his mother, son and others. Psychologists might call it wishful thinking, he says, but for him, it remains a fact: the dead person is at times present in his animal. He says his cats are his "last link to a dying species."

In other places, he speaks of cats entering his dreams to communicate with him.

Can you identify any behaviors in your pets that might suggest psychic abilities, beyond the usual empathy they display? Are they, in some cases, reading your mind?

Have you ever dreamed of your pets? If so, what were they trying to tell you? Burroughs is convinced that his cats dream of him at times. Do yours? How can you tell?

Do you ever see the attitude or spirit of a dead loved one present in your pet as they look at you?

Try to be a telepath with your animal. Give it a mental command or instruction as you hold it or look at it. How often do they respond positively?

Draw a picture of yourself and your animal in your Beat Journal, a childhood or imaginary pet if you don't have one now. Realism is not important. Capture the essence of the relationship.

14 \ The Third Mind

In their book, *The Third Mind,* Burroughs and his collaborator Brion Gysin assert that whenever two minds work together, a third results. Much of Burroughs's work was influenced by this thesis and he was fascinated by the disappearance of individual personality as it became submerged in the "third mind." This of course was a natural outgrowth of his interest in decontrol and of the inherent viruslike nature of words and images used as a tool of control and limitation.

One of Burroughs's friends at the time, Ian Somerville, created a photo illustrating the third-mind principle. He did this by taking a headshot photo of Burroughs and one of Gysin. He cut them in half vertically and then glued them together; the result is a portrait of the third person that Gysin and Burroughs represented in their experiments. The assembled photo itself becomes a deconstruction of image and representation. Here is a "third-mind" photo of myself and my partner, Sarah:

Here is a place for you to glue in your third-mind photo of yourself and another. Burroughs quotes T. S. Eliot as saying, "Who is the third who walks always beside you?" This picture is that third. Recognize it?

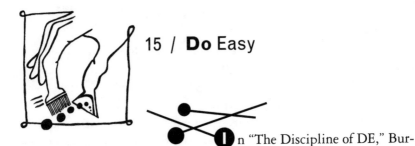

15 / **Do** Easy

n "The Discipline of DE," Burroughs outlines his method of "doing easy." In the essay, he gives advice on how to do ordinary things more efficiently and, well, easily. The best piece of advice I picked up from this was maybe something your mother told you as well, but coming from Old Bill, it really carries authority.

His advice for a clean house is easy: Every time you enter a room, straighten or clean just one thing or surface. Just one. If you make this a habit, your home will be clean with a minimum of conscious effort. Housekeeping Tips from the Martha Stewart of the Beats!

16 / **Reading** Minds

urroughs and his wife, Joan Vollmer, liked to try out some of their theories about the paranormal and psychic. One "game" that they played was to sit in opposite corners of the room, each holding a piece of paper they had folded into nine squares and then unfolded flat.

Both would draw a picture or symbol in each square, comparing them when finished to see how in sync they were with each other, to verify whether some sort of "mind reading" or telepathy was occurring. It occurred often enough to convince Burroughs of the existence of such powers, although he averred that Joan was a better sender and he a better receiver.

Try out the same experiment with someone. Which of you is the strongest sender? Receiver? Do this regularly to see if you get "better" at this form of communication. Use your Beat Journal to do this exercise, dividing a page into nine sections. Give the other person a piece of paper if he or she doesn't have a Journal.

17 / **Nothing Is True**

Burroughs is fond of invoking and quoting Hasan-i Sabbāh, the Old Man of the Mountain. Hasan-i Sabbāh was the leader of a mystical Islamic sect located in what is now northwestern Iran. Possessed of immense power, he lived with his followers in a mountain fortress designed to resemble the Islamic conception of Paradise, replete with rivers of milk and honey and beautiful maidens. His followers, called Assassins, obeyed his every command and were often dispatched throughout the Middle East to do his bidding.

Sabbāh's deathbed statement, "Nothing is true, everything is permitted," occurs in nearly every book by Burroughs and in fact is a nearly ubiquitous touchstone in much postmodern music and literature. Should this be read as a nihilistic statement or as an affirming and liberating one? Your answer probably depends a lot upon the amount of decontrol you've experimented with. Is the reverse also true: if everything is true, then nothing is permitted?

Write out three things that you wish weren't true (the more blasphemous and unreal, the better!):

1) _____

2) _____

3) _____

Now proceed to the second part of this exercise:

18 \ **Everything** Is **Permitted**

If the three things you just wrote out are not true, then what exactly does their fallacy permit? Come on, be creative, even perversely so . . . even criminally! Through adhering to this statement of Hasan-i Sabbāh's you become a virtual deity in your own private universe, the god of your own planet, to quote Mickey Knox in Oliver Stone's *Natural Born Killers*. Aleister Crowley's comment "The whole of the law is: Do what thou wilt!" is in some ways similar to Sabbāh's. So what wilt thou do if nothing is true?

Again, three formerly forbidden or impossible things that are now permitted to you, based upon the "Nothing Is True" exercise:

1) _____

2) _____

3) _____

Some examples from me:

Nothing Is True:

1) There is no God.

2) There is no death.

3) There is no Mel Ash.

Everything Is Permitted:

1) I construct my own morality.

2) I will experience absolutely everything.

3) I can be anybody I want to be.

Apply the "Nothing is true, everything is permitted" technique to any clichés or truisms that are passed your way as wisdom or eternal verities. By reversing common sense, we often come to our senses. By standing truth on its head, we often land on our feet.

19 \ **Cut** the **Word** Lines

This book you are reading is a prerecorded tape; it is a virus and it is manipulating you and your culture. Reading it, you are playing back my sounds of panic and paranoia. You have a choice. As Burroughs repeatedly states, you can "cut the word lines" or continue reading. The next section, on Allen Ginsberg, represents some real-life solutions and alternatives to the intellectual and philosophical problems posed by Burroughs.

Where Burroughs disposes, Ginsberg proposes. Where Burroughs deconstructs, Ginsberg gleefully reconstructs.

Cut the word lines. Word lines the cut. The cut word lines. Lines word cut the.

Nothing is true. Well, maybe some of Ginsberg. Everything is permitted. Especially your active participation in this book.

A Selected **William** S. **Burroughsography**

Books

The Adding Machine: Selected Essays. New York: Arcade, 1993. A collection of short essays that range over most of Burroughs's ideas. Clear, forthright, commonsensical and often funny.

The Cat Inside. New York: Viking, 1992. Nice anecdotes about Burroughs's pets. You can even give this one to your mother!

Cities of the Red Night. New York: Holt, Rinehart, and Winston, 1981. Concept of words as extraterrestrial viruses is treated fictionally.

Electronic Revolution. Bonn: Expanded Media Editions, 1996. How-to handbook for causing trouble.

Ghost of Chance. New York: High Risk Books, 1995. A short recent novel of pirate utopianism and ecological despair illustrated by Burroughs's paintings.

Guns & Painting. Madras and New York: Hanuman Books, 1992. Burroughs's thoughts on art and weaponry.

High Risk: An Anthology of Forbidden Writings. New York: Plume, 1991. Contains Burroughs's "Just Say No to Drug Hysteria" article; also valuable in itself for the other pieces as examples of post-Beat writing.

Junky. New York: Penguin, 1977. Burroughs's first book, a hard-boiled factual treatment of addiction.

My Education. New York: Penguin, 1995. A selection of dreams.

Naked Lunch. New York: Grove Press, 1959. The book that started it all. Much talked of and rarely read. Read it.

The Western Lands. New York: Penguin, 1987. Burroughs's most eloquent treatment of death, writing and other issues. In many ways, a summation.

Recordings

Burroughs possesses one of the most distinctive voices of the century and has made a second career as a spoken-word performer. His recorded work is beginning to rival his published output and he has collaborated with a wide variety of contemporary performers. Often confrontational and offensive on the printed page, Burroughs is nothing short of hilarious and avuncular in his verbal delivery.

Call Me Burroughs (Rhino). Burroughs's first LP.

Dead City Radio (Island). Nice collection of pieces backed by 1940s orchestral music.

Seven Souls (Virgin Records, with Bill Laswell's band, Material.) Readings from *The Western Lands* concerning death and immortality, backed by Middle Eastern/fusion music.

Songs in the Key of X (Warner Bros.). One song recited by Burroughs, backed by R.E.M., inspired by *X-Files* TV show. Another generational homage.

Spare Ass Annie (Island). Stories with hip-hop mix.

The Elvis of Letters (with Gus Van Sant). Director plays guitar behind eerie Burroughs samples.

The Master Musicians of Jajouka (Axiom). Contains liner notes and appreciation by Burroughs and Gysin.

They Called Him the Priest (with Kurt Cobain). Two generations meet on the common ground of heroin addiction. A Christmas CD, believe it or not.

Videos/Films

Commissioner of Sewers (available from Mystic Fire Video).

Drugstore Cowboy, directed by Gus Van Sant. Burroughs plays an old junkie priest.

Even Cowgirls Get the Blues. Burroughs makes a cameo appearance of a few seconds early in this film narrated by Tom Robbins, a Beat heir, from his book of the same name, looking up at the New York skyline, muttering only one word: "Ominous."

Land of the Brave. A performance film by Laurie Anderson; contains the Burroughs-inspired song "Language Is a Virus," along with Burroughs dancing with Anderson. CD also available. Yet more evidence of Burroughs's influence on succeeding generations.

Naked Lunch, directed by David Cronenberg. Based more on Burroughs's life than the novel of the same title. Helps to have read a history of the Beats before viewing. Great sound track by Ornette Coleman.

Biographies

Literary Outlaw: The Life and Times of William S. Burroughs, by Ted Morgan. New York: Avon, 1988. Most extensive treatment. Functions also as a good history of the Beat movement in general.

William Burroughs: El Hombre Invisible, A Portrait, by Barry Miles. New York: Hyperion, 1992. A more intimate look with valuable examinations of Burroughs's cultural influence.

Critical and Auxiliary
Literature

The Job: Interviews with William S. Burroughs, by Daniel Odier. New York: Penguin, 1989. Best overview of the Burroughsian world and cosmic view.

The Letters of William S. Burroughs, edited by Oliver Harris. New York: Penguin, 1994. Intensely personal correspondence to Ginsberg and Kerouac during the Beat heyday.

Ports of Entry: William S. Burroughs and the Arts, by Robert A. Sobieszek. New York: Thames and Hudson, 1996. Large-format book of Burroughs's paintings in full color. Catalog of a show at the Los Angeles County Museum of Art.

William S. Burroughs at the Front, edited by Jennie Skerl and Robin Lydenberg. Carbondale: Southern Illinois University Press, 1991. Collection of academic papers, reviews and commentary on Burroughs from 1959 through 1989. If you want to dig deeper, this is your shovel.

With William Burroughs: A Report from the Bunker, by Victor Bockris. New York: St. Martin's–Griffin, 1996. Collection of transcripts of dinner conversations at Burroughs's home in New York City, with guests such as Lou Reed, Allen Ginsberg, Mick Jagger and Andy Warhol.

Allen Ginsberg

The **Way** of **Spiritual Nakedness**

(*"AH!"*)

*T*he face of Allen Ginsberg has become virtual shorthand for the sixties. Seemingly everywhere at once in that decade, he fanned the fires he had ignited in the fifties, regarding the hippies as natural heirs of the Beats. The most politically outspoken of all the Beats and their unacknowledged organizer, publicist and cheerleader in the fifties, he easily assumed the role of national leader in the sixties and beyond, being at the forefront of antiwar protest, spearheading gay liberation, and early on becoming one the country's most impassioned advocates of meditation and Buddhist practice.

If something is of any cultural note or controversy, chances are that Allen Ginsberg was there first. There's a little of Ginsberg in each of us at the end of the century, like it or not. He's been *that* influential on the lifestyles we all lead and the attitudes we all take for granted.

I realized the entire Universe was the manifestation of One Mind.

In recent years, he fought hard to garner academic and critical recognition of the Beat contribution to America's literature and culture. America's most translated poet and most widely recognized unofficial ambassador, Allen Ginsberg gives permission: permission to explore, to dare, and to be oneself. He kept himself as contemporary as Burroughs, also becoming an influence on the punk movement, even recording with the Clash. On his deathbed, he was busy writing his last poems.

Like all the other Beats, he never advocated a position or lifestyle that he himself had not tried. Like his role model, Walt Whitman, Ginsberg remains an American original, demonstrating in his own life the power of one person to make a real difference. "You don't have be right," said Ginsberg, "all you have to be is candid."

1 / Howling

 saw the best minds of my generation destroyed by madness, starving hysterical naked . . ."

Ginsberg's most famous work, "Howl," like the Minutemen at Lexington, fired a shot that is still heard 'round the world. Its opening line, quoted above, left no doubt as to the intent and rage of the words to follow. Written in the postwar culture of the fifties, in which to be "yourself" was to be different, suspect and often ostracized, Ginsberg's poem was the first to savagely indict the cultural "norm." Regarded as extremely shocking and even criminal, as evidenced by the subsequent obscenity trial for the poem, Ginsberg, nonetheless, shattered forever the suicidal blanket of silence smothering American society by taking it *personally.*

The poem's first part goes on to list, quite graphically, the friends of the poet who had been driven mad or to suicide by the prevailing social order. The poem mounts in intensity as the incidents pile up, savagely indicting the powers responsible for maintaining such a monstrous and inhuman structure.

Years later, psychiatrist R. D. Laing would put forward his theory of "madness" in *The Politics of Experience,* which, in short, is that personal madness is an appropriate response to a mad environment masquerading as "normal." Ginsberg presciently called into question the entire idea of "normality" and instead 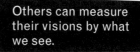 lionizes his friends who responded to the general madness with acts of seeming "madness" as defined by the culture of the time.

Others can measure their visions by what we see.

Some of the acts he lists include throwing potato salad at lecturers, engaging in homosexual sex, doing drugs, staying up all night talking, having angelic visions and hitchhiking nonstop cross-country. Some of these so-called mad friends survived and are now being recognized as cultural prophets and near-saints of a distinctly postmodern spirituality.

The form Ginsberg uses in "Howl" is a long line beginning with "who," followed by a description of the person's unique act or brand of "madness." The cumulative effect is one of a catalog. Your exercise in howling is this:

Write your own list of people you personally know who have acted "madly" or even died in response to their environment. In doing this, you will be forced to examine not only your friends' actions but, more sinisterly, the conditions that precipitated them, perhaps and hopefully leading you to a deeper and more visceral understanding of the "insane" culture that leads to such extreme actions, actions that by their very nature can now be seen as poetic acts of spiritual protest. (By the way, Ginsberg included himself in the poem, so you do the same, including some action of your own that fits the bill. The Beat ethic does not allow for you to be an innocent bystander. Reclaim the dignity of your own experience and howl it out!)

It's helpful for this exercise to have read the poem as found in one of the suggested books. If you haven't, don't fear. Your version will be that much more real for you. What follows are a few lines I made up of my own followed by identification.

who thinking disease an error, mommed and dadded to deathguilt, unable to drown the voices in his head with music books and loves, closed the garage door turned on the car and sat out the rest of his life

who armbroken by father and pretending hetero sex, only blonde haired one in a family of wiry black and brown, came and pulled me like quivering jello from angry attack, later a queer and happy

who at 90 miles an hour stoned beyond stoned headlights off, Blue Oyster Cult beyond decibel count, sheared off his entire right arm as his pickup hit the bridge on a dark Iowa prairie night

who, numbed with junk years beyond gray years, replacing childhood from Lovecraft, cleaned up went sober ten years, finally tested after all good boy time HIV plus, found dangling from a rope in his room, last image in brain an ancient shared needle

who in horror recoiled in touch at man's loving fingertips, remembering father's thudding approach when mere 13, his heavy body bourbon breath entering her, now she enters not but leaves her body, hopes for a permanent solution to this problem every time she reenacts the little girl daddy scene

Whew! My experience is no more unique or horrible than your own, I'm sure. To make it easy to start, write five of these lines, as I just did, in your Beat Journal or in the spaces provided below. Under no circumstance are you to be concerned with "literary" quality or comparing yourself to this world-famous poem. Do be concerned about honesty and the validity and accuracy of your own senses.

Write as fast and uncritically as possible, as did Ginsberg in his "fit" of all-night inspiration, thereby avoiding the interference of your own interior censor. The "mad" and "criminal" truth will escape onto the page, ahead of your mind's police. If you are inspired to go on at length (and I hope you are), please do so on a sheet of paper, or better yet in your Journal.

Be nakedly honest till it hurts, till it hurts as bad as your friends did. Not only is this an act of rage; it is also an act of spiritual exorcism, casting out the demons and doubts that have plagued us all these years, redirecting the rage from our own injured selves to the real enemy without. Think kindly of these people as you write of them. Resolve to change the world that so hurt them. In so doing, you will have already changed yourself.

who _____

_____

_____

_____

who _____

_____

_____

_____

who _____

_____

_____

_____

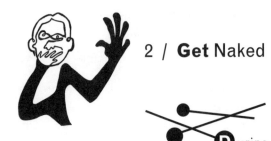

2 / **Get** Naked

uring one of his first public readings of "Howl," Ginsberg was repeatedly heckled by a man in the audience. At the conclusion of the performance, the man demanded to know what the poem was "about." "Nakedness," replied Ginsberg, meaning spiritual and emotional nakedness. "What does that mean?" the man shot back, still confrontational and cynical. Ginsberg began removing his clothes as he advanced on the heckler, throwing his garments at him one by one until he stood before him, naked. This is what it means, he said. If you're so brave, you do the same. The man fled the room, later returning sheepishly for an autograph! A convert made by example, not explanation.

I'll play the heckler for you and ask again: What does this mean? Two things as far as I can determine. I'll illustrate the first with something that happened to me as a Zen student. The old Korean Zen master would see us privately, testing our spiritual practice with questions chosen and aimed as carefully (and as dangerously) as arrows. The first few times I saw him, he would place a glass of water between us on the floor, point at it and ask, "What is this?" I would answer, "A glass of water." "Wrong," he would yell, "that is what it is called. What is it?"

Candor ends paranoia.

This went on for a few sessions. I tried every clever thing I could think of: a cylindrical container made of silica holding H_2O? Every answer was refused. Finally, exasperated and no longer caring about explaining endlessly "What it is," I entered the room where the Zen master sat waiting like a tiger in his lair. "What is that?" he demanded, pointing to the glass of water. Wordlessly, I reached down, picked it up and drank. As I set it back down, he beamed. "Very good answer!"

What did I learn from this? I learned, just as Ginsberg's heckler did, that sometimes things are just as they are if we are receptive enough and that labels, words and explanations often stand between us and the real thing, which is immediate experience, unfiltered or unmediated by language. This is what my poem looks like, this is what water tastes like; this is how this sentence ends. The man should have just listened with an open mind; I should have just drunk; you just finished reading this.

The second lesson lies in this: Ginsberg's heckler became a fan and I remained the Zen master's grateful student. I even have his autograph! By providing instant and understandable yet ultimately compassionate examples removed from the chains of words, we can do a lot more good than simply arguing, intellectualizing and explaining. Life awaits us this very instant. To even have to say so is keeping us from living it.

The Beat ethic always involved spontaneous and immediate expression, even (and especially) to the point of violating "proper" and predictable (that is to say, robotlike) behavior. By doing this, you will, in Ginsberg's words, inevitably "widen the area of consciousness," becoming aware of feelings and experiences you never knew existed.

The exercise is one you learned in elementary school, except in the short version. Remember "Show and Tell"? Forget it. It was one of your first bad teachings, one that you are still recovering from. From now on, show, but *don't* tell!

What is this? asks someone, pointing to your watch. "It's three o'clock," you answer. What do you mean by that? asks the always argumentative friend about your response concerning, say, art and free-dom, always eager for intellectual one-upmanship. Instead of answer-ing, you get up and draw on the wall. Do you still love me? asks your partner. A big kiss! What do you do? you're asked at a party. Continue eating and drinking. Who are you? asks someone else. It's me, you re-ply. Or simply open your arms wide, smiling. As you can tell, there's a fine line here between wise-guy, show-off behavior and truly honest re-sponse. You'll find the line soon enough, believe me!

The sort of spiritual and emotional nakedness and instant physical response demanded by Ginsberg (and the Zen master), if practiced, places us in the here and now, wakes us up from the trance of words, and expands life beyond its constricted boundaries. It is naked in the sense of revealing our true self and responses, unclothed in the clever fashions of words. It is truly the real thing.

And, as in Ginsberg's challenge to the heckler, as he stood there naked: Are you brave enough to do this, rather than just heckling and explaining your way through life at a distance? I think you are.

Show, don't tell. Start today. Try to find at least one opportunity each day to practice until it becomes instinctual. For the next week, do this at least once a day, listing the incidents and responses in the spaces below or on the table you copied into your Journal. Better yet, start right now. I have a question for you. Are you done reading this? Uh-uh, don't speak, even mentally! Hey! Where did you go? Come back!

1) Incident	2) Your Response	3) Other person's Response
Day 1		
Day 2		

Day 3 _____

Day 4 _____

Day 5 _____

Day 6 _____

Day 7 _____

3 / **Get** Really **Naked**

O K, enough of the abstract "as if" exercises. This one is self-evident.

Get naked. Really naked. As in take off your clothes right now.

After doing this exercise, seek opportunities to get naked with others. Perhaps without warning, say, in a safe gathering of close friends or with one friend (not a lover). Examine your feelings and fears as you do this. After you're naked, explain your actions to your friend, blaming it on me and this book if you like.

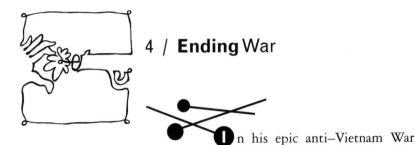

4 / **Ending** War

n his epic anti–Vietnam War poem of the sixties, "Wichita Vortex Sutra," Ginsberg personally declares the end of the Vietnam War. He says as he lifts his voice aloud, he is making "mantra of American language" followed by: "I here declare the end of the War!" Before the actual declaration, he has called upon and named virtually every higher power imaginable, from Christ and Allah to Krishna.

What? One single "unofficial" man declaring the end of the war? Yes, indeed, for not only was Ginsberg hoping against hope that his incantation would actually work, but more important, he was declaring the end of the war within himself, that is, the effects of a spiritually murderous environment that had seeped within his consciousness through media and history.

His thundering declaration makes our modern-day, New Age–type affirmations seem wimpy and tentative indeed. An old Jewish saying is that if you save one person, you save a world. The Zen Buddhist equivalent exists as well, in that if you awaken from suffering, so does the entire globe.

Basically, all this involves is changing P.O.V. (point of view). If you see the world as a hell, then a hell you will indeed inhabit. By shifting the style of your consciousness only a few degrees, you can tilt an entire planet!

Ginsberg had realized that the real power in this information-fueled world is language; that whoever controls the descriptions of reality can control reality itself, to paraphrase Timothy Leary. Just before the declaration, he says, "I search for the language that is also yours—almost all our language has been taxed by war." In an environment drenched with war language and violent imagery, Ginsberg took back stolen human language and images, hurling them back and declaring not only an end to war but a beginning to personal peace as well.

It is important to do this out loud as he did, believing 100 percent in the power of your words, like an angry and righteous Old Testament prophet, calling down divine power. Ginsberg recorded this poem spontaneously into a tape recorder as he drove across the Midwest listening to news reports of the mounting war. Saying it out loud and feeling it reverberate in your flesh and the surrounding air lends a lot more transformative weight to the words.

By declaring an end aloud, you are actually sending out measurable sonic vibrations into the world, just like throwing a pebble into a pond. Who knows how far the ripples will go or with what effect? Ginsberg's words eventually reached millions of people. The war is over. Coincidence?

Refuse to participate in the general madness or be a party to the Big Lie by declaring, like Ginsberg, the end of something equally horrific in your life or world. Call upon divine powers if you are so inclined or do it in the name of your own trembling and mortal flesh, or that of your friends and family.

My own declaration, from my own Beat Journal:

In the names of Thomas Paine, Henry David Thoreau, the girlfriend I lost due to her conversion by evangelists and the Great God Pan, I hereby declare the end of religious imperialism, on TV, on the street, at my door, on my TV and in Washington, D.C.

Here's a fill-in-the-blank form to make it easy for you to start:

In the names of _____, _____,
_____, **and** _____, **I hereby declare
the end of (to)** _____.

The object of your termination could be a war, a job, a feeling of worthlessness, or whatever fits your particular bill. Remember this declaration whenever you become enmeshed in the tangle of poisonous language and feelings. Repeat it aloud from memory as a mantra of protection. Do this until the end has indeed been achieved. I, in the meantime, in the name of my editor, publisher and reader, hereby declare the end of this exercise!

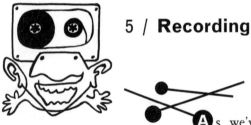

5 / **Recording**

As we've seen above, much of Ginsberg's mid-sixties poetry, including "Wichita Vortex Sutra" and his book *The Fall of America,* was spoken directly into a tape recorder as he drove cross-country. He found this method of "writing" somewhat artificial at first, finally growing comfortable with it as a means of instantly recording the spontaneous motion of his consciousness. You know yourself that many of your best insights and ideas come to you while driving. No matter how hard you vow to remember or write them down when you get home, it's nearly all forgotten.

Jack Kerouac, as well, utilized early tape recorders in the fifties, recording his conversations with Neal Cassady, thereby, in his view, preserving a record of the moment as it actually occurred, without revision or comment. To most of the Beats, the sanctity of immediate experience was paramount and any revision or reinterpretation of it amounted to sacrilege.

The insidious process of second-guessing ourselves and denying the validity of our own experiences can be short-circuited by techniques such as recording our responses immediately, either through tape or spontaneous writing. What you are left with at best is a record of your true, original nature. *Reading or listening to this record of your consciousness becomes a spiritual exercise in returning to your real, spontaneous self; a powerful affirmation of your own life.*

The exercise is apparent to you already. Turn off your radio in the car with its incessant messages of fear and greed. Don't play those CDs or tapes of someone *else's* experience substituting for your own. Reclaim your life from electronically induced hallucinations by providing your own music and personal life news *as it occurs.* Put a cheap portable tape recorder on the seat beside you as you drive. At first you'll feel quite self-conscious about doing this, even foolish, but that's really the point of all this, isn't it? To become *self*-conscious?

Don't make a big deal of this. Just begin by describing what you see as you drive, much as Ginsberg did in *The Fall of America,* describing refineries, other cars, billboards and so on. Doing this, you will begin to notice how much you really notice without being aware of it, **Catch yourself thinking.** paradoxical as that sounds. In Zen and third grade, this is simply called "paying attention" and is really all there is to the process of awakening to spiritual life.

Just look. Just *really* look. Report it to the tape recorder. When you begin to think about different things, think out loud into the recorder. Don't edit or censor yourself. There are plenty of people outside the isolation of your car willing to do that for you. This is your time and space.

Here's a snippet of a tape I made while driving from Rhode Island to visit my sister in Connecticut:

The bridge will be coming up soon. New London. Whales. Ships. Nuclear submarines. There's one now. Remembering the time Berrigan poured his blood on a new sub. Over there: Connecticut College, where I hung out as a teenager, hitched with the dorm to Providence once for an antiwar rally. I live in Providence now. Ahh! Salt air. The shoreline. Long Island Sound. Childhoods at the beach. Old Saybrook Bridge. . . . Can't wait to see Beth . . . I finally see her as a grown woman, a friend . . . so cool to have her as a sister. . . .

You could try this every day for a week using the same tape, noting the day and time verbally as you begin. At the end of the week, listen to it; again with a nonjudgmental and un-critical mind. Who is this person? What are they thinking about? Is this really me? Yes, it really is! If you do this over a length of time, you'll begin to notice a new pattern and even courage in your recordings as you become more confident in your spontaneous nature.

> Follow your breath out, open your eyes / and sit there steady & sit there wise

These tapes also make great gifts to close (and I mean very close) friends: an actual record of your life as it happened. They are also a sound track to go along with your Beat Journal. What could be more precious than that? After all, Ginsberg bravely made his tapes available in book form, proclaiming not only his triumphs but also his very human longings and failures. *The Fall of America* courageously said, "This is who I am!" His gift implies a challenge, doesn't it? Who are *you?*

6 / **Mind** Breathing

In the seventies, Ginsberg became deeply involved in the practice of Tibetan Buddhism. His studies profoundly affected his poetry and politics, resulting in some of the clearest contemporary texts describing the often perplexing experience of meditation. His book *Mind Breaths* contains several poems aptly capturing the feel of meditation. One in particular, "Thoughts Sitting Breathing," is based upon a phenomenon long identified by Buddhist meditators.

The phenomenon is this: that the brain and lungs, only inches apart, are a holistic and organic system. The upshot of this is that breathing profoundly affects thinking. If you can view thoughts as the secretions the brain uses to digest experience just as the stomach's secretions digest food, you're halfway to understanding meditation. You've already noticed yourself, I'm sure, that deep, cleansing breaths will still the turbulent thought waves of the brain.

If you sit quietly, just observing your thoughts as they come and go like clouds in a vast blue sky, you'll soon become aware that there is a definite rhythmical cycle to their appearance, metamorphosis and disappearance. This cycle is determined by your breathing, hence, Ginsberg's title *Mind Breaths.* Paying close attention, you'll notice that your thoughts actually change with each and every single breath. Your breathing seems to be generating the frequency of separate thoughts and indeed it is.

The poem "Thoughts Sitting Breathing" is based on the ancient Tibetan mantra *om mane padme hum.* Ginsberg starts each line (and breath) with one of its syllables, writing down the mental activity he observes during the interval before intoning the next syllable. The poem goes on at length, repeating the mantric syllables, and accurately reporting his thoughts as they arise and transmute.

For beginners, it can be quite alarming to have proof that you really have no control over your thoughts, that they are an almost automatic and autonomous system, having no real solidity or permanence. This revelation inevitably leads one to the the age-old questions of "Who am I really, then?" and "What's real here?" If you persevere with this practice, you'll inevitably arrive at answers.

There's no great mystery or occult science at work here. As already implied, the brain (which we confuse with our real selves) is just another flesh-and-blood organ that responds to stimuli. It is only when we begin to use the brain to examine itself that we become fully human.

Be patient as you do this exercise. Pay close attention to your mind, trying to see the thoughts as separate from you. Have a pencil ready and jot them down as fast as you can in the spaces provided. Don't give up after a frustrating session. Return later and try again. This is an acquired skill, one that has been literally deleted from your operating system by a world hell-bent on material validation and the supremacy of the human mind (and you see where that's gotten us!).

Here are the instructions as based on Ginsberg's poem. Breathe in deeply, thinking or softly intoning "*om.*" Observe your mental state and write it down as you exhale. The thought might be as ridiculous as "I don't know what he's talking about in this exercise!" or "I can't see my thoughts!" Write it down! Keep at it. Pretty soon, you'll see the pattern of your conditioned mind emerging on this worksheet.

Next, repeat with the syllable "Ma," again writing down your thought. Repeat until the end of the mantra. The thought generally won't fill more than the line provided, being the duration of a single breath. Try to do this daily for a great introduction to meditation. You can copy this form into your Beat Journal and do the exercise on a regular basis. It's helpful to repeat the cycle at least three times each session.

OM _____

MA _____

NE _____

PAD _____

ME _____

HUM _____

Looking back, you'll be able identify definite progress. Finally, it'll become nearly automatic and you'll be a lot more in touch with your real, unconditioned self and those around you. Above all, enjoy the experience!

7 / **Losing** It

What would you do if you lost it?" is the title of another poem in *Mind Breaths.* It is a direct quote from Ginsberg's meditation teacher, Chögyam Trungpa. Trungpa challenged Ginsberg with the question as he looked at the black box that Ginsberg carried with him everywhere, full of his poems, books, incense and other "necessary" possessions.

This is, of course, a very Buddhist question and demand. If we define ourselves by our possessions, who are we without them? Even more insidiously, if we define ourselves by our mental constructs and beliefs, who are we really bereft of them? And the ultimate question we will all face: Who are we if we lost this body? Who are we then? Hmmmmm?

This method of mental and physical deconstruction is a well-known Buddhist technique for uncovering our true nature beneath the mounds of accumulated crap, be the crap physical or emotional. Some practitioners even take to meditating in graveyards or cremation grounds (as did Ginsberg during a stay in India), visualizing the decay and loss of their body.

Ginsberg responds to Trungpa's question in this poem by cataloging all the things he stands to "lose," such as his files, old checks, brother, fame, eyes and so on. The form he accomplishes this with is to start each line with "Goodbye" followed by the object, belief, person, emotion or memory that he fears losing. The list starts simply enough with the black box already mentioned and ends dramatically with the loss of his body and mind at death.

What would you do if you lost it? I mean really lost it? What would *you* do? Who would you be without these things? Not sure? No better place to start than by compiling your own list of goodbyes. How secure are we really? How spiritually naked do we dare to get? List your losses honestly, even tearfully.

This is an exercise in learning the art of dying, both literally and figuratively. Right now, fortunately, we're dying "theoretically" and metaphysically, to a small sense of self smothered beneath all these things we stand to lose and guard so fearfully, such as material possessions, self-images, or hopes and fears. Let them go in this list, either here or in the Journal. (The form can also be altered to read "Goodbye to . . .")

Goodbye _____
Goodbye _____
Goodbye _____
Goodbye _____

Now pick one thing from the list and really get rid of it. Freedom lies beyond the loss. For this exercise, I gave away a treasured book I'd had since high school, something I thought I could never part with.

8 / **Self**-Portrait

n the eighties, Ginsberg, always an excellent and avid photographer, took a series of self-portraits, sometimes with a pre-set camera, but more often by simply aiming his camera at a mirror. In some of these photos, he poses unabashedly naked.

If you're the person who always gets stuck taking the photos, this is a great exercise for you. Yes, you actually do exist despite there being no photographic record, except for your thumb over the lens in some shots. For the rest of you, it is still a wonderful way to examine self objectively and document your journey through life.

We are quite often hobbled with an excessive sense of false self-modesty, often nearly bragging about how "modest" we are. You exist! You are unique in the history of the planet! Jewish mystics teach that each one of us is necessary for the completion of creation, like pieces of a puzzle.

Acceptance of our physical form, of sex, of desire, of aging and death, of the validity of our own instincts and direction are all necessary steps toward spiritual liberation. Zen masters teach that this very body (yours) is the body of Buddha; that Nirvana and this life are no different. The mind/body/spirit split is a clever fiction we have constructed to stay asleep, continuing this addictive dream-drama of "suffering." Our complicity in the fiction can be ended by becoming who we already are: divine creatures of flesh and blood on this jewel of a planet.

Document your existence and confront your false sense of self. Take your own photo of yourself. You are a planet unto yourself, a microcosm of the universe, orbiting around the sun of your own shining desires for love and completion. Do it clothed or naked. This is not prurient, exhibitionist or weird. This is who you are. Can spirituality exist anywhere else?

Paste it in your Beat Journal as your "author photo" or in the box below. This is a picture of your guru, your redemption and your desire made real. Kerouac said that we are already dead and in heaven. So stop crucifying your tender angelic flesh. Inhabit your Buddha body completely. This photo is a story, just like your body is a poem made of flesh.

> My interest in pictures was more sacramental than photographic.

Can you speak its language and read between its lines? Said Ginsberg in "Howl": "Holy! Holy! Holy! Holy! . . . The world is holy! The soul is holy! The skin is holy! The nose is holy! . . . Everything is holy! everybody's holy!"

This picture most holy of all:

9 / Chant

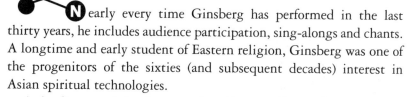

Nearly every time Ginsberg has performed in the last thirty years, he includes audience participation, sing-alongs and chants. A longtime and early student of Eastern religion, Ginsberg was one of the progenitors of the sixties (and subsequent decades) interest in Asian spiritual technologies.

As he discovered that he was primarily an oral poet, that is, that his work is best read aloud, he began strengthening his delivery through chanting. In the early days, this meant that an audience who came to hear him read the famous "Howl" would instead hear only an hour or two of Hindu and Buddhist chanting.

The last time I saw him, in 1996, he asked the audience, composed of primarily college-age students and a few old Beats and hippies (your author included), to sing and chant along with him. For the most part, they did not and seemed embarrassed and too self-consciously "cool" to join in. It is this very quality of "coolness" and isolation that Ginsberg continually attempted to undermine, seeking to bring people together outside of their hang-ups and sullen anger. He lectured us for a while but to no avail. Nevertheless he carried on bravely by himself, sometimes out of tune, and completely unselfconsciously.

Try to sing along with Allen now, even if you refused to at one of his performances or if you feel self-conscious when doing these things with others. The spiritual reasons for chanting are many and I won't belabor them here. Primarily, it feels good and also facilitates group action, something increasingly rare these days.

To make it easy, use that old standard "om." Take a deep breath, and intone it on the out breath slowly, allowing the sound to roll through your chest, reverberate through your rib cage and eventually taper to an end from your lips. Breathe deeply.

☐ **Yes, I chanted om.**
☐ **No, I remain om-less.**

Do it again. Do this for at least five minutes. Do it alone and do it with at least five other people. When done with others, you begin to actually feel yourself part of a larger organism and literally cannot tell who is breathing, you or the group as a whole.

10 / **Make** Love **to** Yourself

In one of his early collections, *Empty Mirror,* Ginsberg closes with a short poem in which he says he made love to himself in the mirror, kissing his own lips, saying, "I love myself."

Much of Ginsberg's work and indeed that of the rest of the Beat writers involves this intensely personal, some would say, narcissistic attitude. It is rather a search for acceptance of self denied, separated and loathed; self commodified and alienated; and a search for divinity in this very body, nowhere else.

Ginsberg, of all the Beats, follows most closely his role model, Walt Whitman, in his celebration of physical self and the location of godhood therein. To have done this in the time in which he grew up was nothing short of amazing, given the corporate and puritanical environment in which sex was often criminalized and physical form either ignored or marginalized.

To find your "true" self, look at your naked form in front of a full-length mirror. Kiss your lips and, like Ginsberg, tell yourself that you love you. And then in Whitmanesque style, name every body part you see, touching its reflection with your hand, saying, "I love my————."

It's an old, shopworn cliché that we can't love others until we love ourselves. This "loving ourselves" is not some abstract, fuzzy warm kind of thing. It's real and it's waiting for you in your mirror.

Who do you love? ——————————.

Which part of your body do you love above all others?———.

Continue making love to yourself in the mirror until you're "both" satisfied.

11 / **Crazy** Conduct

Perhaps the most important factor in the development of Ginsberg's personality and his subsequent role as caretaker and advocate for the abnormal was his mother, Naomi. She became progressively more and more mentally ill as Allen grew up, until finally she was permanently institutionalized and eventually lobotomized.

Being witness to this progression significantly affected his worldview, making him tolerant and tender toward those with different, even bizarrely different, forms of consciousness. He came, in some cases, to view madness as a divine gift. His explorations along the edges of madness through the use of drugs, meditation and his own homosexuality widened the area for acceptance. Occasionally, he would write despairingly that he believed himself to be going crazy, heir to a family madness and paranoia.

Despite all this, however, anyone who has ever encountered him, either personally or through his writing, can attest to having met one of the most centered and sane people who ever lived.

There during Kerouac's descent into alcoholic hell, during Burroughs's own journey through the Hades of heroin and through too many other people's insanities to relate (including the national psychosis of Vietnam), Ginsberg remained sane and more ready than ever to open his arms to all forms of human behavior.

1) Have you ever gone "crazy," even if it was on drugs, alcohol or hormones?

2) Have you received a clinical diagnosis of mental illness?

3) Does madness in any form run in your family? Perhaps a friend? It sure does in mine.

4) Name the form of insanity you fear the most: _____.

5) "Craziest" person you've ever known: _____.

6) Normal and conventional behaviors and beliefs you secretly consider crazy: _____.

7) "Crazy" things you do regularly, perhaps secretly: _____.

If you embrace and don't fear madness, à la Ginsberg, but instead court and experiment with it, it will surely call into question the entire concept of what constitutes "crazy" and "normal." You will begin to wonder just who is doing the describing for you, and if the describers themselves are not actually the mad ones. Compare your "Crazy" list with others whom you encourage to do this exercise. Maybe you're not so alone and crazy after all.

12 / **Patriotic** Conduct

Ginsberg's longtime role as an advocate for social change is perhaps his best-known public persona. People who have never read his poetry are familiar with his image from various protests and rallies, posters and news footage. A central organizer and icon of the sixties rebellion, Ginsberg has never been afraid to let his words (or body) be in the service of change.

His poem "America," found in the early *Howl* collection, is a direct addressing of America, almost as though the country were an actual person. Nearly every line begins with the word "America," followed by some request, lament or statement such as, "America I've given you all and now I'm nothing," or "America you don't really want to go to war."

The poem ends with an affirmation and a statement of purpose: "America I'm putting my queer shoulder to the wheel." Ginsberg of course made good on this threat issued in the late fifties, and later became internationally influential in his active and tireless promoting of countercultural values opposed to the military-industrial-corporate culture.

These days there may not be such obvious hot-button issues as the Vietnam War, but I'm sure there are some things that irk you (and the country) deeply nonetheless. Write your own letter to America in your Beat Journal. End it with your own statement of intent. Whatcha gonna do about all the stuff you wrote about America, your wishes, fears and hopes? This is your new Pledge of Allegiance. Please stand.

America _____

America _____

America _____

America _____

13 / **Sloganeering**

In keeping with his role as agent provocateur, Ginsberg's work has sometimes been condemned as sloganeering rather than "literature." A small book he issued in the early nineties and collected in his *Cosmopolitan Greetings* even bears the title *Mind Writing Slogans*. This is a collection not of original work but rather of actual slogans, mottoes and sayings that he has collected as they relate to the art of writing.

Strung together, they create the feeling of a well-executed collage or assemblage. In keeping with the postmodern aesthetic of appropriation of cultural images and words to create an entirely new work, *Mind Writing Slogans* is composed of eighty-two separate quotes from sources such as Jack Kerouac, Ezra Pound, Walt Whitman, Bob Dylan and even Plato. All the quotes relate in some way to writing, a small primer if you will, to refer back to for inspiration and guidance.

What Ginsberg has in essence created is a small and valuable handbook of his favorite quotations; one he (and we) can easily refer to. How many times have you made a mental note to jot down some cool quote or idea you just read or heard? Of course, we don't usually and we later search in vain for the words.

Create your own slogan collection using the words of others. Dedicate a section of your Beat Journal to this enterprise, setting aside at least five pages on which to record your finds. Make a title page as well before the quotes begin. Whenever you run across a quote that is particularly apt, inspiring or striking, record it. Theme the book as Ginsberg did his, that is, collect quotes that pertain to a subject near and dear to you. Say, sports, raising children, art or even some aspect of your work.

Here are a few examples of my own collected

"Magic Slogans"

"Logic only gives man what he needs. Magic gives him what he wants."

Tom **Robbins.**

"Magic calls itself the other method for controlling matter and knowing space."

Brion **Gysin**

"Magic combines in a single science that which is most certain in philosophy, that which is eternal and infallible in religion."

Eliphas **Levi**

"Magick is the Science and Art of causing Change to occur in conformity with Will."

Aleister **Crowley**

"Magic in action looks like luck."

Donald **Tyson**

To get you going on this work of being a quote curator, choose a topic and write it before the word "Slogans" in the title provided below or preferably on the title page of the section in your Journal. On the lines below the title, record at least six quotes you find illuminating about the subject you chose. They'll be easily found around your house in books, magazines and so forth.

The best quotes often come from friends and family or overheard on the street. By all means, include these "slogans." Fame is most definitely not a prerequisite for inclusion in your list. Quality is.

The Beat spirit ethic in fact demands that you first seek out ideas from sources more home- and handmade, unmediated and distinctly uncommercial. You're creating your own culture here.

_____Slogans

_____

_____
_____

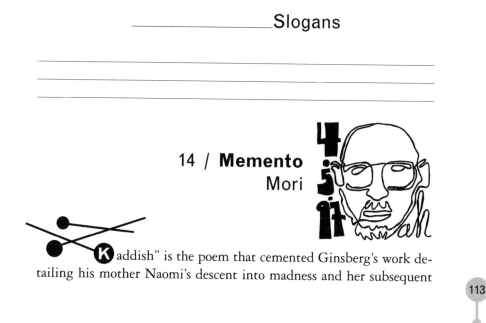

14 / **Memento** Mori

"**K**addish" is the poem that cemented Ginsberg's work detailing his mother Naomi's descent into madness and her subsequent death. "Kaddish" is the Jewish prayer for the dead, hence the title. The poem is unflinching in its detailed examination of the poet's memories of his mother. Ginsberg later wrote other commemorative poems, most notably about his friend Neal Cassady.

Our memories of those who have died are often locked deeply away in our hearts, hurts forgotten and pain lacquered over. Finally, one unspeakably sad and inexorable day comes the time when we can't even recall the sound of the dead one's voice; only the faint echo of longing:

Remember me. Remember me. That's all most of us want. To be remembered. To know that yes, we were actually HERE.

Write out one memory of a person who has died; a person close to you or one deeply loved (or even feared). One incident from the treasure trove of your mind. You needn't use a religious model as Ginsberg did for this exercise. What is important is the amount of emotional honesty you can muster. What is important is remembering and bringing that person to life, however briefly through this alchemical process of memory, emotion and recording.

If you're using your Beat Journal, consider gluing in a photo of this person, as well, or doing a little sketch. Dedicate the Journal to this person. The picture at the beginning of this exercise was done the day Ginsberg died. Believe it or not, I was actually editing this part of the book at the time I heard the news.

Name of person being remembered: _____

_____

15 / **Out** Of **the** Closet

Ginsberg's gay sexual orientation is well known. An early and fearless advocate of gay rights, he has always exemplified an attitude of complete candor regarding sex. His obvious model in this endeavor is Walt Whitman, who unabashedly celebrated every part of the human body and all its manifold potential. While many of Ginsberg's poems are incredibly frank in their use of sexual language and description, some would say they verge on the pornographic. Luckily for us, however, those "some" are most likely not reading this book.

Contrary to the prevailing cultural norms and descriptions of his time (remember, Ginsberg was "out" as early as the late forties), Ginsberg asserted that by accepting his homosexuality, he was becoming normal, obviously the reverse of what he was being told at the time by the "authorities." In fact, one of his early therapists recommended that he "go straight" and get married, something he actually tried to do.

The prevailing belief was (and still overwhelmingly is) that homosexuality is "abnormal," "perverse" and can only contribute to one's depression and mental illness. Ginsberg, however, by fully claiming his sexuality in sharp contradiction to these attitudes, became, by all accounts, robustly sane and mentally well balanced.

The Beat writers and artists championed those on society's fringes, those who differed from the cultural norm, and who represented alternatives to the deadening and gray lifestyles being imposed by the social structure: junkies, blacks, ethnics, artists and gays. An important precursor to today's gay liberation movements, the Beats expanded the palette of possibility and began the erosion of a monolithic and limiting sexual definition.

That many of the Beat progenitors were gay and lesbian is no accident. Even those who were "straight" welcomed the inclusion of the gay Beats and their unique sensibilities to the culture. Many of the "straight" members even experimented with gay or lesbian lifestyles as a means of expanding their consciousness, in much the same way as they did with drugs or spontaneous writing.

The Beat spirit demanded hands-on experience, a full and unmediated involvement with one's life and a reporting back from the battle lines of experience with the media of art, poetry and prose. It's important to always keep in mind that Beat texts and documents do not represent fantasy or fiction, but are usually literal reports of events and states generated and experienced by the writers and artists themselves. The experiences were primary, the texts often secondary.

To participate in the actual Beat spirit calls for much more than consumption of ideas and sterile discussion of "what ifs" and "how abouts"; it is a strident demand of "why not?" It is life lived fearlessly and along the edges of possibility.

Who am I? Who am I really, without socially imposed limitations and brainwashing? Again, the central question of the Beat spirit raises its bereted and goateed head. In order to really find out who we are, we need to eliminate or embrace all possibilities. Direct experience is the only method available to us (and the Beats). You can read about it, argue about it and have opinions about it but there ain't no substitute for actually doin' it.

So . . . how do you know that you're "straight" or "gay"? Does fear inhibit your honesty in these matters? Since gay/lesbian/bi sensibilities loom so significantly in Beat spirit, it's time for us to examine those components in ourselves.

Are you:
☐ straight ☐gay ☐lesbian ☐bi or ☐don't know/care? (check one).

How do you know? Record a same-gender experience you've had as frankly as possible here or in the Journal (if you haven't had an experience, then perhaps a fantasy or recurrent dream):

_____

_____

_____

For straights only: How many openly gay friends do you have (real friends, not acquaintances): _____

On this pie chart or on one drawn in your Journal, indicate how big a slice of your psyche is straight, gay or confused:

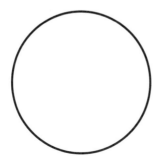

Share this self-revelatory information with a friend you can trust. This is what the Beats did. Constant and fearless self-revelation was the most potent means they had for becoming who they really were. If you're serious about truly exploring the Beat spirit, can you do any less?

16 / **Things** You **Don't** Know

Many of the exercises in this section have been in the nature of lists. This is not surprising, considering the nature of Ginsberg's written work, harkening back as it does to Whitman's "list" poetry, such as "Song of Myself" and "I Sing the Body Electric."

In *White Shroud,* a Ginsberg collection from 1987, we find a poem entitled "Things I Don't Know." I think you already "know" what the poem (and this exercise) is about. The poem is essentially a page-and-a-half "list" of things the poet doesn't know, such as, "What's the size of the U.S. national debt? How do people overcome panic driving cars? What makes electricity in a battery? How make a living, if I couldn't write poetry?"

More than a "cute" collection of questions, this "things I don't know" exercise is, again, a vivid illustration of a primary Buddhist and Beat psychological technique: that of not knowing (and admitting it!).

By listing things we *don't* know, we can begin to know that the only thing we know is what we do not know, thus stretching the limits of both self and potential.

Here are some things that I don't know: why the sky is blue, why people really die, how a CD player really works, how to set the time on my VCR, how to identify edible mushrooms, which constellation is which.

Write out some things you don't know here or in your Journal:

Things I Don't Know

1) _____

2) _____

3) _____

4) _____

Pick one of these things you don't know and learn a couple of things about it. I'm going to learn the constellations.

17 / I Am **Not**

This exercise is the much requested and eagerly awaited sequel to the critically acclaimed exercise you just did, "Things I Don't Know." Now that you're accomplished at composing these "negative" lists, we turn to another *White Shroud* poem entitled "I Am Not."

This is a shorter work and, you guessed it, is a list of what the poet is not; things such as "I'm not Gregory Corso . . . I'm not anyone I know."

By knowing who we are not, perhaps we can at least begin to know who we are. Too often, we confuse ourselves with our role models, be they positive or negative. All this work at negation, that is, things we don't know and people we are not, reduces us to the essential question, the one at the heart of the Beat spirit: Who am I really, on my own terms? And just what are those terms? By eliminating all the negatives, we are left positively autonomous and free.

It is up to us to decide who we are and what we know. Start by writing down who you are not, even ridiculous things, such as "I am not this Beat Journal I am writing in" or "I am not the author of this book":

I Am Not:

1) _____
2) _____
3) _____

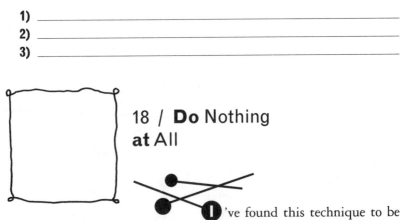

18 / **Do** Nothing **at** All

've found this technique to be one of the most valuable life skills I've yet learned. From the time we're born, we're instructed to DO something. Our business seems to be our busy-ness. We feel guilty when not doing something "constructive."

Just hanging out feels more like hanging, doesn't it? At least it feels that way to me. I'll bet you, too.

Much of the Beat Spirit was formulated, even discovered, during times of hanging out, of just doing nothing; nothing, that is, other than living. Many beginning meditation students experience excruciating mental and emotional stress when they first begin practicing. It is not the immediately stress-reducing, bliss-following experience they believed would come. The first skill they have to learn is doing nothing and having that be OK. After that and only after that can true practice and relaxation begin.

In the recorded live performance of his song "Meditation Rock," performed with Bob Dylan, Ginsberg sings (to laughter in the audience): "It's never too late to do nothing at all."

It's not too late now, either. Before you read the next section about Kerouac, do nothing for a while. Sit. Putter. Ruminate. Scratch your butt. Yawn. Sleep. Go window-shopping.

After all the intense activities in this book so far, don't just do something. Sit there! This is your exercise. Get busy (or not). Here is a space for you to do nothing in:

A Selected **Allen** Ginsbergography

Books

Allen Verbatim: Lectures on Poetry, Politics, Consciousness. New York: McGraw-Hill, 1974. Just what the title says. A lot of information and research also on early stages of the War on Drugs.

Collected Poems, 1947–1980, New York: Harper & Row, 1984. Contains all his poetry to 1980, especially the significant work published by City Lights. Superb notes and commentaries. The ultimate Ginsberg.

Composed on the Tongue: Literary Conversations 1967–77. San Francisco: Grey Fox, 1983. Valuable collection for writers and fans seeking insight into Ginsberg's method.

Cosmopolitan Greetings: Poems, 1986–1992. New York: Harper-Collins, 1994. Recent work.

Indian Journals, March 1962–May 1963: Notebooks, Diary, Blank Pages, Writings. New York: Grove, 1996. Ginsberg's diaries and fragments from his stay in India.

Selected Poems, 1947–1995. New York: HarperCollins, 1996. A less daunting and more current collection.

Straight Hearts' Delight: Love Poems and Selected Letters, 1947–1980. San Francisco: Gay Sunshine Press, 1980. Ginsberg's most public documentation of his sexuality.

The Yage Letters (with William S. Burroughs). San Francisco: City Lights, 1990. Letters and writings by both men concerning early psychedelic explorations.

White Shroud: Poems, 1980–1985. New York: Harper & Row, 1986. Update to *Kaddish.*

Recordings

Ginsberg's poetry is based on an oral tradition and written with the long breath as its measure. After you've heard him once, his poetry takes on a whole new meaning and you'll hear his voice in your mind as you read.

Ballad of the Skeletons (with Paul McCartney, 1996). CD single, also a music video that ran on MTV.

Holy Soul Jelly Roll (Rhino Records). Four-CD set and booklet. More spoken and sung Ginsberg from a forty-year span than you'll know what to do with. Excellent booklet and graphics.

Howls, Raps & Roars (Fantasy). Second CD of the four-CD set is all Ginsberg, his first two LPs.

Hydrogen Jukebox (Nonesuch). A Beat opera with Philip Glass!

The Lion for Real (Island). Modern musicians back some of Ginsberg's best poems.

Videos/Films

Allen Ginsberg. Reading poetry in his apartment, available from American Poetry Review.

Pull My Daisy. Definitive Beat film by Robert Frank with a very young Ginsberg.

Renaldo and Clara. Featured role in this "documentary" of Dylan's 1976 Rolling Thunder tour.

Biographies

Dharma Lion: A Critical Biography of Allen Ginsberg, by Michael Shumacher. New York: St. Martin's Press, 1992.

Ginsberg: A Biography, by Barry Miles. New York: HarperPerennial, 1990. Either biography is extensive and definitive. Again, individual biographies are also excellent histories of the entire movement.

Critical and Auxiliary
Literature

The Jew in the Lotus, by Rodger Kamenetz. New York: Harper-Collins, 1995. Contains a chapter and interview with Ginsberg shedding light on his Jewish/Buddhist mind-set.

Snapshot Poetics: A Photographic Memoir of the Beat Era. San Francisco: Chronicle Books, 1993. Photos by Ginsberg, who made a second career as a photographer, much like Burroughs and his painting. Great historic material plus his handwritten commentary. Ginsberg always archived and documented everything Beat, believing early on that he and his friends were going to be of importance. This collection of photos bears out his belief.

Jack Kerouac

The **Way** of
Spiritual **Spontaneity**

(*"Believe in the holy contour of life"*)

*J*ack Kerouac was a writer," says William Burroughs, adding that "The writer has been there or he can't write about it." Kerouac, of all the Beats, paid the closest attention to both his craft and subject matter: his own life. Although it is his name that is so often associated with drugs, sex and Bohemian lifestyles, in his own lifetime called the "King of the Beatniks," Kerouac himself remained solidly middle class and gentle in his outlook and behavior, a paradox that plagued not only him, but his readers as well.

There are times when the artist and the times intersect most fortuitously, and this was the case with Kerouac, who happened to be in the right place at the right time with the right words. Believing in a kinder world and of a truly devout nature, Kerouac was deeply troubled by what he perceived to be the excesses of the movement he helped father.

The lines between art and reality are often blurred in the pages of the Beats, especially so in Kerouac, who literally wrote a revolution into existence, sending millions of young people on the road in search of enlightenment and kicks. Again Burroughs on Kerouac: "Writers are, in a way, very powerful indeed. They write the script for the reality film. Kerouac opened a million coffee bars and sold a million pairs of Levis to both sexes. Woodstock rises from his pages."

Tragic misreadings or mistaken impressions of Kerouac and the Beats have led to many ruined lives and many shattered dreams; the earnest readers finding misinterpreted justification for any extreme in the pages of their works.

Read me as I wrote, Kerouac might say to us: in awe of the moment, in devotion to life. Then live out your own life as a sacrament. If you want to honor me, then survive and persevere. That's the Beat spirit.

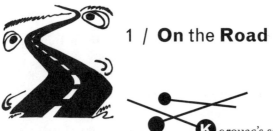

1 / **On** the **Road**

Kerouac's second published novel and the one that started the whole public phenomenon of the Beat era was *On the Road,* an account of his travels and adventures with pal Neal Cassady (Dean Moriarty in the book) in search of God, kicks and adventure. The book inspired countless young people to take to the road in search of Kerouac's America, an America that was already fast disappearing when he wrote the book, which also can be read as a sort of eulogy for a past buried beneath interstates and fast-food franchises and the relentless blue glow of the television (an image Kerouac uses in the book).

The trickle of on-the-roadsters become a torrent by the sixties, when millions of youth took to the road in fulfillment of Gary Snyder's prediction, recorded in *The Dharma Bums,* of a "rucksack revolution, millions of young people taking to the road."

The lure of the road is peculiarly American and figures prominently in our national mythology, from the Pilgrims to the astronauts. The relentless and restless search of Americans on the move became epitomized in its time by *On the Road.* If you're reading this book, then I can also assume you have logged your time on the road à la Kerouac, keeping in mind that there are as many types of roads as there are people.

On the following map or on one copied into your Beat Journal, trace your most memorable road trip, one that mattered the most to you on all levels: spiritual, emotional, sexual, financial, etc., so on and so forth—you get the idea.

Or perhaps you've a got a trip for each category under your belt. Trace those in colored pencil or crayon, a different color for each: a sexual odyssey, a spiritual pilgrimage, a financial flight. If you've got a lot of these, then draw them in as well (and maybe write your own damned book).

Instead of states such as Rhode Island, Iowa or Washington, you could label the areas of the country with the actual states you were in as you traveled: States of Insanity, Confusion, Bliss?

Also label the routes with the mode of transportation used (car, train, motorcycle, thumb . . . sorry, land travel only. Planes don't really provide an accurate experience of America other than courtesy copies of *USA Today* and the mid-flight PG movie).

> Look at your little finger, the emptiness of it is no different than the emptiness of infinity.

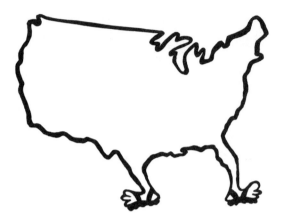

Every step outside your door takes you *on the road* in some way. Experience is up for grabs, anything is liable to happen. Be absolutely open to your local trips, even the ones to the mall, local weekend vacation spots, grocery shopping and driving the kids to school.

Make an effort this week to invest one of these short, usually mundane trips with deeper significance. Pretend, if you can, that it's the first time you've ever done this or been there. Try, if you can, to return home with at least one new bit of experience, information or insight.

Maybe introduce yourself to someone you take for granted beyond the register. Maybe stop at a small store you pass regularly, but have never patronized. Take a different route instead of the same old way you're used to. Walk instead of drive, if the distance is short enough. The "Sacred Drift" exercise by Hakim Bey near the end of this book is another excellent way to get *on the road.*

2 / **Word** Sketching

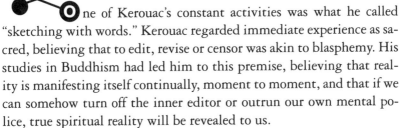

ne of Kerouac's constant activities was what he called "sketching with words." Kerouac regarded immediate experience as sacred, believing that to edit, revise or censor was akin to blasphemy. His studies in Buddhism had led him to this premise, believing that reality is manifesting itself continually, moment to moment, and that if we can somehow turn off the inner editor or outrun our own mental police, true spiritual reality will be revealed to us.

He quoted Buddhist sutras to that effect, saying, "All the Buddhas of the past, present and future have arrived at enlightenment by this very same method: the spontaneity of their radiance." Good Zen Catholic that he was, Kerouac also brought in the Bible to support himself in his assertion, quoting Mark 13:11: " . . . take no thought beforehand what ye shall speak, neither do ye premeditate; but whatsoever shall be given you in that hour, that speak ye: for it is not ye that speak, but the Holy Ghost." To do this with writing demanded a whole reeducation of self, a complete restoration of absolute faith in self-nature. His use of sketching with words was one method he developed to capture the flow of experience as it happened.

To sketch with words, one must be less a writer than an artist. Instead of using lines to capture a portrait, you instead use words. This will feel forced at first, and you will experience a certain amount of resistance to the process. This is the strength of your conditioning against spontaneous trust in yourself and your own responses. Sketching with words is the solvent used to eventually dissolve this artificial barrier to realization.

I'll provide an example of my own before you attempt this exercise. What follows is a word sketch of the computer I'm using to type this book:

beige-square-glowing blue screen like eye in the middle—words & letters appearing across screen like the pawprints of small animals in electronic snow—sound of clakclakclak plastic keys typing—light shine on corners of computer from window beside me—pink plastic brain model centered on top of Mac as decoration or icon—blue & black phone nestled at 30 degree angle beside keyboard—flashing cursor on off on off on off throbbing—page 31 at bottom of screen—time in purple at top right says 2:10—

You can do this with either a keyboard or a pencil or pen. I'd encourage you to do as Kerouac did and carry around a small pocket-size notebook or your Beat Journal to sketch spontaneously as the urge and opportunity arise.

The process is deceptively simple. Just begin writing or typing as fast as you possibly can (even if you're not as fast as Kerouac, who reached speeds up to 126 words per minute), describing what you are seeing or experiencing. If you pause to reflect, the censor/editor in your brain will start its nitpicking and revisions. Just write without regard to quality, grammar or punctuation, using dashes to separate thoughts or descriptions.

OK! Your turn. Get a pencil or pen and write your own spontaneous word sketch in the space below (or in your Beat notebook). Use what I call a "zencil." A zencil is a pencil without an eraser, like those big fat pencils you used as a child in school. There is no eraser because there is no mistake to be made! Also no possibility of correction. Everything is as it *is*. There can be no error!

Put your zencil on the first line below or on a blank page in your Journal and describe this open book as fast and freely as possible:

_____

_____

_____

_____

3 / **Rereading**

One of the ways in which Kerouac immersed himself in Buddhism was to read the *Diamond Sutra* every single day for a few months. Every time he read it, he obtained a new insight, a new angle. These days, a lot of people don't even read, much less *read the same thing on a daily basis.* That people can sit through countless reruns of inane sitcoms or car-chase movies and yet never return to a favorite book is unbelievable to most of us reading this book.

Yet we are as guilty as they are in their avoidance of literary repetition. We often refer in conversation to treasured and influential books in our lives, urging them on others. But how often have we really read them? How much of their import do we really remember? When was the last time we even cracked open that dusty Thoreau from high school or that Dr. Seuss from even earlier? If we are at all honest with ourselves, we will hang our heads in illiterate shame.

Just as repetition is a time-honored practice in Buddhism (the recitation of the same mantra or word over and over again), so too can the same spiritual technology be applied to the written word. By repeating your readings on a daily basis, subtle shifts in consciousness begin to appear. You realize that the text actually changes and grows along with your own grasp of it, reflecting your changing, evolving self like a mirror. What you read when younger will surely carry different meanings for you today. The same rule applies to reading something the next day! You are a daily process, not a finished product of the decades, and rereading is an excellent way to affirm this reality.

In addition, you are also literally reprogramming your mind with the repetition of the material, just as you learned your multiplication tables through constant practice. Kerouac found the *Diamond Sutra* particularly well suited to his own reprogramming. You, on the other hand, might choose material more congenial for your own situation. One book I did this with recently was *Oh, the Places You'll Go* by Dr. Seuss (a spiritual manual for adults cleverly disguised as a children's book). I read it daily for a month and felt a definite improvement in my self-trust.

Kerouac's own *Scripture of the Golden Eternity* is another one I've used for repeated readings throughout the last twenty years.

Your exercise is to pick something to read daily for at least the next week. A Beat text would be most appropriate for this exercise, something from one of the suggested anthologies.

Make sure it's a short piece or a poem, something you can accomplish in a half hour or less. Each time you read it, bring a clear mind to the process, attempting to wipe out any "I-already-know-what-this-is-about-ness" from your thinking. Just read. See what is reflected back.

Below is a record for this experiment that you can copy into your Journal, if you like. This is also a good time to reread what you've already done in the Journal! Now reread this section to make sure you've understood!

Text chosen to read _____
Record of days read: ☐ **1** ☐ **2** ☐ **3** ☐ **4** ☐ **5** ☐ **6** ☐ **7**
Short reaction to text (boredom, illumination, bewilderment, insight . . .):

Day 1 _____
Day 2 _____
Day 3 _____
Day 4 _____
Day 5 _____
Day 6 _____
Day 7 _____

4 / **Zen** Word **Game**

In a magazine article from 1960, Kerouac has this to say about the relationship of words and Zen: "Zen is like looking at a word for several minutes until it entirely loses all its meaning, like you take the word SQUARE, look at it, look at the 'Q', look at that 'S' on one end and 'E' on the other, and such silly combinations as 'QUA' or 'UARE'—Who invented it and what is the location of one's mind anyway?"

Try this with your own name. What does it really mean? What are words really? What is the thing that perceives the words and gives them meaning? Start with the "SQUARE" exercise and then do it again with your name. It takes three or four minutes of attention until you attain the state Kerouac describes, the one in which the word loses its meaning and starts to appear, well, rather *odd.*

SQUARE

Now write your own name in large block type and repeat the exercise. Come on now! Go ahead and do it. Don't be a square.

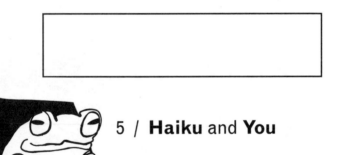

5 / **Haiku** and **You**

If you're like me, you probably grew up with a dread of poetry instilled in you by grade-school teachers who made you write haiku. Even if you wrote what you thought was a really cool one, the teacher made you go back and change it so that it conformed to the right number of syllables. You may remember that haiku are a Japanese form of short poem that classically (in Japanese) have only so many syllables per line.

A traditional Haiku is written in three short lines of seventeen syllables, the first line containing five syllables, the second seven, and the third five. The haiku usually contains a seasonal reference, mentioning snowflakes or blossoms, for example, and attempts to capture one of the aesthetic moods inherent in much Zen and Japanese art: *yugen* (mystery), *wabi* (poverty), *sabi* (isolation), and *aware* (impermanence).

The haiku becomes an object for meditation and should capture the feeling of immediacy and "now." Like Zen paintings with their large areas of white space and spare black brushstrokes, a haiku is more suggestive than descriptive, the bare bones and not a clothed, fleshed-out figure.

Kerouac, as one of the first contemporary Americans to introduce Zen forms into popular culture, wrote a great many haiku, finding them a wonderful way to sketch with words. The spontaneous and descriptive nature of the haiku form particularly appealed to him.

Void of Whole . . .
bursting to pop.

As in so many other literary conventions, Kerouac insisted that we break the rules in order to create something new. He insisted that we need not adhere to the traditional 5/7/5 form, but rather that a haiku should simply consist of three very short, succinct lines. After all, we write in words and English, and not in Asian ideographs.

As in all "poetry" and perhaps even more so in haiku, the poem is literally the bones of the experience you are describing. When someone reads or hears your haiku, they should be immediately transported to the experience, as though they were actually there.

The classic haiku most of us are familiar with is by the master haiku poet Basho:

An old pond
Splash!
A frog.

See what I mean? This haiku, hundreds of years old, transports you to the immediacy of experience, obviously a high value in the Beat spirit. Describing only what IS, we can share in Basho's life. Notice as well, that the 5/7/5 structure is missing in this English translation. The poem is even more pithy and direct.

Kerouac recorded an album in the fifties called *Blues and Haikus,* on which he jammed with two jazz saxophonists, Zoot Sims and Al Cohn. Kerouac would read one of his haiku, followed by a brief and improvised musical commentary by the musicians. As in all his writing, Kerouac brought his considerable feel for music, particularly jazz, to his writing.

The haiku he wrote reflect his always present concern that the moment is sacred and that any art growing out of the moment should be completely spontaneous and unrevised, like good jazz. Once a horn player has blown a riff during a live gig, he can't return to the moment and erase it. He goes with it; swings with it.

Writing haiku is a simple and pleasurable way to begin the actual process of writing and of entering this present moment. They don't have to be immortal pieces of art, can even in fact be viewed as throwaways. Writing them in the spirit of Kerouac becomes a meditative experience as well as a musical one. As Kerouac says in his "Belief and Technique for Modern Prose": "No time for poetry but exactly what is." One of my favorites by Kerouac:

In my medicine cabinet
The winter fly has died
Of old age.

In a separate section of your Beat Journal dedicated only to haiku, or on the lines below, write your first haiku. Time yourself, taking only about ten seconds at the most. In three short lines and with a minimum of thinking, describe what you see in front of you this very minute, no more and no less.

_____

_____

_____

On the next three lines, write a description of what you are hearing right now (same "rules"):

_____

_____

_____

For your final haiku exercise, write a description of your interior emotional state:

_____

_____

_____

Attempt to make haiku writing a habit. Instead of doodling at an office meeting, write a haiku describing some aspect of it. Write one each evening in your Journal encapsulating your day. Use the form as a warm-up exercise before writing letters (or books). Just swing with it like Kerouac, don't look back and by all means—break the rules. Here's my haiku:

Instructions for haiku:
This is the second line.
Here's the third.

6 / **Parlez-Vous?**

Kerouac said that as you age, you get more genealogical. In his case, it meant becoming more Catholic and French-Canadian. Both these factors influenced him greatly. French was his native language and he remained fluent in it all his years. His books are filled, sometimes drenched, with a longing for his boyhood and its lost innocence, and the details of the novels draw deeply on his native working-class Franco-American environment.

One of his last books, *Satori in Paris,* is an account of his travels to France and England in an effort to trace his name and lineage. As he became older, these things, he said, started to matter more and more.

I find this to be true of myself as I grow older, especially now that I have children. They wonder about who their ancestors were, how we got our names, and who they resemble from the remote (and not so re-mote) past.

Kerouac traced his last name through a few variations. Is your last name the one your ancestors had? Have you thought about it and how you came to be so named? My name, Ash, is really an Anglicization of the Norwegian name Aske. My middle name, Thomas, is again an English version of its original Thor (both names were my great-grandfather's as he came through Ellis Island). A nation of rootless immigrants longing for a lost past: Kerouac repeatedly returned to this theme throughout his work.

Part of the Beat spirit is a relentless, probing and unflinching examination of how we got to be who and where we are. This examination is extrapolated from the intensely personal to the national: Who are we as modern Americans, and even to the universal: Who are we as human beings? Nothing is taken for granted. Only then can we decide just who in the world we're going to be.

Create a genealogical section in your Beat journal for this exercise or use the spaces below. What is the origin of your family name?

_____

_____

If you don't know, find out from surviving relatives.

What is your ethnic/genetic makeup? Fill out this pie chart in percentage slices:

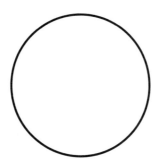

Name a trait you feel you received from each ethnic slice in your personality. Write the trait below the ethnic name in the pie. Here's my pie chart as an example.

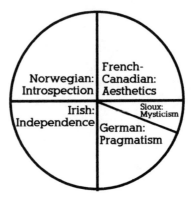

	French- Canadian: Aesthetics
Norwegian: Introspection	
Irish: Independence	Sioux: Mysticism German: Pragmatism

Would you like to get rid of any of your ethnically linked traits? Another possibility: consider changing your name back to its original form. That's the end of this exercise from Mel Thor Aske, experiencing a satori in Oslo.

7 / **Spontaneous** Writing

Kerouac outlined his suggestions for writing in a list of thirty items called "Belief & Technique for Modern Prose." The thirty things he lists not only are good advice for writers, but function as a Beat approach to life as well.

Several of them, however, are definitely exercise material, suitable for challenging our limits and conditioning. One of the most powerful ways to stretch ourselves is by deliberately ignoring what we've been taught, such as unlearning the correct way to write and to begin to right rong.

If we can begin to do this with such innocuous things as writing, perhaps it'll become easier to improvise with other areas of our lives. Transgressing literary conventions is a sign of your impending freedom.

Number thirteen of his list reads:

Remove literary, grammatical and syntactical **inhibition.**

For Kerouac, this dictum came to mean the elimination of much punctuation in his work. He attempted to write as fast as he felt and thought. Pausing for correct punctuation would have meant an annoying (and to Kerouac, sacrilegious) break in his stream of consciousness. To get around this, he indicated breaks in thought and structure with dashes rather than commas—periods or semi-colons—

Another reason for doing away with unnecessary punctuation was his method of writing with the breath. For this, he drew upon the experience of jazz musicians once again—A horn musician can play a line only as long as he has the breath to exhale through his instrument—after that he pauses to inhale and resume blowing—Hence the dash indicating a break—much like pauses in jazz—

In the section on Allen Ginsberg we discovered that our thoughts fairly precisely correspond to our breath—that is—the length of our breath determines the length of each thought—each successive thought—no matter how seemingly similar—is a new and slightly different take on the previous one in much the same way that jazz riffs build and improvise on previous ones—

In addition to the removal of punctuation, Kerouac played with both grammar and spelling—often substituting his own idiosyncratic inventions that accurately reflected the state of his mind—

In order to capture your states of consciousness, it becomes necessary to remove—as Kerouac says—these literary inhibitions—if you try this even once you'll experience a certain amount of resistance—our conditioning about making "mistakes" is so deep and pervasive that it takes a certain amount of practice to become spontaneous and free—practice to become spontaneous? Yes indeed and that is precisely what we'll attempt next—

Write a description of your workday in your Journal or below—this needn't be a fast riff à la Kerouac—what we're looking for here is the purposeful transgression of "literary, grammatical and syntactical inhibitions"—eliminate punctuation or make up new ones# mispel as many werds as you can or reespell them in a creative manner///grammar invert where possible:

bye riting thiz prozaik peeze abowt yr wurk : in a creeAtiV waaay, U kin BGin 2 cents th pozzibiliteez 4 knot only wryTing butt 4 yr LIFE AZ well::::::::: _____

_____

_____

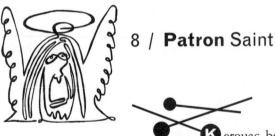

8 / **Patron** Saint

Kerouac believed in saints, not only the wild-eyed bohemian saints he described in his books, but dead ones as well. His favorite was Saint Thérèse of Lisieux, also known as the Little Flower. His boyhood church also was named after this saint and he would often attend the church when he returned to his hometown of Lowell, Massachusetts.

Saint Thérèse of Lisieux believed in the essential goodness of humanity and took as her guideline for redemption Jesus' words that one must become as a child in order to enter the kingdom of heaven. Kerouac, with his Buddhist beliefs coexisting with his Catholic ones and his "safe in heaven dead" philosophy, could only interpret this as meaning that one must maintain a pure, innocent and hopeful heart.

Doing this would open our eyes to the kingdom of heaven which we already inhabit. He never lost this touchingly sweet side of his nature and would often invoke Saint Thérèse to his defense. Like Kerouac, she also died at a very early age; Kerouac in his forties and she in her twenties.

Kerouac believed that Saint Thérèse showered him in his dreams with rose petals to lift his sadness. This idea was taken from the folklore of Kerouac's boyhood and it remained a comforting image to him throughout his life.

Patron saints have fallen on hard times these days. Even Saint Christopher, patron saint and protector of travelers, was "de-sainted" by the Vatican. Most of us, Catholic or not, are familiar with the little Saint Christopher medals people have in their cars. My wife, never a Catholic, credits a Saint Christopher medal with saving her life when she was in a car accident as a teenager. She carries it to this day, despite her Wiccan and Druidic ways. Whatever works.

Most often, our saints (which are really just inflated role models) are chosen for us by parents or indoctrinated into us by early religious or cultural education and we never question their prominence in our lives or their subtle effects on our subconsciousness. They cause us guilt, feelings of inadequacy and unattainability, be they religious, secular or fictional. We just know we'll never be big enough to fill their shoes.

To choose your own role models, to canonize your own saints, to people your own alternative pantheon, to, in short, create your own culture, is very much part of the Beat spirit. To change yourself, also change your templates for living, those mythical, larger-than-life beings who inspire and frighten us.

Do you have a patron saint? Some religious or historical figure who watches out for you and who you, at least spiritually and perhaps secretly, rely upon? There tends to be some embarrassment about this, as we feel that grown-ups should, as it says in Corinthians, leave childish things behind. Part of the Beat spirit is to reclaim our right to childish spontaneity and naïveté.

Do you have a patron saint from your childhood? A Catholic saint, a Hasidic rebbe like the Baal Shem Tov, a Hindu saint such as Sri Ramakrishna, a teacher like Krishnamurti? _____

If you don't have a "religious" figure, how about an historical figure? Increasingly, my patron saint is John Lennon. Important to me as a child and even more important as I age, Lennon is a saint whose presence I feel and invoke, a role model I can attempt to measure myself against at times, a figure who inspires and prods me into attaining all that I can.

For others, it might be Elvis, around whom an entire metaphysics has sprung up. People have even reported near-death encounters with Saint Elvis and he appears in contemporary movies as an occasional spirit guide (see the film *True Romance*).

Name a secular saint important to you: _____

If you've never thought about this, then choose a saint for yourself at this time. Read a book about his or her life and hang a picture of your saint in your home where you will see it regularly.

The saint I adopt: _____

Glue a picture of your saint on the inside front cover of your Beat Journal, both protecting and blessing it.

For lots of people these days, Kerouac himself has assumed saintlike proportions. Saint Kerouac? Why not?

9 / **Respect** Your **Mother**

he most important person in Kerouac's life was his mother, Gabrielle. Despite the public image of all his rootless wanderings, he always returned home to his mom, to a nice clean bed and home-cooked meal. She supported him through the years when he was writing and traveling, working in shoe factories to provide a home for him to return to.

His friends often complained bitterly about her control or joked about Jack, the King of the Beats, being a mama's boy. But Kerouac always revered her to the point of sainthood. Ginsberg, as well, has been shadowed by the specter of his mother and her mental illness and a lot of his significant work (*Kaddish, White Shroud*) is an examination of his relationship with his mother, as we have seen.

Kerouac even allowed his mother, it is said, to edit some of his later work that she found offensive, as well as to manage his money. He had promised his dying father that he would always take care of his mother, and this promise plagued him through the years when he was penniless and wandering. His filial obedience and deathbed promise never left him and he took his vow seriously.

As he descended into his inexorable and terminal alcoholism, he moved to Florida, taking his mother along with him, and she was present when he died. There at his birth (obviously) and there at his death, Gabrielle, for better or for worse, bracketed and, to a large extent, determined the shape of Kerouac's psyche and subsequent life. Never able to break wholly free of her long apron strings, he seemed to find a sort of freedom and security in his maternal bond and not the nooselike suffocation it might imply to others.

In any event, in true Kerouacian spirit, it is not for us to judge the rightness or wrongness or the latent psychological reasons for their relationship. "Just what is" is what Kerouac demanded of his work and just what is is what we'll take at face value: what the relationship was.

Many of us have troubled histories with our parents, and especially our mothers. Despite our histories and feelings about it all, the fact must always remain: we can no more break free of our mothers than we can of our own bodies. Hence, some sort of closure or peace with the situation becomes paramount in the Beat work of discovering who in the world we really are. Your mother is who you are in some very primal ways. Kerouac's was.

If your mom is living, do you get along with her? _____
Name one, just one, way in which you resemble your mother (a way you don't like to admit): _____
Name the one, just one, thing your mother taught you that you find the most valuable: _____
Have you called/seen/written her lately?_____

If that's not possible, because of her state of being "safe in heaven dead," as Kerouac puts it, or an estrangement, then pick someone else's mom, and do something nice for her in lieu of your own birth mother. And in memory of the mother of Saint Kerouac, as well.

You don't have to tell them the reason for your attention. Just do it. Make every day Mother's Day. Who knows? You may be a mother, too.

10 / Up All Night

The very basis of Beat spirit is its insistence that we share our experience with one another. In Kerouac's list of essentials, "Belief & Technique for Modern Prose," is number 24: "No fear or shame in the dignity of yr experience." Of all the Beat statements of "philosophy," this one in particular is the one I find the most liberating, nay, revolutionary, in its implications.

If we take the statement at face value and actually implement its spirit, we become freed of role models we can never live up to, reclaim all our repressed experience and ennoble our often desperately lived lives. Our lives become larger and more generous and not narrowly circumscribed by what Kerouac refers to as the toxins of "shame and fear." Only by this process of confessing and sharing with others like ourselves can we cleanse our spiritual and emotional systems of the fear poisons.

This sharing is at first a risky and threatening process, but soon becomes an exhilarating release. We find that what we thought were our dirty little secrets and irrational fears alone are common inheritances. We discover that although we might be mutants and aliens in certain ways, the entire human race is in some essential sense an alien (or alienated) life-form and that our individual mutations of spirit might possibly portend positive evolutionary states and not shameful, retrograde ones.

Much of the early Beat sharing took place in all-night marathons of excited intimate talking, often fueled, it is true, by drugs. A lot of the subsequent Beat texts are merely the reporting of what was consensually arrived at during these nocturnal explorations of the individual and group psyche.

Kerouac's novels, especially those placed in the Beat era, rather than his childhood, include these scenes of all-night yammering and talking. We've all experienced this, particularly when we're young, perhaps all-night college bull sessions or all-night confessionals with new lovers. Later on, we fall into predictable, even robotic behaviors and forget the lessons of those early and revelatory (and reveling) sessions.

Pick a night when you can sleep in the following morning with no guilt (another toxin to be gotten rid of during the session). Pick a partner (or partners) to go with you on this voyage between suns and spirits. Pick up food, drinks and music to make the verbal voyage more pleasurable. Pick a comfortable place (pad) to do it. (No TV, radio or other media are permitted. Don't answer the phone, either.)

As you talk through the night, attempt to maintain absolute honesty. Attempt to share your experiences as immediately as possible. Perhaps even allot blocks of time to each other so that you can truly listen, and not merely wait impatiently for your turn to talk.

If you run out of things to do or talk about, then do some of the exercises in *Beat Spirit,* using your Beat Journal as a common place to write, record and experiment.

And as Kerouac did with his friend Neal Cassady in *Visions of Cody,* you might consider tape-recording the night, making copies for yourself and your partner(s) as mementoes of the event.

If you do/did this, record the date and time frames in your Beat Journal or here: Date: _____ from _____ to _____.
Person(s) participating: _____

_____

Most important revelation (self or others) _____

Warning: This could potentially be the most dangerous exercise in this book. Be careful. Arrange your environment safely. Agree beforehand on limits and boundaries. And do it because you want to, not because I said so.

11 / **Torah** Bums

By this point in *Beat Spirit,* you've most likely noticed the Beat fascination with the exotic, foreign and even bizarre as means of self-exploration and expression. In forties and fifties America, it didn't take much to pass for different. Xenophobia and rampant smug nationalism assumed a cultural superiority, and any idea of cultural relativity was decades away (and ultimately contributed to by the spirit of the Beats).

Essentially a spiritual if not religious movement, the Beats' fascination with the possibilities of expanded consciousness naturally led them in the direction of seemingly exotic religions and philosophies. At that time, Buddhism was a little-known and stereotyped religion, a cartoon in this country exemplified by the image of staring at one's navel. The great flood of accurate translations and availability of qualified teachers was at least ten years away.

Ginsberg and Kerouac did their research into Eastern philosophy primarily in public libraries at first, swapping knowledge and ultimately teaching themselves meditation and other Buddhist spiritual technologies. Only later, when they traveled to the West Coast, did they encounter a more fully realized form of Buddhism in the persons of Gary Snyder, Alan Watts, Lew Welch and others. California's position as a Pacific Rim territory had naturally led to an early flowering of Buddhism in those parts, enriched as well by the large influx of Asian immigrants.

Burroughs, somewhat skeptical of Buddhism, nevertheless investigated it, as well as forms of yoga, Scientology (ultimately disenchanted) and the mystical forms of Islam, a natural for him since much of his early writing career was spent in Morocco and around his friends Paul and Jane Bowles, fellow expatriate writers. Paul Bowles, in particular, had delved deeply into Moroccan folklore and music.

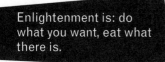

Enlightenment is: do what you want, eat what there is.

As a follow-up to the successful publication of *On the Road,* Kerouac quickly penned *The Dharma Bums,* an account of his meeting with Gary Snyder (Japhy Ryder in the book). *The Dharma Bums,* like much of Kerouac's subsequent work, is deeply informed by his studies of Buddhism. For many of us, reading Kerouac was one of our first introductions to any sort of Eastern philosophy.

Kerouac had found an easy fit with Mahayana Buddhism, correlating it to his native Catholicism, eventually writing much material centered around his interpretations, including the yet-to-be-published *Some of the Dharma.*

Kerouac's idiosyncratic interpretation of Zen became a sort of shorthand for Beat. The two words *Zen* and *Beat* were to become inevitably linked in the public mind. Alan Watts, whom we will look at later in this book, wrote a critical essay examining the phenomenon of Beat Zen in the late fifties.

This exercise is not suggested so much by the Beats' evangelization of Buddhism as by the spirit in which they eagerly explored other forms of spirituality and made them their own. Make it a point to investigate a belief system radically different from your own, one with which you are not familiar. Perhaps one that has intrigued or even repelled you.

You needn't convert. To do this, follow the Beats' example and go to the library or bookstore. I basically grew up as a Zen Buddhist because of my adolescent reading of the Beats, eventually becoming a Zen teacher. In the past couple of years, I've undertaken a study of Judaism, particularly Hasidism and Kabbalah. I've found, as did Kerouac between his Zen and Catholicism, many points and practices in Judaism that deepen my own Zen spirituality.

If you're Jewish, you might want to investigate Zen. If you're Protestant, perhaps Rastafarianism. If you're Catholic, perhaps Islam. If you're Muslim, perhaps Wicca. If you're Pagan, perhaps Atheism. If you're an atheist, perhaps Vedanta. If you're Buddhist, perhaps Theosophy. See the possibilities?

The assignment is simply this: Read at least one introductory book about a religion alien to your upbringing or current practice (or nonpractice). Make sure you do it in a spirit of fun and anticipation. Do it in the spirit of Kerouac. Remember, you're a Dharma (or Torah) Bum, just passing through whatever system you're investigating, not figuring on settling down, looking for a spiritual handout.

Record your new religious experiences below, or keep track of them in what has hopefully become, for you, a personal Bible: your Beat Journal.

The religion/belief system I chose to expose myself to: _____

Book used: _____

Other activities: _____

Things I found useful for my life _____

_____

If you like some of what you discover, then attempt some sort of further contact, perhaps attending a service or seeking a teacher in that tradition. Keep an open mind in some respects and a closed one in others. You don't have to buy everything they'll be selling you. *Mazel tov!*

12 / **Old** Flames

One of Kerouac's nicknames was "the Great Rememberer." Apparently possessed of a prodigious memory, he would quietly (and sometimes not so quietly) observe at parties or meetings and later be able to write in exacting detail everything he had witnessed.

This memory extended far back into his past and became the storehouse for many of his books about his upbringing. Basically a sentimental and even nostalgic person, Kerouac, in many of his books, painted longing and sad portraits of his hometown and family. Despite all the media about the Beats' attacks on morality and family values, they were, as we have seen with Ginsberg and Burroughs, essentially very old-fashioned.

The Beats lamented the passing of an America they grew up in, an America where models of normality disseminated by the media had not yet seeped into the national consciousness, an America before the regimentation of war economy and corporate bottom lines, in short a gentler and slower America, the sort lamented as far back as Whitman and Emerson. Whitman himself was pessimistic about America's future, seeing his beloved country taking the narrower of two roads that he saw forking in his own time.

This is an exercise, then, in remembering: remembering golden sunset ocean glows, the cold snap of fall air and the tentative feel of your first kiss. In *Maggie Cassady,* Kerouac brings to life his first real love and girlfriend from high school. An essentially sweet and innocent book, *Maggie Cassady* runs counter to much of the public perception of the King of the Beatniks.

List ex-flames or lovers by name in your Journal. Following their name, list a color you associate with them and next a season. Finally, an emotional state they call up in you as you do this exercise: melancholy, bittersweet regret, soft smiles, what? This is the effect that Kerouac's memories have upon us when we read them: the soft itch of a girl's wool sweater, the autumnal gray of a rainy sky, the faint brushing of lips. These amorphous feelings are most often the strongest memories we retain, having forgotten dates, sequence of events and so forth. I'll go first. Remember:

Name: Karen

Color: Brown and green

Season: Winter in Canada

Inner State: Smiles, Freedom

Name: _____

Color: _____

Season: _____

Inner State: _____

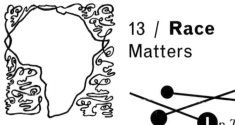

13 / **Race**
Matters

In *The Subterraneans,* Kerouac details a brief affair he had with an African-American woman. This interracial dating and marriage was acceptable pretty much only in so-called Bohemian circles, since in mid-century America it was actually outlawed in many places.

The Beats, while not the first subculture to cross racial lines, certainly drew heavily upon African-American experience, from language to music. Kerouac, while often guilty of sentimentalizing people of color, nevertheless found himself drawn to them repeatedly. Another novel, *Tristessa,* is about his romance with a Mexican woman.

His disgust with white, technological consumer society and his innate nostalgia for the past led to his sincere fascination with what he called the *fellaheen,* an Arabic word for people of the earth, the common people, and especially people of color. His own blue-collar, working-class sentiments also probably tipped the balance of his sympathies to those left behind or cast to the side.

The influence of black jazz musicians on Beat culture cannot be underestimated. The improvisatory and spontaneous nature of jazz particularly appealed to Kerouac, and musicians such as Charlie Parker and Dizzy Gillespie became role models for not only his life, but his writing as well, as he attempted to write the same way that jazz musicians riffed.

If you're not African-American, do you have any friends of color? If you do, have they introduced you to any aspects of black culture that you find valuable in your own life?

If you don't have any black friends or family in your life, why not? Think about this. Is it an accident? A result of your chosen neighborhood? So why not try the following activities to broaden your understanding and experience:

Viewing: Watch an evening of "black" television, such as BET (the Black Entertainment Network on cable) or rent films for a week by black directors such as Spike Lee, John Singleton, Gordon Parks Jr. or Melvin Van Peebles.

Listening: Most cities have at least one black nightclub or music venue where you can still hear jazz being explored and evolved. We have one here, one where my wife and I have a wonderful time. If you're unable to do this, purchase a CD of black music on the recommendation of a black friend or salesperson.

This week, put your home or car radio on an "exclusively" black station, if one exists in your area. In Providence, where I live, the local college radio station devotes all of its Sunday programming to what they call "The 360 Degree Black Experience in Sound," a day during which I can hear gospel, rap and public-affairs interviews.

Reading: Most cities also have a black community newspaper. Providence does. White as I am, I freelanced for them for a time. Pick up a copy of your local black paper and see what's going on with your fellow citizens.

The next time you're at the magazine rack, pick up a copy of *Ebony, Jet* or another black publication such as *Vibe,* along with your *Rolling Stone* or *Newsweek.*

Besides the usual classics by black authors that you should already have read (*Manchild in the Promised Land, Soul on Ice, Autobiography of Malcolm X, Native Son*), there are lot of current black writers out there waiting to speak to you about race, such as bell hooks and Cornel West. Ask your local bookseller for their African-American section or for recommendations.

In subsequent sections of *Beat Spirit,* you'll also find black Beat authors such as Bob Kaufman and LeRoi Jones (Amiri Baraka), who embody the black Bohemian spirit. If you're black, you probably didn't need to do any of these exercises, but will want to begin exploring these personalities. Other black Beat writers such as Ted Joans are also worth exploring.

If you do at least a couple of these activities, I'll bet you've got some black acquaintances by now, if not actual, then intellectually. If you want to be Beat, you've gotta be black as well. At least a little bit.

14 / Jocks

A major and early influence on Kerouac's psyche was not, as is commonly thought, either Buddhism or books, or drugs or dharma-bumming. Quintessential American that he was, Kerouac was, at heart, a jock. As a high school football star,

Kerouac found sports a way out of the working-class fate that awaited him in his hometown of Lowell, Massachusetts.

Enabled to attend Columbia on a football scholarship, Kerouac would never have met Burroughs and Ginsberg in New York without his gridiron stardom, and you and I wouldn't be here at this moment discussing the cultural revolution that resulted.

Not usually associated with the Beats, sports, nevertheless, has a role in the Beat experience. In his first novel, *The Town and the City,* Kerouac writes some incredible and indelible descriptions of his big football game, the one that propelled him into both a scholarship and the kingship of the Beats.

This is the sports section of *Beat Spirit,* its steamy locker room if you will, where you are invited to snap each other with wet towels and give the high five. Being corny, being athletic, being a jock: these things, too, are part of the Beat spirit.

Did/do you play a sport? What is/was it? What sport seems the best metaphor for your life (the mannered, slow walk of golf or the frenzied, masochistic rush of marathons; the straining immobility of weight lifting or the contorting and graceful curve of gymnastics—what?):

If you did this exercise, you are entitled to your Beats sports letter. You can sew it proudly on your black turtleneck or paste it in your Journal, which is fast becoming your Beat yearbook, as well. Here it is:

B

15 / **Comic** Book

Popular culture was an enormous influence on all the Beat writers. Movies, recordings, radio shows and serials and even comic books are some of the raw materials out of which they have woven their own unique tapestry of American culture.

Kerouac especially is finely attuned to the influence of popular culture on his psyche. In his work, he speaks lovingly and fondly of attending Saturday-afternoon movie matinees and of listening to old radio serials. Beat, he says, is composed of these things and their attitudes. Prefiguring the Pop art movement of the early and mid-sixties, the Beat spirit recognized the iconic and ideological power of art for the masses.

Rather than try to escape into the rarefied regions of "literature" and high art, removed from common and accessible experience, the Beat spirit embraced the common and even the repulsive and mundane in its pursuit of truth and possibilities.

One popular form that caught Kerouac's attention as a young person were the cartoons in newspapers and comic books. His early efforts at writing included his own illustrations, usually in cartoon-strip form. One piece of his work that has been widely reproduced is called "Doctor Sax and the Deception of the Sea Shroud." Drawn when Kerouac was an adult, it alludes to both his novel *Dr. Sax* and a character by which he was haunted as a child: the Sea Shroud.

The character of Dr. Sax is based upon his childhood fantasies and fears of a mysterious man who lurked around his hometown. The book itself is very unlike his other novels and filled with palpable terror and hallucinatory imagery, much like that experienced by a child with an active imagination.

The cartoon he drew of Dr. Sax as an adult is amateurish and crude compared to professional standards, but that really wasn't the point. Kerouac's ethic of trying anything unashamedly and freely led him to experiment with this form of cartooning. Dr. Sax, and the cartoon illustrating it, are unabashed celebrations of what the world regards as some very childish things.

In panels you draw in your Journal, celebrate one of your American heritages. Draw your own comic as Kerouac did, connecting to the dense and fertile underbelly of American culture (and your own newsprint-sodden childhood). Subject? If you can't think of one, then maybe an incident at work or involving your family. Make it personal and based upon your experience.

Don't worry about your art ability or absolute lack of it. As I said, Kerouac's was not all that polished. This isn't for publication in the Sunday paper. This is for you and maybe your friends. This is about you. *This is a way to discover who you really are.* It may be a funny paper, but there's nothing laughable about doing it. Have fun.

16 / **Better** to **Burn** Out . . .

. . . than fade away, sang Neil Young. My, my, hey, hey, haven't we heard this before? In one of his most oft-quoted pieces from

On the Road, Kerouac says that the only ones for him are the mad ones, the ones who burst and flare across the sky like roman candles.

Sadly and prophetically enough, Kerouac himself was one of those who flared across the American sky, burning out alcoholically at the age of forty-seven in front of a TV set in Florida in 1969. It has been said that America kills its heroes and then canonizes them; the hall of fame of those who died young, of those who flared majestically and then im- or exploded in public grows longer every year: Kerouac, his friend Neal Cassady, F. Scott Fitzgerald, James Dean, Marilyn Monroe, Joplin, Hendrix, Morrison, Kurt Cobain. The list is too long and sad.

"Hope I die before I get old," sang the Who in the sixties, composing a motto (or epitaph) for an entire generation of promising young artists. In our examinations of Burroughs and Ginsberg, both elder statesmen of Bohemia and entitled to senior-citizen discounts on the purchase of their own books, we were presented with models for aging, growing and surviving within a conscious countercultural framework.

It behooves us to pay attention to these elders who have discovered ways to hold on to their visions and integrity, people who became more open and radical as they aged and not more entrenched and conservative, as is the usual path for people as they grow more, ahem, mature (Kerouac himself grew increasingly entrenched and reactionary in his thinking as he aged, even to the point of renouncing the movement he had helped found and turning on his old friends). Using Kerouac's reversal of the Four Noble Truths technique, perhaps we can begin to sing, "Hope I get old before they die."

Accept loss forever.

You, I'm sure, have friends or family who exploded across the nighttime sky of your life, only to burn out and fade away all too soon. Make a list of them in your Journal or below, eulogizing them by writing a few words that describes their life, a word such as the "incandescence" of a roman candle:

Name	Life Qualities
My example: Curt	**Brooding, absent, smiling, enigmatic**
Yours:	

Now visualize these people had they lived. What would they look like, in your mind's eye? Speaking out loud (if you're comfortable doing this) tell them the three most important things they've missed since they've been gone, personal things about yourself or their friends and family, not elections and the like, but joyous, life-affirming things such as births, surprising careers, and marriages.

In doing this, you not only honor and remember the dead, but remind yourself as well of how very good it is not to explode and burn out, but to hang around, lighting the way.

17 / **Sea** Sounds

At the end of *Big Sur*, his harrowing book detailing his descent into alcoholic madness and delirium tremens, Kerouac appends a poem entitled "Sea." The location was, of course, in Big Sur, California, that wildly rocky, mystical and cliff-hanging section of coast made famous by Henry Miller, Esalen Institute and many other countercultural luminaries.

Kerouac was staying at City Lights publisher Lawrence Ferlinghetti's Big Sur cabin when he underwent the experiences he chronicles in the book. His constant companion during his stay there was the always present roar of the nearby Pacific Ocean. As we've seen in previous sections, Kerouac's main operative belief about both writing and spirituality was accurate apprehension and reporting of the moment, that is, the attainment of a Zen state of mind in which one simply reported things as they are, or as in Kerouac's words: "No time for poetry but what is."

Nearly at the end of his physical and metaphysical ropes at Big Sur, and in the throes of a crisis brought on by sudden fame and alcohol, Kerouac turned at long last to listening to and recording the primordial sounds of nature, perhaps the closest thing we have to the voice of God; especially the ancient and soothing sound of ocean waves.

In the poem, Kerouac attempts to record the sound of the sea near Ferlinghetti's cabin. In a poem that runs twenty-three pages, he intersperses stream-of-consciousness English-language fragments with the sounds of the ocean represented by syllables such as these: "posh l'abascroosh . . . Ker plotsch. . . . Shoo-Shaw-Shirsch . . ."

Michael McClure, also a character and participant in the happenings at Big Sur, was already experimenting with these seemingly nonsensical syllables in the form of what he called "beast language," an attempt to recapture the pure sound beyond the limits of words (a somewhat Burroughsian idea: sounds as pure expression, drained of their "meaning" and symbolism).

> Thalatta—Merde—Marde
> de mer—mu mer—mak a
> vash
> The ocean is the mother

The section on McClure will include a closer examination of this sort of expression, but it's significant that the Beat writers had pushed language to the limits of what they thought it could accomplish and took the final (and logical) step into pure sound, something that kindred Zen spirit and avant-garde composer John Cage was doing with his "musical" compositions that utilized random found sound rather than organization and artificial structure.

To move beyond language, to reach what Burroughs calls "the end of words," become a conduit for earth spirit, and accurately report things as they are, please do as Kerouac did and mimic sounds of nature. How to do this?

You can either first write them down in your Journal and then read from them, or simply start vocalizing aloud with no prepared script. Some ideas: sounds of the ocean, birds, a storm (thunder, lightning, then rain), wind blowing through trees. Be creative. Write/perform a nature sound poem for at least three minutes.

Record your nature sounds in your Journal or below:

Title (Sounds in imitation of: **)** _____

Sounds: _____

_____

_____

Again, as with all the exercises in this book, this will prove most effective and fun when done with others, perhaps as a dinner party icebreaker or as an alternative in your family to nightly videos. Kids love this one and so will you. Who are you? You are first of all natural. Howl like Ginsberg. Roar like McClure. Attack the language like Burroughs. Whooosh shoo whoosh caw caw like Kerouac. Thunder and pour like yourself.

18 / **Be** in **Love** with **Yr** Life

s number four of Kerouac's list "Belief & Technique for Modern Prose" and possibly the best piece of advice he ever wrote. As we've seen throughout *Beat Spirit* and particularly with Kerouac, it is the dignity and truth of one's own experience that mattered most to the Beats (and, I hope, to you as well).

In a world increasingly dominated by secondhand, vicarious experience provided by TV, videos and film, reclaiming our own lives the way we choose to live them is the most subversive, transgressive and ultimately liberating possibility.

Who are we? We are what and who we love, and we are the *way* in which we choose to love. If we don't love our own lives and live them as though we meant it, then we have lived life as spectators, consumers and victims.

Victory is attained when we fall deeply in love with all that we experience and learn to flow with it, spontaneously, not afraid to make it up as we go, improvising wildly like a jazz musician, throwing away predictable scripts written for us by religion, business or state. "Be in love with yr life," demands Kerouac. Being in love with our lives will turn out to be all the truth, God and meaning we will ever need. That is all that the Beat spirit demanded.

And it is also the last request I have of you in this sad and sweet section about Jean-Louis Kerouac, a working-class boy who had his heart broken by the world, confirming his belief that life is, indeed, sorrow. His spirit, however, remains defiantly at large. Capture a bit of it as you list the things you love about your life:

I love: _____

1) _____

2) _____

For the next couple of days after this exercise, ask other people the same question: What things do they love most about their lives? They might be a bit taken aback at first by such a strange and forward question, but generally will warm to the subject quite fast.

Their responses might even suggest areas of your own life that you've overlooked. You can love things about their lives, too, once they've shared so openly, just as Jack Kerouac did.

A Selected **Jack** Kerouacography

Books

Big Sur. New York: McGraw Hill, 1981. A harrowing account of Kerouac's alcoholism. Also contains "Sea" poem.

Desolation Angels. New York: Perigee, 1980. Best firsthand account of Beat years, friends and travels.

The Dharma Bums. New York: Viking, 1972. Introduced Zen Buddhism and Gary Snyder to America.

Good Blonde and Others. San Francisco: Grey Fox, 1993. Collection of Kerouac's essays, columns and oddities. Contains his "Essentials of Spontaneous Prose."

Heaven and Other Poems. San Francisco: Grey Fox Press, 1987. Contains Kerouac's Doctor Sax comic.

Maggie Cassady. New York: Penguin, 1993. His sweetest book, about a high school crush.

Mexico City Blues. New York: Grove Press, 1985. Jazz and Buddhist inspired poems.

On the Road. New York: Penguin, 1985. The book that started it all.

The Portable Jack Kerouac Reader, edited by Ann Charters. New York: Penguin, 1995. The best buy and most representative sampler for anyone, especially the neophyte.

The Scripture of the Golden Eternity. San Francisco: City Lights, 1994. Long unavailable, the best Beat take on Buddhism.

Selected Letters, edited by Ann Charters. New York: Viking, 1995. The raw material of Kerouac's books.

Visions of Cody. New York: McGraw Hill, 1989. Acclaimed as a masterpiece and largely unread. The sourcebook for *On the Road.*

Videos/Films

Heartbeat. A fairly decent Hollywood look at Kerouac and Neal and Carolyn Cassady, cameo by Jan Kerouac.

Kerouac: A Documentary. Available at most video rentals.

Recordings

The Jack Kerouac Collection (Rhino WordBeat). Three CDs and booklet, includes all of Kerouac's fifties LPs as well as live TV appearances. Kerouac is a joy to listen to, his phrasing and rhythms naturally jazz-like. Listening to him, you learn how to read his books like a music score.

Kerouac kicks joy darkness (Ryko Voices). Tribute CD with music and readings by Lydia Lunch, Johnny Depp, Joe Strummer, Matt Dillon, Michael Stipe, and Kerouac himself.

Biographies

Desolate Angel, by Dennis McNally. New York: McGraw Hill, 1979. Not only a biography, but a history of the Beat Generation as well.

Memory Babe, by Gerald Nicosia. New York: Penguin, 1983. Critically acclaimed and exhaustive biography.

Kerouac, by Ann Charters. San Francisco: Straight Arrow Books, 1973. The first biography of Kerouac and still the clearest and easiest read by someone who knew him and the scene. Charters remains his most dedicated editor and a dependable partisan of Beat literature.

Auxiliary and Critical
Literature

Jack's Book, by Barry Gifford and Lawrence Lee. New York: Penguin, 1979. An oral history of Kerouac and the Beat Generation era.

Kerouac at the Wild Boar, edited by John Montgomery. San Anselmo, Calif.: Fels & Firn Press, 1986.

The Kerouac We Knew, edited by John Montgomery. San Anselmo, Calif.: Fels & Firn Press, 1987.

The two books above contain personal memories of Kerouac by friends, plumbers and bartenders. Valuable for a nonprofessional, very human look at the real man.

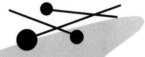

Exodus: **West** Coast

Burroughs eventually departed New York for years of self-imposed exile in Tangiers, Paris and Mexico, returning to the United States in the early seventies. Kerouac and Ginsberg traveled extensively as well, visiting Burroughs in Morocco to help assemble the manuscript of *Naked Lunch.* Both men also put in their time in Mexico, a favored Beat destination, admired for its authenticity and cheapness of living, and liberal, if not nonexistent, vice and drug laws.

Ginsberg, after leaving New York, moved to Berkeley to attend the state university. It was in the Bay Area of San Francisco that the transcontinental Beat deal was made, when he fell in with the poets and personalities of what has come to be called the San Francisco Renaissance.

Dating back to salons held by Bohemian elder statesman Kenneth Rexroth, the Renaissance was exploring many of the same ideas as had the small group in New York. San Francisco, with its long tradition of tolerance and being a safe haven for the eccentric and adventurous, was an ideal breeding ground for the seeds of a nascent counterculture.

Just as New York's Greenwich Village had become the "hip" locale for East Coast Beats, San Francisco's North Beach area became the West Coast destination for the world-weary and woebegone Beats. In short order Ginsberg met Gary Snyder, then a student at the university who was about to depart for an extended stay in Japan to study Zen Buddhism.

Ginsberg also met and befriended the young Michael McClure, born in 1932 in Kansas, who had originally come west to study painting, but had instead turned to poetry and the Bohemian culture he encountered.

Ginsberg, in typical fashion, was soon at the center of all this activity and quickly organized a public reading of a group of poets that included himself, Snyder, McClure and others who went on to Beat fame. Kerouac had by now made the scene and was present the night that the famous "Six Gallery" reading was held in December of 1955.

It was that night that Ginsberg gave his first public reading of *Howl.* Ferlinghetti and others present have said that they were aware that poetry had been changed forever. That night marks the public introduction of the Beat movement, as well as the marriage of the East and West Coast groups. Ginsberg and Kerouac didn't settle in San Francisco, but returned often. Kerouac in particular was deeply influenced by Snyder's Buddhism and recounts those experiences in his second published book, *The Dharma Bums.*

Lew Welch, an old friend of Snyder's, returned to the West Coast from Chicago and became active in the poetry scene. Alan Watts was also an early participant in forming the unique West Coast Beat consciousness with his lectures on Zen and his friendships with most of the writers.

These West Coast Beats form a consciousness as unique and independent as that of their East Coast brothers and sisters. The West Coast's natural beauty and its proximity to Asia and still-living Native cultures gave it a definitive flavor as distinct as the cynical, urban and intellectual thrust that the New Yorkers brought. Together, the two styles meshed to form what we identify today as the Beat spirit.

Gary Snyder

The **Way** of Spiritual **Craftsmanship**

(*"In our minds so be it."*)

An attractive and rugged combination of scholar and lumberjack, Gary Snyder grew up in the woods of Oregon and worked in forestry as a young man. Born in 1930 and attending Reed College in Oregon, he had become friends with Philip Whalen and Lew Welch, both destined to become pivotal West Coast Beats in their own rights.

Snyder, in retrospect, seems the very archetype of the sixties hippie, with his interests in Zen, Native American culture and ecology. It was his natural cultural "template" that so impressed both Ginsberg and Kerouac when they encountered him. In meeting him in the fifties, they had seen the face and spirit of the sixties and beyond.

He returned to the United States in the late sixties after having lived as a Zen student for a number of years in Japan, just in time to contribute to the changes that were sweeping the country. Appearing at the Human Be-In in 1967 in San Francisco's Golden Gate Park along with Ginsberg and McClure, Snyder took his rightful place as elder hip statesman of the hippie movement he had helped inspire.

Snyder's concerns range from craftsmanship and a strong do-it-your-self ethic that helped inspire the "back-to-the-earth" movement to examinations of female deity in his later work. In his essays and poetry examining the necessity of wilderness, both actual and mental, Snyder becomes an eloquent spokesman for the natural world.

Gary Snyder continues to write forcefully in defense of the environment, tours nationally, continues his Zen practice, and teaches writing at a college in California, as well as maintaining a homestead in the northern part of the state. A natural heir of Thoreau, his advice is now sought by elected officials and pundits alike on matters both artistic and environmental.

1 / **Non-Human** Minds

Snyder's world is this very world that we live in, that is, the world of nature. Throughout his writings and philosophy, he continually returns to his insistence that we reenter into an immediate and reciprocal relationship with natural processes. Humans once had this relationship, he says, but it has been torn asunder by the recent rise of Western technology, nationalism and religions that not only justify, but command man's domination of nature. Hence our alienation and spiraling toward ecological disaster.

One of the ways in which we can reconnect with nature and our own place in it is to begin to communicate with what Snyder calls non-human minds; minds and forms of consciousness that have been marginalized and even exterminated by the human assumption of superiority and its consequent hatred of non-human forms.

In the past, shamans, witches and yogis were able to communicate with non-human minds, entering the consciousness of animals and plants. Snyder quotes Chan-jan, a Chinese monk, to the effect that even inanimate things possess the Buddha-nature. In one of his poems, Snyder takes America to task for never having given mountains, rivers, animals and other non-humans a vote.

Snyder asks, "How would one learn this sweet interspecies attention and patience? What practice would tune us in not just to dreams but to their songs?" How can we become proxy voters and begin to bring equal representation to the wilderness? The way of the shaman is one such way, he says.

The shaman regards the wilderness, or the area outside man's domination, as the actual unconscious. By locating the unconscious, a basically "spiritual" domain, in nature, the shaman becomes capable of communicating with what is essentially her or his true nature. The Cahuilla Indians, says Snyder, say that if you listen closely enough you can hear a little voice from plants. Poetry is another way of communication with the natural world, a way of opposing the forces that have sought the destruction of natural human interaction with non-human beings.

To get in touch with your larger, unconscious self, the silent self that has been shouted down by modern alienated machine society, attempt to listen to some of these "little voices" that non-humans speak in. Find a quiet, secluded spot, perhaps in a park or state forest. Sit down near a plant or tree. Quiet your thoughts, close your eyes, and become sweetly attentive to the life-force beside you. Do you "hear" anything? Place your hand slightly on the entity. This "hearing" might possibly take the shape of emotions, images or even physical feelings that you receive, even almost imperceptibly.

Listen with all of you. Listen *to* all of you. Then record your observation in your Journal or below.

The non-human I listened to: _____
What I "heard": _____

The "voice" you hear might be a subtle feeling—emotional, physical or spiritual—perhaps a tingling of the hairs on your arm, a slowing of your heartbeat, vague and unfamiliar mental images that float through your mind, a slight breeze that springs up out of nowhere, a sudden drop in air temperature.

Don't dismiss anything like these as products of your "imagination," wishful thinking or coincidence. Just pay attention. Non-humans speak in non-human ways. Humans can learn to listen if they use their entire being as an open ear.

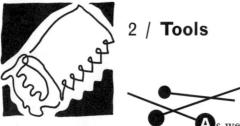

2 / Tools

As we've seen in the previous exercise, Snyder's spiritual vision is anchored around some very concrete and everyday metaphors. Trained in Japan in Zen Buddhism as a young man, Snyder epitomizes the Zen ethic of discovering the sacred in the seemingly mundane and in its insistence that a day without work is a day without eating.

Snyder makes his spiritual visions come alive not only in the forms of poetry and prose, but in actual building and craftsmanship as well. His own home in California's Sierra Nevada, Kitkitdizze, was lovingly built by him and friends years ago. One of his hobbies is maintaining and repairing things around his homestead.

Snyder's care for tools is well known and he owns several tools for taking care of each tool. He calls virtually everything he owns "tools" and he prizes the utilitarian value not only of actual tools, but of metaphysical ones as well. Even his choice of Zen Buddhism, a very practical and present-based technique, reflects his interest in do-it-yourself sustenance and fine craftsmanship.

How we believe and live will inevitably be reflected in the products of our hands as well as our minds. Sloppy, careless use of tools, be they beliefs or axes, will only result in sloppy, unattractive and potentially dangerous craftsmanship, be it a house, furniture or ideology. Snyder's Zen attention to detail and process informs nearly everything he attends to, and we would do well to attend to these lessons as well.

We're looking at an awful lot of metaphysical tools in this book, so let's take a well-deserved break from our work and attend to the care of tools. Not all our exercises in so-called spirituality need be high-flown imaginings. Snyder's example teaches us that spiritual satisfaction and even insight can be found in such simple acts as woodworking and small engine repair.

By giving these acts our full and undivided attention, we invest them with the dignity of a job well done and accomplished. Once again, something considered "old-fashioned" rears its head in *Beat Spirit,* a book ostensibly about crazy beatniks and reckless abandon. Burroughs's MYOB attitude, Kerouac's sentimentality and Snyder's craftsmanship all point to a Beat insistence on some eternal values in human consciousness.

Take a breather and do this very simple thing:
Find a tool you use regularly in your work or hobby, such as a hammer or pair of vise grips. Commonplace tools that serve us well and we take for granted make good subjects for this exercise: your lawn

mower, electric drill, a rake or even a coffee grinder. Spend at least five minutes cleaning, examining and oiling it or whatever is needed for proper maintenance. Perhaps your computer's keyboard needs a good cleaning.

When doing these activities just get lost in the form and function of the tool, appreciating its utility to you. Do not make it into a fetish or art object. Appreciate it for what it is. When you're through, return it to its proper storage area. If you're like me and most people, you'll have to search to find that tool, because of our habit of undervaluing its place in our life.

This time, make a special place for it and always return it there. You know the rules: If it's dirty, clean it. If you take it out, put it back. If you break it, fix it. Now you know that these are actually Beat rules for living a well-organized and craftsmanlike life.

The tool I maintained: _____

Place I store it: _____

(Now if you forget where you put it, you can refer back to this book or your Journal. Pretty useful, huh? *Beat Spirit* is a tool. Please take care of it.)

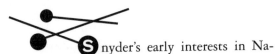

3 / Find Your Place

Snyder's early interests in Native American culture and religion prefigured an entire generation's interest in the same subject, and predated as well the modern uprisings of Native Americans in defense of their lands and ways of life. Growing up as he did in the Pacific Northwest around Native peoples, his interest was a natural one that informed his deep and abiding advocacy of wilderness and older, earth-based spiritual paths.

His college thesis (and subsequent book), *He Who Hunted Birds in His Father's Village,* is an examination of a Haida myth. In much of his poetry and philosophy, he freely includes images and ideas from native culture and thought, alongside his pervasive Zen attitudes.

His Pulitzer Prize–winning collection of poetry, *Turtle Island,* is for the most part dedicated to examining this concern about place, tradition and our roles in it. The title *Turtle Island* is the native name for North America, referring to the myth that the land sits upon the back of an enormous turtle. Snyder also dates his work in an earth-based fashion, eschewing the A.D. system commemorating the death of a Middle Eastern messianic cult leader. Instead, he dates his work in its distance from the first cave drawings, that is, the first known creative activity of humans.

The idea of place looms large in Snyder's worldview. The sense of connectedness and rootedness are values that he esteems highly. Lamenting the fact that modern Americans are so largely *ignorant of their land,* he often poses a few questions to illustrate his concern such as:

1) Do you know where your water comes from?
2) Do you know the type of bio-region you live in?
3) Have you ever seen your area in a topographical map?
4) Can you identify at least one wild plant food native to your bio-region?

5) Do you know anything about the Native people who preceded you here? The name of their tribe? A couple of words from their language?

6) How did local features such as mountains and rivers get their names?

In short: where are you on this planet, besides being caught up in the tortuous geography of your convoluted brain?

To become more rooted in your bio-region, try to find the answers to the questions posed by Snyder. If you can't dig this up in the library, then try to get the translation of Native names in your area. Older people often know this sort of stuff and will be glad to talk with you about it.

For example, my birth state of Connecticut means "long river." Where I live now, my city water is actually from a lake/reservoir in the wooded northern part of the state. Visit your watershed or supply if possible once you locate it. They're usually nice places for picnics and hikes if public access is allowed.

Until we acknowledge that we are relative newcomers to Turtle Island (and ungrateful guests, as well) we can't begin to come home to the places we already inhabit. To become more than a thin layer of parasitical vermin on the continent, we have to begin the process of knowing our place and our places in it.

Native name of my region is: _____

The meaning of the name: _____

Try also to learn at least one "myth" pertaining to your bio-region from your research. Write it in your Journal in your own words.

Other ways to be where you are: eat as much locally produced, in-season food as possible. Wear articles of clothes produced locally. Find out what minerals are found in the largest concentration around your habitation, as well as any medicinal plants that can be easily foraged. Bring home a rock or mineral that you have identified.

Local historical societies, chambers of commerce and nature organizations are excellent sources for research as well as libraries. Try to do at least one of these things this week. "Think globally, act locally." It's a lot more than bumper sticker philosophy. It's exactly where you are right now. Get up and look out the window at it.

4 / **Home** Zendo

At his home in the Sierra Nevada, Snyder constructed his own zendo. A zendo is a dharma center, a building for Zen basically, akin to a church or synagogue. Miles from anywhere, his zendo is not a luxury but a necessity, considering Snyder's emphasis on regular meditation practice. Visiting Zen teachers as well as masters of other traditions lead sessions and retreats at the zendo, which is called "Ring of Bone," after one of Lew Welch's best poems.

The zendo, a short walk from his home, makes spiritual practice not only convenient, but probably inviting as well. Many of us, if we go to an organized house of "worship" at all, do it only on the proper days. Despite our good intentions, our home practice (whatever that might consist of) is often desultory and most often nonexistent. Remedy this by constructing your own zendo at home.

It needn't be a separate building of course, like Snyder's. Perhaps you can allot a corner of a room, if not an entire room, to the the practice of some spiritual discipline such as meditation, dancing or reading. Don't use the area for any other activities and try to spend at least a portion of each day in the space. If you're at a loss for what sort of spiritual pursuit to pursue in your new "zendo," then start with this book, placing it on a desk along with your Beat Journal and allied books you'll want to refer to in the course of your studies.

Name your area in the spirit of Snyder's "Ring of Bone," making it special and personal. Snyder's ideas about place and reinhabitation point not only to the globe at large, but our more intimate spaces as well. Reinhabit your home and spirit at the same time.

In my own home, I keep a meditation cushion and bench in my sparsely decorated library/writing room. Since I spend a lot of time there anyway, the cushion beckons me to sit with its very availability, relieving me of the need to schedule meditation. In the room, I have a small statue of Kuan Yin, the female bodhisattva of compassion; a stone gargoyle; a stained-glass pentangle on the window and an abstract expressionist print. I call my home zendo "Right Here." Describe your sacred space in your Journal or "here." Perhaps a floor plan would be nice too.

Area used for spiritual study: _____

Decorations: _____

Name given: _____

5 / **Your** Own **Prayer**

uch of Snyder's work is written in a reverential, even prayerful attitude. Drawing upon his wide experience studying comparative religions, this attitude exemplified the devotional aspects of his spirituality, a devotion most usually centered around nature.

Some of his poems are actually prayers for the well-being of the planet and its inhabitants. Others can be read in that manner, and have been done so in churches around the country. Rigorously secular and religious at the same time, Snyder's prayer/poems also serve as stimuli to meditation and contemplation. In this regard, he stands influenced by his own Zen and Native traditions.

Native people, of course, had prayers and benedictions for most occasions, such as killing prey, harvesting plants and so forth; prayers that were really intended as communication with the non-human world, a way of *tikkun olam,* which in the Hebrew tradition means to "heal the world."

Zen Buddhism as well, despite its atheistic sheen, is rife with rituals and rites for nearly everything. Zen "prayers," mantras and invocations serve much the same purpose as the Native ones. By making mental or verbal note of occasions or action with formulaic words, one is forced to pay attention to what is going on or to the consequences of one's action upon a larger world. The prayer becomes an illumination, an anchor and a behest to act responsibly and in full consciousness, rather than on automatic, unmindful pilot.

Most of us have grown up with prayers that have become monotonous, meaningless invocations to wrathful male deities and as a result
have a built-in block to undertaking powerful and ancient activities
such as prayer. Again, as Snyder demands, we must reinhabit these old
and degraded customs, reinventing them anew as tools for healing and
connecting.

One of Snyder's best-known prayers, "Prayer for the Great Family,"
based on a Mohawk prayer, is excerpted below:

Gratitude to Mother Earth, sailing through night and day—
and to her soil: rich, rare and sweet
in our minds so be it

Gratitude to Plants, the sun-facing light-changing leaf
and fine root-hairs; standing still through wind
and rain; their dance is in the flowing spiral grain
in our minds so be it

Gratitude to Air, Bearing the soaring Swift and the silent
Owl at dawn. Breath of our song
clear spirit breeze
in our minds so be it

Snyder's prayer goes on to include Wild Beings, Water, Sun and the
Great Sky. I have heard this done beautifully on a number of occasions
in Unitarian churches and at family gatherings.

At the close of my first book, *The Zen of Recovery,* I close with a prayer
I wrote commemorating those who have died from compulsive dis-

eases. To my surprise and gratitude, it has been adapted for use at a local annual AIDS healing service. Others report having heard it recited at memorial services and at the close of discussion groups. I've included an excerpt of the poem/prayer, "The Bones of Others," here as yet another example of homemade ceremony.

> If you are here to read this,
> think of those who aren't.
> Pray for them: good thoughts for those
> who lost their minds, love and years
> to compulsion, addiction and fears.
> Think of their great sacrifice.
>
> We recover on the bones of others.
> Wrap your loving thoughts around them:
> alone no more.
>
> Remember them as you sleep;
> remember them as you wake.
> Only a thought is the difference
> between you and the bones of others.

In accordance with the do-it-yourself attitude of Snyder, and indeed of all the Beats, I encourage you to compose your own prayer. You can use this daily in your home zendo, or share it at occasions such as Thanksgiving. Keep it short. Address it to whom- or whatever appeals to you personally. Perhaps you can post it in written form in your zendo or kitchen. If you're at a total loss on how to begin this exercise, then write it out as a wish list or base it on the form of a prayer you grew up with. You could write your prayer in your Journal near the picture of the saint that you glued in earlier during the Kerouac exercise.

These wishes, however, must be for the benefit of other beings, preferably non-human ones, such as: "I pray [wish] for the protection of ancient groves of tree-beings; I pray for the restoration of the ozone layer, the breath of the mother earth" and so on. Don't worry about being too hokey or New Agey about this. You don't have to share it with others if you don't wish. It is my prayer, however, that you do.

6 / **Just** Three Letters

Early in his life, Snyder studied classical Chinese, becoming accomplished at both translation and calligraphy. He applied these talents to his translation of Han Shan's Cold Mountain poems, short poems written by an eccentric Zen monk (or Dharma bum) centuries before. The poems were literally written on the mountain and cliffsides in their original forms.

Many of the Beats experimented with learning Asian calligraphy as part of their spiritual practice. Burroughs dabbled in an abstract ink calligraphy that closely resembles Chinese or Islamic script. Ed Sanders, a second-generation Beat poet, founder of the sixties band the

Fugs and editor of *Fuck You: A Magazine of the Arts,* includes classical Greek letters and ancient Egyptian hieroglyphs in many of his poems. Just knowing a few letters or characters of another alphabet is one of the ways in which we can reinhabit our wider sense of what it means to be human. Learning other forms of writing is also a good Burroughsian deconstruction of the words, as the "new" alphabet looks so alien to you that it carries little propaganda or symbolic value (at least in the beginning).

Learn and practice another written language. Chinese. Hebrew. Cyrillic. Whatever appeals to your spiritual sense of aesthetics. Learn these by asking someone to teach you. Perhaps the Korean shopkeeper on the corner, your friend who still complains about Hebrew school or the Greek guy who pours your coffee in the morning. Choose, let's say, three letters of a script significantly different from that of English or Western languages, ones that carry a spiritual impact for you. Write them in the spaces below or in your Journal along with their translation.

Three Letters:

Other benefits of asking someone to show you the words or letters is the risk you take in (1) asking, (2) encountering a different culture and (3) expanding your limits beyond your provincial language. Different scripts encode different and sometimes alien forms of wisdom. Learn to decipher them as you crack the linguistic code that you are.

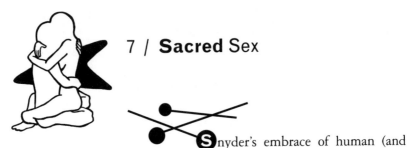

7 / **Sacred** Sex

Snyder's embrace of human (and planetary) potential extends to every transformative tool imaginable. Obviously, sex has a long and honored tradition as a sacred technique in cultures not infected with that curious Western shame over biological function. Sex is one of the ways in which Snyder believes we can reinhabit our bodies and spirits.

In *The Dharma Bums,* Kerouac writes about a sexual encounter he witnessed at Snyder's shack; a ménage à trois. In the book, Snyder speaks of the act's (and arrangement's) spiritual significance. Other references in the book also allude to "Yab Yum," or the slow and sacred sexual intercourse as taught in Tantric traditions during which the male and female partners visualize themselves as deities.

In "Yab Yum," orgasm is not so much the goal as it is a slow and ecstatic unleashing of sacred energy as a result of the union and an ultimate realization of the divinity that dwells within each of us. Tantric philosophy and practice, of course, appealed to the Beats, what with their emphasis on the body as the battleground and launching pad for awareness. That the Tantric philosophy was part of the Buddhism and Hinduism they eagerly embraced was a more than comfortable fit.

In an essay on cultural change, Snyder avers that "Any person who attempts to discover in practice what the real values of sex are, and what marriage really means, will be called immoral or obscene." In this statement, we can again witness the Beat insistence on actual hands-on experience and practice.

Never theoretical, Beat values and conclusions were drawn from real-life risk taking and limit pushing, in sharp opposition to the passive spectator/consumer society in which they found themselves. Any truths or values we claim, say the Beats, must be arrived at consciously and by dint of our own courageous efforts.

Sex remains one of the last frontiers of human consciousness, a frontier on which the culture has installed No Trespassing signs, alarm systems and guards. Exploited in the media and manipulated privately, what most other cultures regard as a divine gift is demeaned and shrouded in shame. You can use sex to free yourself from conditioning, limits and shallow self-definitions.

The instructions for sacred, tantric sex can easily be found these days in many excellent books such as the ones by Margot Anand: *The Art of Sexual Magic* and *The Art of Sexual Ecstasy,* and in newsstand magazines such as *Tantra.* If you're at all interested in attaining "heavenly," transformative sex, look these up.

Otherwise our assignment is this: next time you have sex, agree beforehand with your partner on a time limit beyond what you usually maintain. Make love extremely slowly and sensuously, visualizing your partner as the other half of yourself. Orgasm should be delayed until the end of the time set or not even reached. Your assignment is to have incredible sex.

Can you do this? Put this information in the "Sex" part of your Journal, the same place you wrote out your sexual fantasy and explored your gender identification in earlier exercises.

Did you do this exercise? Yes ☐ No ☐
Length of time (no exaggeration): _____
**Any emotional, physical or spiritual insights attained during
sex:** _____
_____

**Have your partner fill this out as well. Same question re-
garding insights as previously:** _____
_____

8 / **What** You **Need** to **Know**

Of all the Beats, Snyder is the
most accomplished at outlining his objectives: cultural, personal and
professional. In *Regarding Wave,* published in 1970, we a find a poem/list
entitled "What You Need to Know to Be a Poet," excerpted below.

> all you can about animals as persons.
> the names of trees and flowers and weeds.
> names of stars, and the movements of the planets
> and the moon.
>
> your own six senses, with a watchful and elegant mind.
>
> at least one kind of traditional magic:
> divination, astrology, the *book of changes,* the tarot . . .

children's games, comic books, bubble-gum,
the weirdness of television and advertising.

real danger.   gambles.   and the edge of death.

What you should know about this list is that it is also a recipe for being a complete human being. Snyder obviously approaches his work as a poet with the same pride in craftsmanship that he brings to construction projects and tool maintenance. I posted Snyder's poem above my typewriter (pre-Mac dark ages) when I became serious about writing. In my darkest hours, struggling with the very dull and often excruciating loneliness of the actual job of writing, just a glance at it got me through.

A few of us are fortunate enough to do what we love, but for many it is an arbitrary and often draglike way of living. We must reclaim even the most seemingly mundane job from the clutches of mundanity and soul-sucking clock-punching in order to reinhabit our alienated sense of humanity.

Snyder is a poet. He wrote a list of what he regarded as the elements of fine craftsmanship in his job, which is creating poetry. What's your job? What do you need to know in order to do it joyfully and well? Forget the technical and political aspects of your work. Snyder doesn't really dwell too much in his "Poet" list on technical aspects of "poetry." Here's my own list of "What You Need to Know to Write a Book":

a fear of loneliness. and a need to be alone.
the delete key. good, long pieces of music: raga, klezmer, & coltrane.
how to decipher your editor's scrawls in the margins
as though it were a foreign language. which it is.
sudden exhilaration and just as suddenly: black depression.
a love of reading.

how to work for days at a time without a break, swept away.
and more important: how to *not* work for days at a time, no guilt.
not writing being harder and more important sometimes than writing.

good answers ready for: "You do what?"
and "Yeah, everybody tells me I should write a book. Easy work, eh?"

places they'll hold your check for a couple of days.
friends who don't care that you're a writer.
a mate who does.

Try to be really creative when compiling your own list, drawing upon other facets of your life that lend themselves to your work. Have you ever thought about this? Does being childish at home help you relate to people in the office? Do your readings in Beat literature make you more tolerant at the social services agency? Is a knowledge of cooking helpful to an architect, a familiarity with basketball an aid in being a minister?

Write out five things you need to know in order to do your job; five things you wouldn't normally associate with it. Things you need to know to be a _____:

1) _____

2) _____

3) _____

4) _____

5) _____

Doing this, you'll begin to draw different areas of your life closer, granting dignity to each area. Perhaps you'll even identify talents you didn't realize you had. Perhaps another career direction is suggested by the list. Can you postulate a different career based upon your list? What else do you think you're qualified for? Are there areas that need improving in order to do your "real work" more fully?

Snyder has called the the job of waking up and becoming a complete human being "the real work." Doing this list is like doing a search of the human toolbox that you are as you go about your work.

A Selected **Gary** Snyderography

Books

A Place in Space: Ethics, Aesthetics and Watersheds. Washington, D.C.: Counterpoint, 1995. Essays.

Axe Handles. San Francisco: North Point Press, 1983. One of his later classics.

Earth House Hold: Technical Notes and Queries to Fellow Dharma Revolutionaries. New York: New Directions, 1969. Essays, journals, Zen teaching and sixties-style manifestos. Very influential at the time.

Mountains and Rivers Without End. Washington, D.C.: Counterpoint, 1996. Forty years in the making. Snyder's masterwork.

No Nature: Selected & New Poems. New York: Pantheon, 1992. If you're going to have one Snyder, this is it.

Old Ways. San Francisco: City Lights, 1977. Essays on North Beach, nature and Coyote, the Native America Trickster.

The Practice of the Wild (essays). San Francisco: North Point Press, 1990. Snyder's most mature and extensive essays on wilderness and ecology.

Riprap and Cold Mountain Poems. San Francisco: Grey Fox, 1980. Delightful translations of early Zen poems. Early scholarship.

The Real Work. New York: New Directions, 1980. Collected interviews with Snyder.

Turtle Island. New York: New Directions, 1974. Pulitzer Prize winner. The quintessential Snyder.

Recordings

Turtle Island (Living Music Records). Cassette of live recordings with the Paul Winter Consort.

The Teachings of Zen Master Dogen (Audio Literature). Two cassettes of Zen teachings read by Snyder.

Biography

Gary Snyder: Dimensions of a Life, edited by Jon Halper. San Francisco: Sierra Club Books, 1991. An excellent anthology of tributes by Snyder's friends arranged as a biography.

The Dharma Bums, by Jack Kerouac. New York: Viking, 1972. Snyder is the main character, known as "Japhy Ryder," in the book.

Michael McClure

The **Way** of
Spiritual **Rebellion**

(*"I AM A MAMMAL PATRIOT."*)

orn in Kansas in 1932, Michael McClure came to San Francisco in 1954 to attend art school. Falling in with the writers of the area through his association with Bohemian elder statesman Kenneth Rexroth, McClure soon turned his attention to poetry and the emerging counterculture. His first public reading took place at the famous Six Gallery event along with Ginsberg and Snyder. McClure also remained active in the visual arts community, becoming one of its most cogent observers and advocates, particularly of the Assemblage movement in California, which we will examine in a later chapter.

In the years since, McClure has developed a unique sensibility of equal parts science and mysticism. Fascinated by the natural world and an informed and acute observer, McClure's writing is an unabashed celebration of physicality in all its forms, believing as he does that flesh is divinity and that consciousness is as real "as the hoof of a deer."

Like the other Beats, McClure adapted easily to the changing times of the sixties and became even more influential in the new hippie counterculture of the sixties, assisting Jim Morrison with Doors' lyrics, co-writing a song with Janis Joplin, collaborating on a book with the Hell's Angels, writing taboo-breaking plays such as *The Beard,* and attaining a high visibility at countercultural events such as the Human Be-In. Dennis Hopper, himself associated with the Beats before his movie career, said, "Without McClure's roar, there would have been no sixties."

One of the only Beats to become an accomplished playwright, he remains vigorously contemporary, most recently reading his poetry to the keyboard accompaniment of his friend Ray Manzarek of the Doors in clubs around the country, finding a new, younger audience for his words of revolt, mammalian celebration and "bio-alchemical" wisdom.

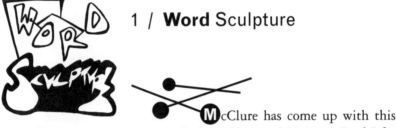

1 / **Word** Sculpture

McClure has come up with this cool exercise in consciousness called the "Personal Universe Deck" for his writing students. The complete and extensive instructions for this can be found in his collection of essays and interviews, *Lighting the Corners.* I'll just give a basic overview of the method and encourage you to look up his full instructions and explanations:

Make a card deck of fifty blank cards, say three-by-five index cards. McClure says to carefully choose a hundred words from your vocabulary, words that will represent your personal universe, past, present and future. Also the hundred words should sound "good" together.

Eighty of them should be divided evenly between sight (my examples: Black, Clear . . .), sound (Thunder, Guitar . . .), taste (Curry, Salt, Blood . . .), touch (Sand, Skin, Granite, Cold . . .) and smell (Pine, Sandalwood, Ozone, Sweat . . .); sixteen to each sense. Be creative and personal.

Then ten words of movement, such as Swim, Walk, Fly, etc. The remaining ten words are assorted choices such as names of heroes (Kerouac, Buddha, Elvis . . .), invented personal words (GooGoo), birds (Falcon . . .), plants, totems, symbols (Crucifix), favorite dinosaurs, personal obsessions, one word delegated to abstractions such as God, belief, etc., whatever is meaningful in your personal universe. None of any of the hundred words should have endings such as -*ing*. At least one of these last ten should be two body parts significant to you, either your own or someone else's. McClure says that's really putting your cards on the table.

Says McClure about all of this, "Stay away from troublesome speculations. Forget philosophy and forget poetry. Give yourself over to the rules (of creating the deck). They're simple if you don't confuse them. It's about you."

Now write the words at the ends of the cards, one at each end, like the Kings in a suit of cards. Shuffling them and picking three out at random, you will suddenly see the words and beliefs that arrange you arranged in a new way.

Says McClure in conclusion, "There are lots of things to do with the cards: play games with them, make conversations with them, tell jokes with them, make sound poems with them . . ." He even refers to the exercise as a "word sculpture," an apt term, I think.

A random card deck poem from me: "Swim Black Buddha! / Green Brain Moan! / Stroke Skin Moss." Here's what one should look like:

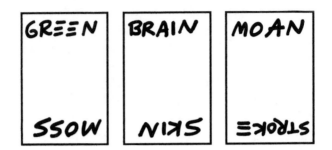

Doing this exercise, one can begin to experience all of what McClure calls the sensorium, or the entire perception-receiving mechanism of the body. The words include textures, colors, smells: all analogs for all the senses. In a Burroughsian sense, the exercise, with its elements of randomness, reclaims words as representations of what they actually represent, not what we might like them to represent.

Let's try it: Garlic? Smell it? Wool? Feel it? Orgasm? Remember it? Sure you do, and this exercise, far from being a mere literary parlor game, should become an actual extension of your physical mammalian and sensual self, reaching out in a caress (or kick or penetration) of the universe you grew out of, much like an apple on a tree.

Dedicate a page in your Journal to record the poems you "write" with your deck. Do this exercise with other people, as well. A great postmodern icebreaker at parties and gatherings. Let them record their poems as well.

2 / **Mindless** Biology

 **T**hese are the instructions for a body-discovering exercise described by McClure in *Scratching the Beat Surface:*

"In privacy allow the muscles of the body to do anything they please, to twist and turn as a baby does on a rug in the sunlight. The eyes are closed and the vocal apparatus begins to respond to the pleasure of the societally negated postures of the body (as one groans automatically under the hands of a masseur). The eyes are closed or squinted, and there is little or no visual stimulation.

"At first it is difficult to writhe purposelessly, twist, groan, cry, sing, chant, kick, twist, moan, weep, or laugh. Eventually, and after a number of trials, a mindless biological state is found. It then becomes easier to find the state, and one may exercise there longer and longer. If one develops this capacity up to thirty minutes or an hour, he finds on reclaiming his social person that he is in a euphoric state—a high.

"The senses see the brightness and auras and colors of objects around them, and there is a feeling of physiological well-being. The experimenter will have been in a place where he, or she, was flying no banners but was a mammal—the universe experiencing itself."

Doing this exercise in "letting go," one is again thrown back into the body. McClure even says that the body is the shape of reason, the depository of all truth, knowledge and beauty. In other places, he states that "WE ARE OUR DEEP BEHAVIORS."

In a world that has alienated us from our physicality and natural health, surrendering artificial, conscious control over our very meat machines helps to shake off the inhibitions and illness that limit and roboticize us. Rebelling against the uptight ways in which we carry (or rest) ourselves is one of the ways in which the Beat spirit can manifest itself.

Loosen up. Let go. Shake, rattle and roll. Twist and shout. Let it all hang out.

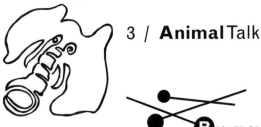

3 / **Animal**Talk

Return to the roots of mammalian expression by roaring your emotion, ecstasy and pain, cutting loose from limiting syllables and clever mental codes of control. Says Michael McClure in *Ghost Tantras,* "Poetry is a muscular principle and a revolution for the body-spirit and intellect and ear. . . . To dim the senses and listen to inner energies a-roar is sometimes called the religious experience." *Ghost Tantras* is written nearly entirely in "beast language," to be read best aloud. Here is an example of McClure's beast language: "OH! NAH OOH!—EHH! GRAHHR—ROOR!KAHR MEEST ROOOHR, BYE THA MEE NORR OOH WEET MEE TEV VOOON NAHHR."

Let your muscles and bones and spirit roar, revolting against the limits of symbolic language. Try writing a paragraph in beast language and then roar it aloud, either alone or with others. "Who you really are" is in your muscles, mammal, not in heaven or hell or this or any book or word. Who you really are is the revolt of your body against the ownership of words and "logic." Roar right now, spontaneously. Just let it out, even a fake lion roar.

To get warmed up or to break down your inhibitions about acting animalistically, maybe you could just start with some cute little meows or precious little barks or cartoonish and idyllic chirps and whirs. After you get used to expressing your non-human mind (see Snyder), then become the queen or king of the jungle and roar.

You already do these very mammalian things. Sighing releases a lot of muscular tension and emotions stored deep in your meat. Yelling when you hit your thumb with a hammer is a spontaneous exclamation of the mammal, beyond symbols and logic. Moans and groans during sex are another way your flesh has of making itself heard when it is played and pounded like a keyboard by the hands of a lover.

You already do these things. Just do them a little bit more extravagantly. Above all, McClure's work constantly reminds us that we are warm-blooded mammals "dancing in our desires" in a very real and beautiful and terrifying universe.

Write a beast-language roar in your Journal or below, at least a dozen different vocalizations. Like the deck-of-cards exercise, this is fun with other people. A mammalian choir! Obviously, you needn't worry about grammar and spelling (or meaning). It means exactly what it says. Roar it aloud.

4 / **Dirty** Words

cClure's early poetry was frequently punctuated with what were regarded as obscene or filthy words, words such as *fuck, shit, goddamn, cock, cunt,* you know some of these words, am I right? I don't want to look like an asshole, so I'll stop writing this shit and tell you what this fucking exercise is all about.

In the late fifties this was regarded as quite shocking and even actionable by legal authorities and self-appointed guardians of the public morality, as if words that everyone is familiar with could corrupt them, or as if words that accurately describe functions and forms could be somehow "inappropriate."

We've already examined how this definition of "obscenity" and the Beats' reaction to it loomed so largely on the cultural stage of the fifties. While we may seem to live in more "liberal" and tolerant times, I don't have to tell you that the cultural war is anything but "cold" these days. Words remain the most potent weapons and talismans for both sides in the war to determine exactly what shape our culture will assume.

In one sense, the Beats attempted to reclaim ordinary language as it is spoken and commonly understood from the cultural elites through their use of "obscenity." William Burroughs, who carried "shocking" language to its extremes, has commented that these days it takes a lot more than the use of the word *fuck* to shock people.

McClure himself has commented that his use of these words, usually at the beginning of a poem, functioned much like a cathartic for the system. The words were usually capitalized and boldfaced, implying that these words were being shouted. You yourself have done this, yelling a "profanity" when "stuck" or "frustrated." After the exclamations, McClure goes into the poem, often one that is quite lovely, in stark contrast to the opening. The use of the magic words (*fuck, shit,* etc.) has, as it were, cleaned out his tubes and the "stuff" can start to flow, unimpeded and spontaneously.

Obscene and profane words do indeed have the stench of power and the scent of magic around them, being culturally forbidden or at the very least, frowned upon. Most often, they are indeed used as invocations, supplications or expressions of ecstasy during orgasm or anguish over pain, emotional or physical. Overuse of them, as Burroughs says, strips them of their incantatory and arcane power.

You were most likely punished when you were younger for doing what I will now assign you. If you get caught, tell "them" it's your school assignment. I want you to write "dirty" words in a book. This book. And in your Beat Journal. A whole page of them. Big, bold, filthy, shocking, even sexist words. Write out a long spontaneous string of them as they enter your mind. Do not censor or edit yourself. Use a bold, permanent marker. It's OK to feel a certain sense of delight in doing this transgressive activity. After you write out your words, say them aloud. With feeling. Again, another group exercise presents itself.

Even a little bit of this activity lessens the hold of words over you. Perhaps their forbidden allure as well. If so-called dirty words lose their power with repetition and usage, perhaps you'll start to realize that obscenity is in the mind of the beholder. These obscene words mean nothing really.

If you use "obscenity" a lot in your normal conversation, like many modern Americans, perhaps this exercise will make you rethink its use. Save those big, bad words for when they're *really* necessary. Like those times when you need big-word mojo to batter down the walls of self, as in McClure's use of them. Otherwise, they lose their power to shock at the same time that they get power over *you.*

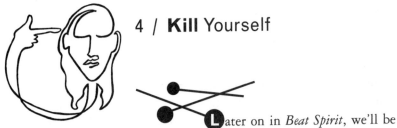

4 / **Kill** Yourself

ater on in *Beat Spirit*, we'll be writing our own suicide notes as part of another exercise. This particular look at suicide, derived from McClure's *Meat Science Essays,* is a prelude to that act. In an essay in the book, he examines the meanings of suicide and death, saying that if there must be such a thing as suicide, then "invent a new Death." The possibility of suicide, he says, must be eliminated before suicide is even possible; every last act must be performed: "Put Heaven and Hell into life before *adieu,"* he says.

The essay is not a glorification of suicide, although McClure does come up with some cogent reasons for it. It is rather an examination of the causes that would lead a conscious organism to self-destruct. Part of the reasons he intimates are "repressed love-emotions and knotted reactive muscles."

The suicide has but one main cause for suicide—"the exhaustion and disillusion that follow the denial of his sexuality. Early love is blocked or turned into a mockery of love by authority and government. The urge to fly outward and make experience is dammed and it returns to contort the human physique."

As in all his philosophy, McClure here remains consistent with his insistence that the actual mammalian body is the place of both liberation and enslavement. Release of the body's natural energies equals health—mental, spiritual, sexual and emotional—leading to creative and godlike acts. Repression of the body's natural desires leads to the ecological and ideological devastation we see all around us. Repression of the body itself can be viewed in McClure's "system" as a very real form of "living" suicide.

In the essay, he even lists numerous things that he regards as suicide. Alongside such mundane suicidal acts as hanging, sleeping pills and fire, he lists "accepting authoritarian demands is suicide, war is suicide, existence without human feelings is suicide, cynical impossible demands from self are suicide, performing the expected is; becoming a martyr for half-felt ideals is. . . ."

These are the things that a suicide *is*. Here are the things he says that suicide is *not:*

"It is not an act of immortal life; it is not a living but a sacrifice of life." The alternatives? Says McClure, "Changing reality is the greatest life. Men who conceive of suicide should first try pleasure. Pleasure may lead to freedom and make the death unnecessary."

Most of us have threatened to kill ourselves at one time or another, usually as a means of gaining attention or as an "I'll show them; they'll be sorry when I'm gone" sort of act. Some of us even know people who have killed themselves. Usually they're the ones who don't give advance notice.

In any event, despite all our grandiose and meaningless threats of suicide, we are *already* committing slower suicides daily. Can you think of two ways in which you have already committed (or are committing) suicide (killing your "true" spiritual and mammalian self)? Refer back to McClure's list to remember some of the more subtle and insidious ways.

Two ways I kill myself and why (habit, guilt, fear, upbringing . . . ?):

1) _____
2) _____

Alternatives to killing myself:

1) _____
2) _____

Here's my example:

I kill myself over my children. Why? Guilt. Do I spend enough time with them? Do I really listen when they talk to me? Do I provide a good role model? Guilt in all its varieties is, by McClure's definition, lethal, lessening the quality of our lives and removing us from the "now." In some cases, guilt can and does lead to actual suicide.

An alternative to this suicidal guilt: I will set aside time to listen to my kids, telling them I'll be quiet for five minutes as they speak, attempting to really listen before I respond. I'll ask them what they like about other fathers to determine the qualities they admire. And every time I get guilty, despite all my good intentions, I'll make a mental inventory of the good things we did that week. Then I'll get on with my life as they do with theirs.

6 / Revolt!

Perhaps the most significant aspect of McClure's work and philosophy is his preoccupation with the necessity for revolt. The idea and act of revolt run like threads throughout all his thought, undergirding his other concerns. For McClure, without revolt, there is no measure of a life truly tested and lived to its fullest potential. For support of his thesis, he draws heavily upon the natural sciences that he so well knows and loves.

For McClure, revolt is far more than a political or ideological stance or attitude. It springs, he says, from biological necessity, and he uses illustrations from the natural world to buttress his claims. He defines revolt as "a desire to experience normal physiological processes that give pleasure of fullness and expansion." Again McClure locates the physical body and universe as the locus of action, not some high-flown and abstract battleground of ideas. Revolt is never political, he claims. It is personal and must be enacted within ourselves before we can begin to revolt against the larger forces that bind us.

Remembering his early years, McClure writes, "I used poetry to revolt against society during the fifties Cold War, but equally as important was to rebel against my own customs and habits. I believed that spirit was one and the same as the body." He insists that the impulse to freedom has biological roots.

As we've seen in doing some of the McClurean exercises, his intent has always been to free the body and, by extension, the mind and spirit. In this regard, he is at one with the Beat spirit of revolting against personal conventions and habits that reinforce our unknowing and often willing slavery.

Nearly all the exercises in this book aim toward the same effect: to force us to revolt against our composite "selves," subvert our own conditioning, transgress artificial limits, transform into who we really are and transcend our small, limited and suffering sense of self. In this McClure returns us again and yet again to the very place that we are: our bodies. Here, he seems to say, is where the battle lines are drawn. Cross them.

The act of revolt will surely marginalize one in terms of wider acceptance. Can freed people ever mingle comfortably once again with slaves? Again remembering the early years of the Beat movement: "We were treated like outlaws and we were happy to be outlaws in the brutal society of the fifties and sixties and seventies. In the political system of the eighties, everyone with feelings of humanity and love for nature was an outlaw."

If you're still reading this book, then you are by definition one of these "outlaws" McClure speaks of. You are looking for ways to revolt and become yourself. Your revolt at some point isn't a conscious choice, but has become a biological imperative, a calling to freedom from somewhere very deep down in your very meat.

Pick one major thing to begin revolting against in your life. I mean, *major!* A cap gun revolution will make a lot of noise, a fine-tuning will make some cosmetic change, but the Beats, and particularly McClure, are asking us to be a lot more imaginative, courageous and optimistic than that.

This is really the place in *Beat Spirit* for you to write your own exercise, the do-it-yourself part where you finally lay down the book and make the abstract real, something demanded by the Beats of all their readers: make your own living poem/art/literature by putting heart and soul on the front lines of the battle.

In my own life, opposition to war and violence became a defining value during the Vietnam War, and like many at the time, I put my body and freedom at risk at rallies, marches and protests.

Years later, the war a receding memory, I found myself head of the art department at a factory that made trophies and awards. During my brief time there, the Persian Gulf War erupted and the factory began taking orders for the yellow ribbons that became an emblem of support for the war. It was good for morale and even better, it was good for business at the plant, which turned out the ribbons by the mile.

I was stunned at the nearly unanimous approval of the Gulf War, and by the lockstep mentality of my neighbors and fellow citizens. It seemed that to most people, to even question the war was tantamount to treason.

Anyway, everyone at the factory wore the ribbons, even on the job. I kept silent about my opinions, but didn't wear one of the yellow ribbons. In short order, I was called on the carpet by the owner, both my patriotism and corporate loyalty questioned. I was instructed to wear a ribbon. I refused and was soon unemployed.

My revolt was silent, a negative one, really. By simply *not doing* something as silly as wearing a ribbon, my revolt became extremely threatening. Yes, I paid a price, and yes, I kept my peace of mind even while peace was being lost elsewhere in the world.

Pick something to revolt against that everyone takes for granted, that everyone assumes to be universal, like those ribbons (where are they now?). Your negative act will soon have people questioning you, even angrily. The hardest part of all this is to stick with it, even in the face of disapproval and, yes, possible job loss.

Perhaps your revolt will simply mean changing the way you make love, restricting your TV time, eliminating things from your diet, or becoming vocal in the presence of common and insidious things such as sexism, anti-Semitism, racism or homophobia, instead of maintaining an embarrassed silence. This isn't about being "politically correct," either. It's about being a human with some dignity and integrity.

Make any revolt a habit. Commit yourself to it for the long run. Prepare to suffer consequences. These are simply affirmations that you are making waves and changing your life.

In your Beat Journal, dedicate a section to your revolt. It'll probably be something that you already think about anyway, something that's always irritated you deep inside. You've probably already made public or private statements in connection with it. Think back and see if you can't discern a pattern. Record any memories you have of your revolt prior to this exercise.

Keep a new record of reactions to your revolt and how it impacts upon your life. This book, *Beat Spirit,* can be seen as no more than one of the side effects of a decision I made a long time ago to revolt. You have a story and a book inside of you, too. Begin writing it in your Journal. Start here:

The personal revolt that defines me: _____
A major life consequence of the revolt: _____

A Selected **Michael** McClureography

Books

The Adept. (Novel.) New York: Delacorte Press, 1971. Dust jacket description: "Reflects the post-psychedelic generation."

The Beard. New York: Grove Press, 1967. The cast was regularly arrested for performing this play.

Ghost Tantras. San Francisco: City Lights, 1964. Aaaargh! Bea(s)t language!

Lighting the Corners. Albuquerque: University of New Mexico, 1993. Excellent, thoughtful, wide-ranging essays.

Meat Science Essays. San Francisco: City Lights Books, 1963. Sex, drugs, revolt . . . an early manifesto.

The New Book/A Book of Torture. New York: Grove Press, 1961. Rants, peyote poems and jazz.

Rebel Lions. New York: New Directions, 1991. "McClure's roar (of the sixties) has become a scream of the nineties."—Dennis Hopper.

Scratching the Beat Surface. San Francisco: North Point, 1982. Essays on the beginnings of Beat and looks at natural science.

Selected Poems. New York: New Directions, 1986. Essential McClure.

Simple Eyes. New York: New Directions, 1994. Nineties McClure. "Looking at the world *directly.*"

3 Poems: Dolphin Skull, Rare Angel, Dark Brown. New York: Penguin, 1995. Early, middle and modern McClure.

Recordings

Ghost Tantras. Cassette; also featured in excerpt on last disc of *Howls, Raps & Roars* CD set.

Love Lion (Shanachie). Energetic CD with Ray Manzarek. Also on video.

Critical and Auxiliary

Secret Exhibition, by Rebecca Solnit. San Francisco: City Lights, 1990. History of Beat-allied artists in California, including McClure's involvement in Beat visual arts.

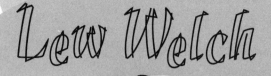

Lew Welch

The **Way** of
Spiritual **Reinvention**

(*"Harnessed jelly of the Stars!"*)

ne of the most concise of the Beat writers, Lew Welch, born in Arizona in 1926, had done his thesis on the writings of Gertrude Stein. A college classmate of Gary Snyder, he lived, during the early Beat days, in Chicago writing catalog copy. Excited by the activity in San Francisco, he returned to the West Coast, becoming an active participant in the Beat subculture of the time.

He became involved early on in the Haight-Ashbury hippie movement and provided a valuable link to the older Beat culture, as did the examples of Snyder and McClure, who both threw themselves fully into the new counterculture of the sixties. Articles and poems by Welch were featured in the hippie underground press of the time.

One of the least celebrated of the Beats, Welch nonetheless exercised a profound influence on many of them and is often the subject of their writings. He is featured in Kerouac's *Big Sur* as "Dave Wain," and is often referred to by both Ginsberg and Gary Snyder, who has said of Welch's work, "The words stop, but the meaning keeps going on." Welch's writing, with its economy of language and extraordinary clarity, shows his debt to his study and practice of Zen Buddhism.

Welch struggled long and hard with depression and alcoholism, and was settling in to build a house near Snyder's in northern California when he walked away into the woods with a gun in 1971 at the age of forty-five, leaving only a note behind, instructing his friends as to the disposition of his literary estate. His body was never found. His collected poems, *Ring of Bone,* were published soon after his disappearance.

1 / **Step** Out **onto** the **Planet**

Here is one of Lew Welch's best-known poems and a superb Beat exercise as well. Read it for not only its poetic content but its instructional value as well. In fact, read all poetry in this manner!

> Step out onto the Planet.
> Draw a circle a hundred feet round.
>
> Inside the circle are
> 300 things nobody understands, and, maybe
> nobody's ever really seen.
>
> How many can you find?

This piece is nearly always reproduced in Welch's own beautiful calligraphic script and illustrated with a Zen-type circle he painted with a brush. There are two ways in which you can approach the "doing" of this activity. First, do as he says, and mark off a large area outside (doesn't have to be a hundred feet—try maybe ten or twenty). Follow his instructions. What do you become aware of? How many can you count?

The second way is to make a small circle shape. Maybe use a paper plate, cutting the round raised center out, leaving a doughnut shape. Place this stencil on various places on the ground (or even on a floor in your home). How many different, unusual things do you notice?

This exercise in simple and surprised attention is typical Welch, who as an early Zen student in the fifties was attracted to the idea of just paying attention to "what is." His longtime friendship with Gary Snyder, dating back to their days as college roommates at Reed College in Oregon, is also apparent in this poem/exercise.

Much of Welch's work, like Snyder's, is centered around an acute and unromantic consciousness of nature. In another poem, "Notes from a Pioneer on a Speck in Space," he describes the planet earth as though he were talking to someone (an alien perhaps) who had asked for a description of the planet.

The things framed and revealed by your circle or stencil compose an earth poem made of found objects. Hold it up and peer at distant mountains or the sky. How many beautiful things do you see? Count them out loud. Now look through it at a mirror. Can you see one beautiful thing? Who is it?

2 / **Reinvent** Yourself

A s you've most likely concluded by now in your reading and doing of *Beat Spirit,* the main intent of both this book and the Beat paradigm itself is to rediscover who we really are and, failing that, to *reinvent ourselves,* usually in opposition to the prevailing cultural hypnosis.

The process of reinvention is not one that occurs instantaneously or without a certain amount of pain or real work, as Snyder describes it. The spiritual, emotional, linguistic and even sexual technologies utilized by the Beats (and presented in *Beat Spirit*) all have this process of insight and transformation at their very heart.

Welch, in both his poetry and life, attempted to work out the parameters of this self-reinvention through the persona of an invented character and alter ego he calls "the Red Monk," a wise (and often wiseguyish) Zen cleric. Here is "Entire Sermon by the Red Monk," which concerns itself with Welch's prescription for reinvention of self:

1.
We invent ourselves.

2.
We invent ourselves out of ingredients we didn't choose, by a process we can't control.

3.
The Female Impersonator, and the Sadistic Marine can each trace himself back to the same stern, or weak, father.

4.
Usually, it's less dramatic; he was only indifferently a basketball player. Now he is selling cars.

5.
The baby on the floor cannot be traced, forward, to anything.

6.
It's all your own fault then.

7.

On all kinds of baby purpose, you invented whoever you think you are. Out of ingredients you couldn't control, by a process you can't control.

All you really say is, "Love me for myself alone."

8.

It is also possible to *uninvent* yourself. By a process you can't control.

9.

But you invented Leo. Forget it.

Essential to an understanding of Welch's process is the idea that the process cannot be "controlled" (in the "Sermon," "Leo" is Welch's pseudonym). We obviously "invented" our personalities out of elements we were exposed to as children, elements and influences we never chose.

As adults, we believe (but rarely try) that it is possible to undo these early formative experiences and reinvent ourselves. We usually fail because we attempt to control and tailor the process of uninvention (or unknowing and unlearning). And just what is it that is doing the controlling? Why, the accidental things that formed us in the first place. So you can see that we are using damaged tools to fix damaged goods. What is needed is a new tool or, better yet, no tool at all, but a trust in the uncontrollable process of uninvention.

For Welch (as well as for Snyder, Kerouac and the others) Zen Buddhism provided a technique of uninventing one's suffering and limited self. The Zen student learns early on the necessity of letting go of the illusion of Control, indeed, of surrendering any expectations of any results from the process of uninvention.

The urge to Control, in both Welchian and Burroughsian terms, is the bugaboo that keeps us from true happiness and freedom; those interior control mechanisms that preordain our every move and action. But how do we begin to lose control of the process? Haven't we heard that "losing it" is not only embarrassing, but the fastest road to the asylum?

Through exercises such as McClure's roaring and lying on the floor, through Burroughs's cut-ups, Kerouac's spontaneous prose, Snyder's trust in nature, a strong theme resounds throughout the Beat spirit. To become free, free yourself of predictability and Control. Spirituality of any sort is to be found in the joy of the process and not the product, the actual doing and not the done, the journey and not the destination.

"You invented whoever you think you are," says Welch late in the "Sermon."

List three things in your Journal or below that you didn't choose as elements from which you invented yourself (parents, religion, be specific): _____

Now list three things you do choose to influence you in your reinvention (this book, a friend, a therapy? Again, be specific): _____

Now list three things beyond your control that could harm you (this is easy—earthquakes, war, whatever): _____

_____

Now apply the "earthquake" attitude to the three things you chose as aids in reinvention and forget about them. The process is already under way and out of your control. As is this book. You're already about to start on the next exercise.

3 / The Red Monk

. . . was Welch's literary invention of a personality separate from his own. In the monk's "voice," Welch was free to pose Zen-like questions and pontificate on other subjects. Another alter ego in his work is called "Leo," a pseudonym for himself, closer in personality than the Red Monk (although Welch had red hair).

In his work, he could use these personalities to explore his own as measured against these "fictional" voices. We all probably have secret alter egos. Perhaps, in your daydreaming, you're a bushy-haired Druid priestess, or a rapscallion French painter on the Left Bank. Name and describe in a few words the "fictional" counterpart of yourself, your shadow adviser and other-dimensional role model.

I've played with this one a lot. My favorite alter ego is an author and near-hermit from the mid-1800s, a lot like Henry David Thoreau. He's very eccentric and cranky. I've named him Zachariah. Sometimes when I'm thinking through an idea I want to write, I'll assume his personality and see if it rings true with his personality. Occasionally I'll even write notes from him on my works in progress, his acerbic comments and withering critiques something I would like to attain one day, oblivious as he is to fame and approval. The one piece of advice I treasure from Zachariah is this: "Write for yourself in a language of your own invention. Then teach others the language."

This is a good way to begin a process of reinvention. First invent a fictional person. Then begin to find ways to move closer in actuality to that model. Make sure the new person is like you in significant ways. (Welch's hair was red and he was interested in Zen; his name, like Leo, began with an *L*.)

Name of my alter ego: _____

Brief description: _____

_____

_____

One line of life advice from my alter ego: _____

You could introduce friends and family to your new personality, signing letters in the new name. Draw a sketch in your Journal of what you imagine your alter ego to look like, or find a photo in a magazine or newspaper that resembles your new personality.

4 / Riddle Me This

The Red Monk appears in a few of Welch's pieces he calls "Riddles." More than riddles, they are actually Zen koans, and Welch is said to have been one of the first to write Western koans. A koan is a paradoxical question that cannot be answered rationally. In order to answer, one must make an intuitive leap into *direct action,* exemplifying the spirit of the question, demonstrating physically, without words and beyond conditioned thought and symbolic language.

The most famous and hackneyed one heard in the West is "What is the sound of one hand clapping?" Zen students are asked these koans in private interviews with Zen masters and must respond immediately or risk being whacked with a stick. Answering a koan indicates a breakthrough to reality and enlightenment.

Among Welch's koans or riddles are "The Riddle of the Hands," "The Riddle of Bowing" and "The Rider Riddle." In "The Rider Riddle," the question is this:

If you spend a lot of time on a mountain, the mountain will give you a being to ride. "What do you ride?" is the koan. Welch says there is only one right answer for every person and only that person can know the answer.

Each riddle by Welch has a commentary by the Red Monk appended (this is classic Zen form as well). In this case, the Red Monk comments that Manjusri, a Buddhist saint, rode a tiger. Says the Red Monk, the mountain will show you.

Quickly now! I am holding a big stick over your head. What being do you ride? A dragonfly, a cat, a dragon? What? _____
Don't write the answer or say the name. If it's a cat: *Meowww!*

Here's a koan of my own invention:

You are caught between a rock and a hard place. Quickly! Show me rock, then the hard place!

Possible answers: Hit the floor or ground (the rock is earth). Then pat the hard place (your head).

Make up your own koan here. If you're stuck, proceed from a cliché like I did:

_____

_____

_____

_____

Ask others to answer. (Don't hit them! Unless they ask, of course.) Afterward, ask for their reactions and record their commentaries about it here or in your Journal:

_____

_____

If attempting to answer the previous "riddle" has you going in circles and on the edge of insanity, good! That's the intended purpose: to force a surrender of the "sane" controlling mind and make it leap into a sudden apprehension of truth, of "exactly what is." What did we learn from this? That learning often happens irrationally, illogically and in the most unexpected of ways.

5 / **Go** Sane

If you need a respite or time out after the previous exercise in what Alan Watts calls "Beat Zen," then here's a reentry into reality for you from Mr. Welch, his Zen-like prescription for centering, balance and gaining perspective on your life. It's titled, "Small Sentence to Drive Yourself Sane":

The next time you are doing something absolutely ordinary, or even better

the next time you are doing something absolutely *necessary*, such as pissing, or making love, or shaving, or washing the dishes or the baby or yourself or the room, say to yourself:

"So it's all come to this!"

Again, the Beat Zen insistence on experiencing this very moment right where we are. Welch's exclamation is one that I have actually memorized and used to great advantage when my brain is taking me away from my life. Right now, yes, this very moment and right here where you actually are, put down this book, consider what you're doing, and say out loud: "So it's all come to this!"

6 / **Real** Speech

Welch, along with the rest of the Beats, constantly stressed the importance and primacy of "real speech" in his writing and philosophy. At the time of the Beats, written language was far removed from the way language is usually spoken. It reflected rather the imperatives of a cultural and economic elite that used language, in the Beats' view, to impose Control, inhibit the body and cement the power structure. The Beats' use of "obscenity," spontaneous writing, colloquial phrases and willful misspelling and odd grammar were all assaults upon the citadel of the "linguistically correct" and a reclamation of our most basic tool and weapon: our words.

Predated in this by Walt Whitman and Thomas Paine, who both wrote in the language of the "common" man, the Beats used common language to impart dignity to everyday experience and, as in Kerouac's dictum, to remove the shame that so often surrounded "normal" people's experiences.

The dread that many people feel when exposed to poetry or indeed any "literature" stems from this removal of the word from the sphere of a shared world. The Beats wrested control of the word away from its captors and freed it upon a world held in thrall by propaganda and ideology, all in turn, based upon artificial and constructed uses of the magic power of words.

Welch recounts a significant experience he had regarding the power of spontaneous and "normal" language. Welch was on a tour of a California winery. The guide, he says, droned on and on, in the rehearsed, homogenized and corporate voice we've all grown so accustomed to from similar tours. Suddenly the guide interrupted his spiel to yell: "Whose kid is that?!" as he saw a small child about to fall into a vat of wine.

Welch says that the force of "real speech slammed against false speech" was as "startling as a thunderclap." Welch vowed never to publish a poem that didn't have the same force of language as the guide's "Whose kid is that?!" exclamation.

Listen this week. Listen well in a world of contrived and rehearsed and polite speech. Collect at least one example of "Whose kid is that?!," an example of real, direct and spontaneous speech. Make it immortal by recording it here. The speech should have the awakening power of an unexpected firecracker or car backfire, lifting you from the hypnosis of rote hearing. Look for short, spontaneous phrases. Make a daily record in your Journal or here:

Monday: _____

Tuesday: _____

Wednesday: _____

Thursday: _____

Friday: _____

Saturday: _____

Sunday: _____

Start to examine your own speech for robotic patterns, automatic clichés and outright artifice. For example, do you automatically say "Have a nice day?" when saying goodbye or receiving change at a store? Do you always say something like "What's up?," "What's new?" or "How ya doin'?" or one of its variants, not really expecting an answer? Eliminate these phrases. Invent new ways to say hello and goodbye. You might find one in the list you compiled above. But don't make habits of your new phrases, either.

Can you record one instance of automatic speech here that you resolve to extinguish from your verbal behavior?

7 / **Mozart's** Watch

Welch never really was able to "make a living" at his real job, which he considered being a poet. Sound familiar? In an essay called "Bread vs. Mozart's Watch," he insists that his job is to be a poet, saying that he's a lousy carpenter. Besides, he says, nobody is asking a carpenter to write his poems.

Mozart's watch refers to the syndrome of rewarding "artists" with things such as engraved watches (so that they can't pawn them, says Welch), feeling it would be an "insult" to dirty their hands with money. Artists and poets are also constantly asked to appear at "benefits," their pay being perhaps their name on a poster.

Burroughs has said to remember that you can't eat your fame. Welch was incredibly frustrated most of his life at the small amount of recompense he received for his art, having to spend upwards of sometimes twenty hours a day at hard manual labor to support his poetry, only to come home too tired to write.

At the end of the piece, Welch vows that henceforth he will pay his bills only through being a poet, secure in his belief that there are thousands of people out there who value what he does.

Some questions:

1) Do you get paid to do what you love and are accomplished at? (Fear not: carpentry and parenting can be a calling, craft and chosen art form, too.)

2) Have you ever received any money for something creative that you did?

3) Have you ever starved (or its equivalent) because you wouldn't/ couldn't find/get a job because you were/are a full-time artist/writer/ dancer/what?

4) Do you have any feelings of shame about receiving money for your craft? Fear of success is the artistic person's personal demon.

And the biggest question of all: Are there ways to begin moving your life in the direction of supporting yourself full-time at your craft?

A small assignment: next time you pass a street musician or performer, throw a buck or two in the basket or hat, not just spare change. Next time you're given the chance to buy a self-published text or poem, buy it. Seek these out in bookstores, usually a dusty bottom shelf in the back.

Do it in memory of the Red Monk, Lew Welch, who one day walked away into the California woods with a gun, deeply depressed and despondent over a world that offered up accolades but no rent money.

No body was ever found. His death was never confirmed. Who knows? Maybe that Xeroxed poetry leaflet you buy for a dollar or so is by . . .

A Selected **Lew** Welchography

Books

Ring of Bone: Collected Poems 1950–1971. San Francisco: Grey Fox Press, 1989. Reading this chronological collection is like hanging out with Lew Welch whenever you want.

I Remain: The Letters of Lew Welch and the Correspondence of His Friends. San Francisco: Grey Fox Press, 1980. As good a letter writer as a poet. Letters from other Beats included.

Trip Trap. San Francisco: Grey Fox Press, 1973. Collaborative haiku written with Jack Kerouac and Albert Saijo on a cross-country trip.

How I Work as a Poet and Other Essays. San Francisco: Grey Fox Press, 1983. Contains insightful advice for writers as well as hippie-era articles.

On Bread and Poetry. San Francisco: Grey Fox Press, 1977. Interviews along with Gary Snyder and Philip Whalen.

Recordings

Welch is featured on Disc 4 of the *Howls, Raps & Roars* CD set.

Biographies

Genesis Angels: The Saga of Lew Welch and the Beat Generation, by Aram Saroyan. New York: Morrow Quill, 1979. Written in a Beat style.

Critical and **Allied** Material

The best appreciation is to be found in Gary Snyder's loving preface to Welch's *Selected Poems.* San Francisco: Grey Fox, 1982.

Alan Watts

The **Way** of Spiritual
Gamesmanship

(*"This is it!"*)

lan Watts, born in England in 1915, became interested in Zen at an early age, writing his first book as a teenager. Eventually emigrating to the United States, he became an Anglican minister while still a Buddhist at heart, believing he was called to be a spiritual leader, and that the liberal Anglican church would provide a safe cover for his exploration of spiritual frontiers.

He left the ministry after a short time to become a writer, lecturer and, as he called himself, a "philosophical entertainer." Possessed of a rich and hypnotic voice, he became a popular lecturer on Eastern philosophy and a vocal advocate of the new humanistic psychology.

Watts had settled in the Bay Area at the time of the Beat exodus from New York and was acquainted with Snyder, Ginsberg and Kerouac, who used Watts as a character in *The Dharma Bums.* His essay "Beat Zen, Square Zen and Zen" was an examination of not only the issues in the title, but of his own inner conflicts over the evolving counterculture.

By the sixties, however, Watts had fully embraced the Beat-inspired hippie subculture, writing eloquently in favor of the psychedelic experience, as well as associating freely with Beat elder statesmen. Watts became the counterculture's nearly official guru, appearing on campuses and syndicated radio shows.

Alan Watts died in 1973, having fallen victim to alcoholism, but his books remain perennial sellers, keeping his spirit very much alive. Gary Snyder, speaking of Watts, said, "He blazed out the new path for all of us and came back and made it clear. Many guides would have us travel single file, like mules in a pack train, and never leave the trail. Alan taught us to move forward like the breeze, tasting the berries, greeting the blue jays, learning and loving the whole terrain."

1 / **Laugh** Like **Hell!**

We'll start this section on Watts with a great warm-up exercise for any occasion, especially something as serious as "spirituality" or an examination of your "self," two things that Watts regarded as the biggest jokes ever played on us.

One of his favorite forms of meditation was invented, he claimed, by Taoist masters and is the laughing meditation. When we think of meditation, we usually have an image of high seriousness, of the stereotypical lotus-positioned and grim monk or hooded and contemplative Franciscan. Watts, as usual for him, insisted through his exercise that life is what the Hindus call *lila,* or play.

Ideally, in Watts's view, meditation is being, acting and doing, rather than a cerebral and inactive examination. This playful and light attitude infects much of his work. Meditation, he says, should be like making love or listening to great music.

In doing these things, one (hopefully) isn't attempting to rush to the end; that is, to the orgasm or to the final note of, say, a Bach concerto. No, insists Watts, life and its activities are a dance and a process, not a product. One seeks ways to immerse oneself in that process. Laughing is a great way to jump-start this attitude.

The instructions are simple: start laughing, perhaps a forced chuckle at first, then artificial guffaws and even feigned belly laughs. At first it'll feel completely foolish and idiotic. Persevere. It's our sense of false dignity and uptight control that is often the wall between us and freedom. Keep on trying to laugh. Persevere. Keep it up for at least three minutes. As you begin to be taken over by the process of laughing, you'll begin to actually laugh, often until tears stream from your eyes. All that stress and emotion that you store all day long in your muscles and psyche are being blessedly drained away as you laugh out of control.

Try this with a few other people, with you leading the laugh. I've done this, yes, feeling completely foolish as I laugh alone until the others get with the program. We're so uptight and fearful of what others might think that there's an incredible amount of resistance to this. One group I was leading, when they finally began to laugh for real, was unable to stop, getting bellyaches, their faces streaming with tears. For the rest of the workshop, any little thing would send them into paroxysms of hysteria.

Feeling sick of it all? Laughter is your best medicine.

2 / **Can I Please** Have **Your** Complete **and** Undivided **Attention**?

This exercise is also called the "snow treatment" by Watts. Much of Watts concerns our very real everyday lives and his search for ways to become more sensual and more in touch with our physicality. We lack, he says, the sense of "experimental adventure," saying that we never ask ourselves, "What sort of life could we live? What would be a new way of living?"

He says that with all our technology, medicine and money, we don't live gracefully or with imagination. Instead most of us work all day only to return home to watch an imitation of life—the TV—and to eat unimaginative food before repeating the whole process again. No wonder most of us feel unfulfilled and that there's something lacking in our lives: *there is.* We have, he says, a "dangerous incapacity for pleasure." The "snow treatment" is one of his antidotes for reclaiming a fully sensuous life.

The "snow treatment" consists of this: You devote yourself to another person for an entire evening. You cook dinner for the other, setting it out beautifully, with your best china, etc. Then give a massage, perhaps a bath with incense and candles. For that evening, you lavish incredible and mindful attention upon your partner.

This is real, says Watts, and not prepackaged synthetic experience; living becomes an art form, and you the artist. Surprise someone tonight. You'll surprise yourself. Watts also says that we somehow feel guilty when doing these very sensual things, that our culture has warped us into feeling that only work and consumption (of products or entertainment) are "approved" and therefore "moral" activities.

Languidly and elegantly push away this artificial guilt that keeps you a robot, and not the sensuous, loving and spiritual animal that you are.

3 / **The** Smell **of** the **Spirit**

As one of the West's first meditation teachers and popularizers of Asian traditions, Watts also introduced many of the props we now take for granted in the practice of meditation. One of these, now ubiquitous in even convenience stores, is incense. Smell, says Watts, represents our repressed sense. Certain scents we associate with certain states of mind, and these states of mind can be evoked merely by smelling the associated scent.

Watts says that we always talk about seeing, touching and hearing, especially in regards to God. But, he asks, what about "smelling" God? If we lose use of our sense of smell, we are as good as blind. Most mammals rely primarily upon their sense of smell as their guides.

We are, he says, ashamed of our sense of smell. We have plenty of adjectives for taste, such as sweet, but only a handful for describing things we smell. The evocative power of smell makes life truly three-dimensional and represents a spiritual aspect of life in this very place and body. Watts describes such evocative smells as leaves being burned on an autumn day, freshly roasted coffee in the morning and frying bacon as particularly strong childhood memories encoded as smells.

It would seem that our memories and responses are stored not only in the lining of the brain but in the lining of our noses as well. Reclaiming this often-repressed sense, we can become truly human and enjoy a fully sensuous life.

The best examination of the links between spirituality and scent is *Jitterbug Perfume* by Beat heir Tom Robbins, an epoch-spanning look at a very smelly subject. If you find that scents have a powerful and transformative influence on you, then *Jitterbug Perfume* is required reading.

Think about this for a minute or so. What scents or smells immediately evoke memories or states of mind for you? Your father's shaving lotion makes you feel like a child again? The scent of patchouli puts you in the middle of Woodstock? Burning wood into Girl Scout camp? List at least two memories that you have stored in your consciousness as odors.

1) _____

2) _____

Now that you're thinking with your nose, light a stick of incense and inhale deeply. Whenever you smell this again, you'll remember this book and exercise. If you're not in the habit of burning incense, go buy some.

4 / **Clothes** Fake **the** (Wo)man

Head in the clouds and feet firmly on the ground" seems an apt description for the teachings of Alan Watts, who in addition to his philosophical prescriptions and ponderings wrote extensively about everyday living. Turning his attention to clothes, Watts had much to say and suggest. Always concerned about the illusion of our "ego," which he considered to be conditional and a construct, he claimed that our modern tight-fitting clothes serve as a barrier and reminder of our limits, of our "existential authenticity," a reminder that we are truly *here,* and a fabric fence prohibiting our flowing over *there.*

The tight formfitting feel of the fabric against skin, the shape-hugging cut of slacks and skirts, the bondage of a necktie all serve to remind one of where one's body begins and ends. The ego, so fragile and subject to the vagaries of the outside world, finds solace and comfort in being trussed up, almost as if the soul were placed in bondage.

On the other hand, Watts asserts that loose, free-flowing garments aid in personal liberation and an enlargement of self-image and the area of potential. The boundary between self and other is less clear, less easily defined. The body is free to shift, hang, move and even undulate in its natural fashion. Referring to the Roman- and Greek-type togas, he reflects that the drapery of loose fabric flatters the human form and enhances its aesthetic qualities. He himself says he favors the loose kimonos of Japan for wear about the house.

Just look at who wears what, he asks. Military, police and uptight businessmen wear tight "uniforms." Holy men, gurus and monks wear robes. Look as well at some of our clichés about human behavior such as calling someone a "stuffed shirt," "caught with your pants down," "wearing an expression," "covering yourself" and so forth. These expressions show the intimate connection between who we are and what (or how) we wear.

Along with the tightness of dress goes its unrelenting uniformity. People, he says, are afraid of standing out and hence all nearly dress alike, dreading the different or colorful or flamboyant. Is this because no one wants to seem conspicuous, because one is engaged in a game of "I'm more modest than you" or because at root, one feels oneself to be a fake? Watts calls this conformity in dress a "crypto-masochism" and heartily endorses the idea that we begin to add color and even eccentricities to our wardrobes.

Examine your own style of dress for clues as to who you really are. What messages are you sending your body (and spirit and ego) by its coverings? Try to loosen up your style of dress, becoming less "uptight." Start by wearing loose clothes around the house and oversize clothes when you go out, perhaps forgoing underwear. You might feel some resistance to this at first, as your sense of self is threatened by the body's unaccustomed freedom of movement. Throw away one constricting item from your closet today.

View clothing as masquerade, an elegant, graceful and playful costume party. Wear something unusual or flamboyant today. Have a picture taken of youself in your looser clothing and paste it in your Journal. Who you really are is longing to shed those tight artificial and drab skins. If you feel as though you're hanging on by a thread, then let go of the threads entirely.

5 / **Insecurity** Is
Good

In *The Wisdom of Insecurity,* Watts examines the desperate search we engage in for something to hold on to, something unchanging and immune to erosion by time and death. It is our basic sense of insecurity that makes us prey and easy targets for facile beliefs and schemes for ego aggrandizement. We try to buy time or immortality through work, money, sex and power. And yet eventually and inexorably all these things and the life that lived them slips away. Despite all our best efforts and intentions and the worst of our fears, things pass away and the ground we walk on is revealed to be transient and transparent.

Our rigid defense of self and boundaries at first provide us with a limited sense of security, and yet the more we have, ironically, the more we fear its loss. You know the equations: more money, more fears about losing the money; more health, more fears about illness. In the words of Lao-tzu: One who feels deflated must once have been a bubble.

And we are all essentially bubbles as we pass through this phantasmagoric and flowing ocean of awareness and life. There is no solidity, nothing for sure. We can disguise this fact and even fool ourselves most of the time, but basically our position is extremely insecure in the terms in which we understand it.

Watts proposes that we take an entirely different attitude, that we embrace and even celebrate our basic insecurity, learning to flow freely with change and exchanging our existential fears for a moment-to-moment exhilaration and expectancy. In accepting our insecurity, we paradoxically become secure for the first time in our lives, freed of stress, fears and dread. One might consider this to be a form of optimistic fatalism, but Watts's prescription is far more than that. It is an injunction to become the process that we are rather than the tubelike products we believe ourselves to be.

What are some simple ways to confront and experience insecurity in an effort to become conversant and comfortable with it? Start easy and safely. There's no need to quit your job or give away all your money (yet). The mental and spiritual attitudes are far more important than the material aspects. Try these things:

1) Leave the house without any ID, such as a driver's license. Who are you without the proper documents? How does it feel?

2) Leave the house with no money. This will restrict your experience to "consuming" free things such as sights and sounds rather than manufactured things.

3) Do the Sacred Drift exercise by Hakim Bey (see page 296), spending a day with no goal or destination in mind.

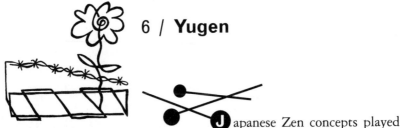

6 / Yugen

Japanese Zen concepts played a large part in the formation of Watts's philosophy. One of these is the idea of *yugen,* a nearly untranslatable concept to which Watts attaches great significance. He renders it as an emotional state of perception. The basic visual symbol of yugen would be a tree growing out of rock.

We've all seen something similar to this. Watts describes this as something unexpected, improbable, mysterious and contradictory, even paradoxical and surreal. *Yugen* was also the name of a Beat magazine run by Hettie Jones in New York City in the fifties. The sense of yugen, of surprise, informs much of the Beat spirit, even in its publication.

Yugen is a sudden sense of surprise and awe; a spontaneous discovery that runs counter to your usual sense of how things should be. Yugen experiences have the feeling of cold water thrown in one's sleepy face, of a sudden awareness that life, despite its monotony and routine, remains spontaneous and unscripted. Look for such symbols in your life.

A couple of urban examples I've experienced: a flower growing out of a storm grate at the side of the street; grass breaking through an asphalt parking lot, a beautiful short poem spray-painted alongside the usual graffiti on a highway underpass. For this exercise, find an example of grace amid degradation, of the unexpected in the midst of the "taken for granted." Record it here or in your Journal. Share it with other people. Make yugen-hunting and awareness a habit.

My yugen: _____

7 / **Listen** Up!

Much of Watts's career was devoted to the teaching of Zen meditation. Explicit and detailed instructions for meditation abound in his books and tapes. Possessed of one of the best voices I've heard, he simplifies and demystifies the entire process, making it seem as natural as a cat taking a nap.

Again and again, he begins his instructions with the simple injunction to "just listen." In this, he is encapsulating the entire thrust of Zen. Basically, Zen consists of nothing more than simply paying attention, without the intervention of one's beliefs, opinions or expectations. Sounds easy, right? But for anyone who has ever attempted to do this and only this, it seems at times like torture. Learning to be present and pay attention is a reeducation in the abilities we once possessed as children and that our pets still possess.

Our brains are too busy being obsessive, says Watts. And what are they obsessed with? Symbols, rather than the reality they represent. And Zen is nothing less than simply entering reality. Our brains, he says, interpret everything in symbols. These symbols take the form of thoughts. Eventually, with age and conditioning, when we believe we are experiencing life, we are actually just thinking thoughts about thoughts. An endless loop and one from which there is no escape except for the one secret your third-grade teacher attempted to teach you: that's right, listen up! Just pay attention. Or else you'll paying your karmic debt instead with missed opportunities, stress and angst.

Watts's instructions for listening are easy, so listen up and pay attention. I'm not going to repeat myself: Sit quietly and begin to listen. Let the air and sounds play with your ears. Don't try to name the sounds. If a car goes by, don't say to yourself "car." Just listen. Don't grasp attractive sounds, and don't become annoyed by unattractive ones. Your brain, the thinking, obsessive one, is what names them good or bad. There are, in actuality, no good or bad sounds. Just sounds. Just listen.

Don't become disturbed by intrusive or "unscheduled" sounds. Again, it's your thinking patterns that make concepts such as schedules and so forth. *Nothing* is unscheduled or inconvenient. You can no more control the process of sounds occurring than you can dam the Colorado with your hand. An obvious but important lesson. Just listen to sounds and let go of the illusion of control as you would allow the water of a river to flow around and wet your hand as you immerse it.

These sounds: are they the same as you or different? Without the physical existence of you and your ears, there literally wouldn't be any sounds; no experiencer in the form of "you." "You" are creating these sounds. You are responsible for them. They are the same as you. No different. You are an extension of sound and the sound an extension of you. Your skin is not where "you" stop.

If names, judgment and thoughts arise and grip you while you're listening, that's OK. Don't hold the thoughts. Let them go. Deny the thoughts attention and pay attention to the sound. Don't think: Oh, I'm a bad Zen meditator. There is no good or bad in this, only the experience, only be here right now, comfortable or uncomfortable. How does it feel?

Listen to the sounds as you would to music. For the time period that you do this, say ten minutes, pretend you're listening to a postmodern concerto composed of real-life "randomized" sounds. Just listen. And who is the composer? Just compose.

8 / **Hide** and **Seek**

Watts adapted Hindu philosophy as well as Buddhist in his quest for meaning. From the Hindu scriptures and mythology, he derived one of his favorite metaphors. He called this teaching "Hide and Seek." In the Hindu cosmology, Brahman is pictured as All. That is, there is nothing besides Brahman, the universal and primordial Cause of Being. Simply put, Brahman becomes bored being all alone, and seeking some drama and amusement, breaks himself into countless fragments of consciousness, setting into motion a great game of self-discovery.

Each fragment, be it human, plant, animal and so forth, is in actuality a part of Brahman. To make it really interesting, Brahman sets this rule: each piece will forget that it is part of Brahman and believe instead that it is unique and isolated from all the other fragments.

The aim of this game of cosmic "Hide and Seek," according to Watts, is for each fragment of consciousness to wake up and remember that it is actually God, or Brahman, and recognize itself in each other piece of the shattered Godhead. When all the pieces remember, then the game is over, and all the fragments return to One, reconstituting Brahman.

Remember, even Brahman itself is gone during the game, having obeyed its own rules and even forgotten that this is, in reality, a game. In this way, Brahman experiences every conceivable form of consciousness, every delight, every horror, every pain and ecstasy. It can take millions of years and countless galaxies for this dramatic game to be played out.

Remember this when you greet someone. Saying "Hello" is essentially shorthand for actually saying "Hello in there, you rascal. You can't fool me. I see you hiding in there. You're part of God, just like me. This is really a game we're playing, pretending I'm me and you're you." The Hindu greeting, or commonplace equivalent of our "Hello," is "Na-

maste" and literally means, "I honor the divinity in you that is also within me."

Say hello today to someone you don't know. Introduce yourself, maybe to the clerk you always buy your paper from, or the gas station attendant whose name you've never bothered to learn. In Watts's view, they're all part of you. Acknowledging them, you're on the way to winning the game of Hide and Seek. Most of us hide behind masks of civility and formality, or even feigned indifference. Stop hiding in there. Seek the others out there who complete you.

A Selected **Alan** Wattsography

Books

Become What You Are. Boston: Shambhala, 1995. Palm-sized book of excerpts.

The Book: On the Taboo Against Knowing Who You Are. New York: Pantheon, 1966. Perhaps his clearest and most useful book.

Cloud-Hidden, Whereabouts Unknown: A Mountain Journal. New York: Vintage, 1974. Mountain journals and short essays.

Does It Matter? Essays on Man's Relation to Materiality. New York: Vintage, 1970. Essays on food, clothing and the material world.

The Essence of Alan Watts. Millbrae, Calif.: Celestial Arts, 1977. Mini-essays; like it says: essential, a good starting place.

Joyous Cosmology. New York: Vintage, 1962. Psychedelic Watts.

Nature, Man, and Woman. New York: Vintage, 1970. On love and sexuality.

Talking Zen. New York and Tokyo: Weatherhill, 1994. Radio Zen.

Tao: The Watercourse Way, with Al Chung-liang Huang. New York: Pantheon, 1975. His last book, reflecting the mature sage.

The Way of Zen. New York: Vintage, 1957. The classic introduction to Zen.

The Wisdom of Insecurity. New York: Vintage, 1951. Advice written in the fifties, more necessary than ever in the nineties.

Audio

Alan Watts Live (Shambhala).
Alan Watts Teaches Meditation (Audio Renaissance).
Om (Infinite Zero).

Video

Many videos of Alan Watts are available, as well as a complete catalog of audio recordings from Electronic University, P.O. Box 2309, San Anselmo, CA 94979.

Biographies and Critical Material

How the Swans Came to the Lake, by Rick Fields. Boston: Shambhala, 1986.

In My Own Way: An Autobiography, 1915–1965, by Alan Watts. New York: Pantheon, 1972.

The Portable Beat Reader, edited by Ann Charters. New York: Penguin, 1992. Contains "Beat Zen, Square Zen and Zen."

Zen Effects: The Life of Alan Watts, by Monica Furlong. Boston: Houghton Mifflin, 1986.

Prophets

The **Way** of
Spiritual **Diversity**

"THE ONLY WAR THAT MATTERS
IS THE WAR AGAINST
THE IMAGINATION!"

Diane DiPrima

In addition to the "major" Beat writers we've just hung out with were a great many other Beat personalities, not all as high-profile, prolific or as widely influential. Nonetheless, they were (and are) all, in their own rights, progenitors of their own traditions, prophets of the future, and authorities in their own fields of expertise.

Scattered across the country and from a diversity of gender, ethnic and spiritual backgrounds, these people rounded out the Beat agenda, and even advanced it further than it might have gone, especially in the areas of feminism, African-American consciousness and Judaism. In this, Beat represented one of the first truly representative literary and spiritual movements, reflecting the cultural diversity that is/was America in sharp contrast to previously all-white, all-male, all-Protestant groupings.

That so few women are represented among the Beat nucleus cannot be ignored, however, but only explained as a function of the times, that no matter how "revolutionary" a group or philosophy might appear, it remains nonetheless in unconscious adherence to cultural norms so pervasive that they are taken for granted. The original Beats, often accused of misogyny, nonetheless provided the philosophical platform for many women to empower themselves in a fiercely patriarchal culture.

As can be seen in the "Latter-Day Saints and Heirs" chapter, women in modern times have moved front and center, virtually dominating artistic and literary fields formerly deemed exclusive provinces of the "Bohemian" male. In this light, the pioneering work of Diane DiPrima gains more and more visibility as the years pass, establishing her as a Beat writer of the first order and one too often overlooked at the expense of the more media-drenched male writers.

Most of the Beats in the "Prophets" chapter were acquainted with one another, collaborating on projects, often traveling to see each other, and occasionally sharing living (or loving) space. They were all encouraged in their work by not only the major Beats, but each other's examples as well.

The selection that follows is, I believe, representative of their central spiritual and cultural concerns. Divided into two sections, it also includes samples of Beat visual-art activities. You'll most likely identify strongly with at least one of the personalities or themes, and I'd encourage you to learn more about them when you finish this workbook.

The Writers

1 / **Bop** Kabbalah

A contemporary and fellow traveler of the Beats, Jerome Rothenberg has made the study of language and spirituality his lifework. In his books, he examines the intersections of the two and engages in unique experiments to illuminate the often powerful interface. In works such as *Technicians of the Sacred,* an anthology of "third world" shamanistic poetry and ritual, and *Poland/1931,* a book of linked poems based upon Hasidism and Kabbalah, Rothenberg pushes the envelope, spiritually and linguistically. One of his most recent books, *Gematria,* is based entirely upon a principle of Kabbalah, or Jewish mysticism. The poems in the book are devised using gematrical manipulations and principles.

Gematria involves, first of all, the recognition of letters as inherently "sacred," their use and manipulation producing actual corresponding manipulations in this "real" world. In traditional Hebrew gematria, each letter is assigned a numerical value. For example, the first letter of the Hebrew alphabet (*aleph-beth*), being *aleph,* **א**, is assigned the quality and number of 1.

All sorts of mystic significances and hidden meanings in Torah can be brought to light in this manner. For our purposes, however, I'd like you to just find out the gematrical equivalent of your name. Here's a handy key for you to use:

A-1 B-2 C-3 D-4 E-5 F-6 G-7 H-8 I-9 J-10 K-11 L-12 M-13 N-14 O-15 P-16 Q-17 R-18 S-19 T-20 U-21 V-22 W-23 X-24 Y-25 Z-26

My own name, Mel Ash, when gematrically transposed, becomes:

13-5-12   1-19-8

and when added up :   30   28
when the first and last names are totaled: 58

These numbers are somehow significant for me and my unfolding karma in this *gilgul* (Hebrew for "incarnation"). I will remember them as they appear in my life (or if I ever decide to play the lottery). I already know that I moved to Rhode Island and took my most significant employment at age twenty-eight and stopped drinking at age thirty, precipitating a life previously unimaginable. What will happen at age fifty-eight? Or maybe the numbers stand for other things? What other words (or names) add up to the same number as your name (spouses, job titles, deities)?

In the space below, do the same thing with your own name, studying the results intently.

Letters of name:

_____

Numerical equivalent:

_____

Total of first name: _____ **Total of last name:** _____
Total of both names _____
Observations: _____

_____

_____

Another way to gematrically transpose letters is simple rearrangement. A Brazilian embassy attaché in one of my D.C. workshops did just that with my name. "Mel Ash," after her transposition, became "Shalem." She found this significant. I found it immensely flattering, as she said it could be pronounced as *shalom,* or "peace" in Hebrew. (Would that it were so!) The difference is in the *O* replacing my original *E* in "Mel." The numerical difference between the letters is 10 (E=5, O=15). Somehow, I've got to come up with 10 more spiritual points to achieve peace. Later on, I discovered that *shalem* is the Hebrew word for "whole" or "complete," so I guess I'm safe.

Try rearranging the letters of your own name and see if any hidden meanings are revealed. As in my case, feel free to change an occasional letter, or even omit one if it renders the result clearer. You can do this in the space below or in a more efficient manner by writing your name on a separate piece of paper. Cut out each letter, like Scrabble® squares, and perform a series of recombinations. Write the result in the space. If you get no immediate results, try just one name; both; include middle name; explore all possible avenues until you arrive. Remember your new, secret spiritual "handle." Live up to it. What's in a name?

Here's an example of name-play from Jeremy Tarcher, publisher of *Beat Spirit* and other fine books :

Jeremy is my name.
Rumi is my favorite poet.
Silence the "Je" (or "I"), the ego,
and Jeremy and Rumi are the same sound.

Results of recombining name letters:

_____

_____

Put your "new" name on the cover of your Beat Journal.

2 / **Suicide** Note

The name of LeRoi Jones's first book of poetry was *Preface to a Twenty Volume Suicide Note.* Jones was one of the few African-Americans associated with the Beat Generation. Based in New York, Jones was also associated with Beat poet Diane DiPrima in pioneering small press publications. Now known as Amiri Baraka, he has produced many award-winning plays as well as becoming a forceful voice for minority rights.

I've read elsewhere that all the literature produced in a writer's life is really one long suicide note. This was obviously Jones's intention in thus entitling his first collection, foretelling his long and prolific career.

The exercise suggested by his title should already be apparent to you, especially if you're at the end of your rope with this book. You needn't write a lifetime, or even twenty volumes, for this exercise, so fear not. All I'm asking for is a short note; perhaps the most important note you'll ever contemplate writing: a suicide note.

In doing this, you'll be forced to really evaluate your reasons for dying in a conscious fashion. (After all, this is all that any good writing is about, anyway.) After writing and reviewing it, I hope you'll also have arrived at some reasons for living! Do it in the handy suicide-note form provided or in your Beat Journal.

(Important: this is not a real suicide note; it is just an exercise, so *please* don't leave it lying around where others can see it and probably freak out! Also, be serious when you write it; no "Goodbye, cruel world-isms," OK?)

Suicide Note

_____

_____

_____

_____

Now write a similar note, a note about why you decided *not* to commit suicide, the things you consider worth living *for.*

3 / **Silence!**

Bob Kaufman, born of Jewish and African-American heritage, lived most of his life in San Francisco's North Beach, the quintessential fifties Beat scene. Friends with nearly all the original Beats, Kaufman was regarded as a genius (the "black Rimbaud") in France for the quality of his poetry while virtually ignored in his own country. Considering himself a Buddhist and strongly influenced by jazz, Kaufman took a vow of silence at the time of John Kennedy's assassination.

He kept silent for ten long years, finally emerging from his self-imposed cocoon in 1973. His writings and thoughts from that time were collected by his wife, Eileen, and other friends in the form of scribblings on napkins and even toilet paper that he would throw away.

Kaufman's reasons for keeping silent for that length of time were his own, but no doubt influenced by his Buddhist beliefs about the invasive power of thoughts and words. Keeping verbally silent often triggers the process of inner silence. In that unfamiliar space, we can begin to actually hear what is going on, rather than interpreting it according to our own usually distorted lights.

The barbed-wire fences that we build of our endless words and conversation keep life at a proper sonic distance. If you've ever tried to keep silent, even for a small amount of time, you know how extremely hard it can be to simply shut up and observe what is, rather than describing what you think it is.

Try to keep silent for an entire day, in the spirit of Bob Kaufman, from waking to sleep. If you find it necessary to communicate at all, carry a small pad and pencil but attempt to keep your communications to a minimum. While keeping silent, also refuse to write out your thoughts or reaction to the silence. This is an exercise in disengaging from *all* forms of abstract expression, a detoxification from the Burroughsian word viruses that keep us at arm's length from true life. Keeping silent is not being *something,* it's simply being.

If this worked for you, maybe you can attempt to integrate this practice into your daily life, perhaps observing silence one day a week, an hour a day, or by simply talking less and listening more. Keeping quiet, you can can begin to hear what the Quakers call the "small voice within" speaking to you. This is who you really are.

4 / **The** War **Against** the **Imagination**

Diane DiPrima began her Bohemian lifestyle in the early fifties, at a time when women were particularly oppressed by societal expectations and stereotypes. Always politically active, her journey has taken her from her birthplace in New York and her association with early Beat publishing to a longtime Buddhist practice, as well as teaching feminine spirituality and magical wisdom in San Francisco.

An important link to the hippie counterculture of the sixties, as was Lew Welch, DiPrima was active in the struggles of that era, living communally in Haight-Ashbury. She continues to explore alternative forms of spiritual wisdom and eroticism, as well as being a warrior in the battles against imaginative freedom.

One of her finest statements of intent, and one often quoted by other Beat writers, is entitled "Rant." Its repeated statement, in capital letters, is "THE ONLY WAR THAT MATTERS IS THE WAR AGAINST THE IMAGINATION!"

She goes on to say that "There is no way out of the spiritual battle/There is no way you can avoid taking sides/There is no way you can not have a poetics/no matter what you do: plumber, baker, teacher."

DiPrima's insistence that we each have a poetics is fully consistent with the Beat approach to life as a self-determined sculpture of self, an artwork in progress. This is the inner meaning of her "poetics," that is, the style and the intent, the artfulness with which we choose to love out our lives.

The right to determine our own poetics, our own styles, to use our imaginations to their fullest, is, says DiPrima, always under attack. The war, she says, is the "war for the human imagination and no one can fight it but you/& no one can fight it for you." People die for lack of imagination, she says, and there are indeed other casualties in the war against the imagination, from the persecution of wise women accused of witchcraft to the demonization of modern artists and musicians by politicians and self-appointed cultural elites.

As children we get very overt messages about what is considered "weird" or "abnormal," and soon adopt the gray dullness that passes for creative thinking in this atmosphere of cultural warfare. Relinquishing our imaginations, we surrender the best weapons we have in the fight for personal liberation and spiritual freedom.

Can you identify any minor (or major) skirmishes from your childhood war against the imagination? Can you remember a teacher, parent or other "adult" figure giving you strong messages about "growing up," about being "weird"? If so, record it here or in your own imaginative Beat Journal as a first shot in your revolution: _____

_____

Can you name any current national events or activities that figure in the war against the imagination? These events affect us all, no matter how remote they may appear, impoverishing the very real imaginative atmosphere we breathe and depleting the realm of possibilities. An example I can think of: the PMRC/Tipper Gore attack on recorded music that led to CD labeling; the attack on the National Endowment for the Arts by right-wing cultural warriors; the banning of books as innocuous as *Tom Sawyer* in various politically correct school districts.

Much of the information/art in question is attacked simply because it calls the prevailing cultural paradigm into question or makes someone in power uncomfortable. The very best information, and the art most valuable for us in its transformative nature, is precisely uncomfortable. List any current wars you are familiar with:

_____

_____

Now go view some controversial art or film, or purchase a reviled CD or book. Put your money where your mouth is. Spend your money with imagination as well using it as a weapon against those who would make you die for lack of wonder and outrage. The Beat spirit is nothing if not confrontational and insistent upon the absolute primacy of the imagination: yours, mine, everyone's.

5 / **Holy** Erotica

DiPrima's autobiography, *Memoirs of a Beatnik,* is an excellent example of Beat erotic writing. The Beat ethic regarded the body and sex as holy, not as a source of shame or guilt. The Beat women, in many ways, were braver than the males in their transgression of cultural taboos regarding sex, particularly when writing about it.

Poet Lenore Kandel's *Love Book* was seized for obscenity when first published in 1965. Friends with most of the Beats and associated with Lew Welch in the sixties, Kandel was another link to the nascent hippie community of San Francisco. Her erotic poems, unabashedly celebrating the intertwining and inseparability of sexuality and spirituality, no doubt alarmed those who preferred to keep the two miles apart and at war.

These attitudes, typically Christian and industrial, run counter to the vast weight of human experience, which celebrated sex as a divine gift. Orthodox Jews long ago would reserve the Sabbath, a day when no work could be done, for sexual activity. Since God so obviously created sex for people to enjoy, sex was a way of worship of the Creator on the Sabbath.

Kandel defended her book in court as a "twenty-three-year search for an appropriate way to worship." She went on to state that she believed "sexual acts between loving persons are religious acts."

Her attitude is not surprising, considering her Buddhist background, with Buddhism's acceptance of sexuality as a divine path, as in the practice of Tantra, the merging of small self into an archetypical other. In her erotic poetry, Kandel followed not only her own lights but those of ancestor Whitman, as well, who was deemed pornographic in his day for his refusal to separate flesh from spirit.

Kandel, like Whitman, used words that people really use, which was perhaps the greatest sin, to report experience as directly as possible, words such as *cock* or *pussy.* The central belief of Buddhism (and the Beats) is that everything is equally holy and simultaneously mundane. No word is less holy than another. It is only the spin our minds give them that makes them so.

Write your own erotic poem in your Journal or on the following lines. Use real language, no euphemisms. If poetry writing is too high-falutin for you to bear, then just describe a loving, hopefully transcendent sexual act you've participated in. Read or show it to the partner(s) in the poem (or perhaps yourself).

As you write it, try to maintain an attitude of reverence and even sacrality about the experience, leaving snickers and smirks where they belong: with those who would deny us the right to worship as we please; with those who fear the body as a land mine in the war against the imagination.

_____

_____

_____

6 / **Poem** Bombs

Poet Gregory Corso was/is one of the original Beat authors, having met Ginsberg, Kerouac and Burroughs in early-fifties New York. Corso educated himself while in prison as a young man (serving time for an ill-advised theft). Having grown up in the rough-and-tumble streets of New York City, he saw poetry as his savior and studied it assiduously, displaying an immediate and natural genius. Of all the Beat poets, it is Corso who seems to garner the most critical respect, despite his slim output.

Observers continually refer to Corso as the prototypical "beatnik," in both mannerisms and behavior. Unlike the other founding Beats, Corso never really became publicly involved in the larger social issues of the day or in the investigation of exotic philosophies, choosing instead to comment in works such as "Power," "Army," "Marriage" and "Police."

An important religious exception is his "Geometric Poem." Published as originally written in his own handwriting and hieroglyphs, it is an examination of ancient Egyptian themes.

The poem that firmly established Corso in the public mind was his broadside "Bomb," a paean to the atomic bomb. Corso, obviously intending it as a tongue-in-cheek surrealist exercise, nonetheless earned the wrath of some audiences when he performed it, as they believed he was actually singing the praises of the bomb. In an odd sort of way, we might consider Corso the first to stand up against humorless political correctness, a role he continues to this day.

"Bomb" was published originally as a long one-page fold-out in order to accommodate the unique format of the poem. The words of the piece were arranged in the actual shape of an atomic mushroom cloud. Hence, the poem "Bomb" looked like the real thing that it was about. In other places, this is called "concrete" poetry, that is, the written piece designed in the shape of its subject. Doing this gives added life to the subject as well as further attacking the power of written words, using them not only as symbols, but as actual building blocks to describe *what is.*

In the box provided or on a blank page of your Journal, write a description of something in your life in its own shape.

Are

you sad?

Say so in the

shape of a large

teardrop.

This exercise should force your awareness into new and delightful shapes.

7 / **Publish** Yourself

Because of their position outside the mainstream, the Beats relied upon independent and often minuscule publications for the first dissemination of their art and thoughts. Many of them started their own small magazines and presses dedicated to the publication of this then-marginal and transgressive material. Diane DiPrima and LeRoi Jones in New York with their *Floating Bear,* Hettie Jones with her *Yugen,* Bob Kaufman's San Francisco–based *Beatitude,* artist Wally Berman's *Semina* and scores of other tiny, mimeographed publications, done for the love of it, spread the Beat gospel.

Paperback books were a novelty in the early fifties, but were nonetheless a powerful, inexpensive and democratic way of spreading the written word. The first bookstore dedicated solely to paperbacks was started by poet and anarchist Lawrence Ferlinghetti and his then partner, Peter Martin, in San Francisco's North Beach.

Naming it City Lights after a Chaplin film, the store has become a world-famous mecca for the hip, literate and simply Beat-curious. Ferlinghetti soon branched out into publishing the works of his friends and others neglected by mainstream publishers, starting the Pocket Poets series with his own *Pictures of the Gone World.*

The publication of Ginsberg's *Howl* in 1956 and its attendant trial for obscenity put City Lights on the map and established it as the granddaddy and ultimate blueprint of small, courageous avant-garde presses. Commenting on his endeavor, Ferlinghetti says that "from the beginning the aim was to publish across the board. . . . I had in mind rather an international, dissident, insurgent ferment."

Ferlinghetti, now devoting much of his time to painting, became known primarily for his book *A Coney Island of the Mind.* City Lights has gone on to publish most of Ginsberg's work as well as books by Kerouac, Burroughs and most of the other Beats.

The DIY (do-it-yourself) ethos of the Beat movement, formulated out of both necessity and belief, revolutionized publishing, empowering writers and poets to publish and distribute their own work. Despite the pervasiveness of all forms of media today, the centralized control of the means of production and distribution means that the situation has not really changed all that radically for those experimenting with different ideas or unpopular art forms.

On the music front, this has led to the establishment of small independent shoestring record labels that spread the early punk gospel. Small presses as well continue to spring up and vanish like mushrooms, spreading the words and ideas of modern rebels.

As we've witnessed throughout *Beat Spirit,* Beat is nothing if not the actualization of thought; that is, one must take real-life action in real deeds, rather than allowing others to produce for you, especially in the realms of art, spirituality and transformation. In short, you become both the creator and the market, forming your own often insular community well outside the safe and predictable mainstream.

Many of the exercises thus far have been personal in nature, not easily observable or critiqued by the outside world. It's now time for you to fully enter the Beat world by becoming, like Ferlinghetti, publisher of your own heart's delight, distributing your essence to a wider market, one defined only by your own audacity and ambition.

Below is pictured the pattern for a small booklet you can "mass"-produce yourself on a photocopier.

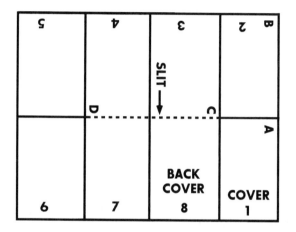

Fold an 8½-by-11-inch piece of white paper as shown, reopening it. You'll see that you have eight separate boxes. On the side labeled (A) you will start your book. In space 1, create your "cover." Start your poem, essay or diatribe on 2, using graphics, handwriting, typesetting or collage. When you reach 5, turn the paper around and continue to 8, which will be the last page or the back cover of your book.

Slice or cut as shown along the line in the middle of the page (from C to D). Fold the paper lengthwise and push it together. The cut will balloon the paper open, creating a diamondlike shape. Push the pages in and crease, creating your own book (see illustration).

Possibilities: copy lots of these to give as presents, sell them at small bookstores or use them as I do. I always carry a few to leave on subway seats, on shelves in stores or to hand to people in the street, especially those trying to hand *me* stuff, such as religious or political propaganda.

In doing this, you yourself stop being a consumer of culture and become a creator, a virus in the media bloodstream through the covert distribution of your own samizdat (Russian word for homemade underground oppositional literature). Who knows? Maybe you'll even get discovered like many of the Beats.

8 / **More** Dirty **Words**

enny Bruce gained fame and infamy as a stand-up comic and satirist in the fifties and early sixties. Continually arrested and harassed for his supposedly obscene language as much as for his acerbic social commentary, Bruce was a contemporary of and influence on many from the original Beat nucleus. The speed of the social change started by the Beats was such that only ten years after Bruce was arrested for saying the word "cocksucker" on-stage, the movie *Deep Throat,* starring Linda Lovelace, became a legal cult hit across the country.

Words that could get you thrown in jail back then are commonplace today. Burroughs has said that it's become shocking to *not* hear obscenity; that the old taboo words were taboo for a reason: their repeated usage drains them of their shock value and incantatory power. These supposedly obscene words take on the nature of holy words in their limitation and power to evoke emotion, image and feeling.

Bruce used so-called obscenity to wake people up and make them take notice. "The word's suppression gives it the power, the violence, the viciousness," explained Bruce. His use of obscenity usually took place in a trenchant social statement aimed at the mainstream that oppressed minorities and creativity. His heirs today—comedians, that is—seem to wallow in the now mundane obscenity, substituting crudeness for originality of thought and humor.

While the battle over language still rages, the war for the most part has long been over, thanks in large part to Lenny Bruce, who died in 1966 at the age of forty. Says Eric Bogosian, "Saint Lenny died for our sins." Others claim he was murdered by an uptight society.

Two ideas spring from these reflections. The first is this: if you've gotten this far in *Beat Spirit,* chances are you occasionally (or habitually) use "obscene" or profane language on a daily basis. If you do, then try not to say any of these words for at least a day; experiment with other ways of shocking expression. What was shocking in Bruce's time is, to say the least, boring and conformist today. See how the pendulum swings? To be really different and nonconformist, don't swear for a day!

Second: what is the filthiest word you can think of? No, not the usual "F"-type bathroom words, but some word that's used regularly around you or that you hear in the media; a newsspeak-type, Orwellian dirty word, perhaps such as *outplacement* or *downsizing,* or truly obscene words such as *ethnic cleansing* or *police action.*

Generally, these obscenities are euphemisms for something nasty that the user wants to mask. Write your dirtiest postmodern word here or in your Journal: _____. Saint Lenny thanks you.

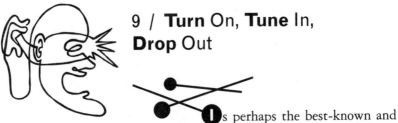

9 / **Turn** On, **Tune** In, **Drop** Out

Is perhaps the best-known and most influential slogan of the century (along with, of course, Make Love, Not War, Kilroy Was Here and Where's the Beef?).

Timothy Leary, the man who coined this phrase, was affiliated with most of the Beats by the start of the sixties, having introduced both Ginsberg and Kerouac to LSD, and traveled to Morocco to confer with Burroughs. In many ways, Leary became an evangelist for the Beat gospel of personal transformation and revolt, continuing until his death in 1996 to share both podiums and writing with most of the principal figures.

The slogan "Turn On, Tune In, Drop Out" was arrived at with the help of media theorist Marshall McLuhan. From the outset, Leary intended to "sell" his psychedelic revolution in the good old American style of "product," slogan and promised result. This is what made him such an absolute threat to the established cultural powers, leading then President Nixon to call him "the most dangerous man in America."

Dangerous because he knew how to use the American system of media and salesmanship. In America, things don't really exist unless they're in the media, and they exist even less without a label, slogan or logo; a popular shorthand for the often too complex ideas behind it. "Turn On, Tune In, Drop Out" was the right finger pushing the right button at the right time.

What exactly did Leary mean with this phrase? Was he completely serious in his intent? Many of the era (and since) have taken the advice quite literally. Should we? Let's examine each component of the expression:

Turn On. The immediate meaning of "turn on" is of course the obvious one: to turn on with drugs, specifically LSD. But the deeper meaning of "turn on" is also not so murky. To turn on implies a state of being "turned off," of sleep and hypnosis, of idleness and inertia. LSD was merely the catalyst in a process of turning on that can be started as easily with meditation, sex and other "peak" experiences.

Leary himself says that we must turn on to our untapped potential—our hidden divinity, if you will—in the same spirit that his friend and contemporary Alan Watts encouraged us to come out and play in the game of cosmic Hide and Seek.

Tune In. Once we're "turned on" to our true inner light and come out of our darkness, in the sense of being excited and aroused, we begin to "tune in." Tune in to what?

Have we been tuned out or poorly tuned? Yes, says Leary. In fact, to use electronic metaphors (as he frequently does), we've been tuned in to a frequency and channel chosen for us, the entirely wrong one, a life-stealing and soul-sucking channel and script masquerading as reality.

Tuning in means to fine-tune your reality and re-create it accordingly. Tune in to the incredible cellular wisdom of your body and the elegant and mysterious electrical energy of your brain. Therein lie the answers. Says Leary, "The only way out is in." Whereas turning on took fearlessness and an almost foolhardy courage, tuning in requires a faith in one's own path and innate wisdom.

Drop Out. Many people took this injunction quite literally, dropping out of school, marriages and careers. This radical step was (and is) quite necessary for many people, who had a great need to alter the contexts of their lives, as well as the texts.

Leary cautions, however, that this is not the only meaning of dropping out. Having turned on to one's potential and tuned in to one's own powers, one must now drop out of robotic behaviors and stop acting in poorly written scripts. If life, as the Hindus believe, is play, perhaps it is also *a* play. The play we act our roles out in is a turned-off and tuned-out one, designed only for the profit of the writers and directors. Dropping out of the play means waking up to reality and writing one's own script; or even better, no more acting at all, in short: real life.

The dropping out can be as simple as performing some of the exercises in this book, a gentle no-saying through words and actions. It can be as simple as refusing to buy certain products, or as dramatic as attempting honesty in a relationship. Dropping out and running to a commune in the country in search of some Arcadian utopia isn't really feasible for most of us since we take our scripts and roles along with us, dooming the entire enterprise.

Right here and right now is the place where we drop out. In so doing, you'll find to your surprise that you're really dropping *in*. Into your own real life for perhaps the first time.

So how do we turn on, tune in and drop out without acid? Other types of mind-altering substances abound, some of them in the forms of actions, beliefs and commitments. As we've seen in Burroughs, absolutely everything conditions and even addicts the mind. Conversely, nearly everything can be used as a drug of liberation and a means of detoxification.

How will you choose to turn on? Are you already? Turn on today by meditation (use some of the Alan Watts exercises we've already looked at), transcendental sex or by any other means you think up. Name it:

_____

Tune in today by listening to your body and brain. How do you feel? Guilty, tired, ecstatic, expectant? Describe your nervous system's activity at this moment as accurately and honestly as possible: _____

_____

Drop out by calling in sick today and going to the woods, by not watching TV and reading a book, by not reading the paper and by writing a letter. Drop out by: _____

Make this threefold process a daily habit. Record it in your Journal. Now drop in to the next exercise:

10 / **Karma** Repair

Richard Brautigan was yet another link between the fifties and sixties countercultures, and still another suicidal casualty of alcoholism in the eighties. Often called the last of the beatniks due to his young age in the decade of the fifties, he was a fixture in Haight-Ashbury, providing along with Lew Welch and Lenore Kandel an elder-statesmanlike presence in the new paisley Bohemia of the sixties. Although Brautigan is best known for his *Trout Fishing in America,* his novels and poems are filled with a dry and surreal whimsy that for a time perfectly captured a moment in the gestalt of America's countercultural youth.

The following poem is taken from Brautigan's collection *The Pill versus the Springhill Mine Disaster.* Your job is to complete the poem, which is reproduced as he wrote it. What is your entry for number 4?

Karma Repair **Kit**: Items **1–4**

1. Get enough food to eat, and eat it.

2. Find a place to sleep where it is quiet, and sleep there.

3. Reduce intellectual and emotional noise until you arrive at the silence of yourself, and listen to it.

4.

If you can fill out number four, and live out the first three, consider your karma repaired.

11 / **Fast** Speaking

he book that brought Anne Waldman to national attention and firmly established her place as an early heir to the Beat lineage was *Fast Speaking Woman.* Co-founder, along with Allen Ginsberg, of Naropa Institute's Beat-oriented Jack Kerouac School of Disembodied Poetics, and tireless friend of the older Beats as well as an anthologizer and foreword writer for many of their books, Waldman represents a transitional generation, one that not only keeps the Beat spirit alive, but invigorates it with new energy.

"Fast Speaking Woman" runs for twenty-three pages in *Helping the Dreamer,* her selected poems, and is basically a variation and repetition of one formula: "I'm a fast speaking woman." The line is repeated in machine-gun fashion, the adjective changing with each recitation. Some examples from Waldman: "I'm an elastic woman, I'm an abalone woman, I'm the transparent woman, I'm the rippling woman, the antediluvian woman, a solo woman. . . ."

This poem is best performed aloud with fervor. By writing out your own similar list of personal adjectives, you might discover some previously unknown attributes, as well as weaknesses. In doing this, you will have created a verbal map of your spiritual, emotional and physical state. Fill in the blanks as fast and unself-consciously as possible. If you wish to go on in lengthier fashion, devote a few pages of your Beat Journal to this endeavor.

When you're done, read it aloud to others. Have them do the same thing in return with their own list. Not only is this a great exercise in self-examination and affirmation, but also a great icebreaker at parties or dinners, and a bewildering answer to the question *"Who are you?"*

I have provided a multiple-choice gender selection at the end of the lines, so read what seems appropriate. (If you're not sure, then you need to be reading a book other than this one.)

I'm a _____ woman, man, person.
I'm a _____ woman, man, person.
I'm a _____ woman, man, person.
I'm a _____ woman, man, person.
I'm a _____ woman, man, person.

The Artists

Overlooked in all the hoopla and media about the Beat writers were their visual equivalents, the artists and sculptors who formed their own version of the Beat spirit in paint, steel and glue. Friends with the literary Beats and present at many of the same events, as well as collaborating with the writers on published projects, the artists, regarded as shocking, sick or insignificant in their time, were, like the Beats, prophetic in their exemplification of the postmodern spirit. The media and ideas they explored, regarded as exotic and outré in the fifties and early sixties, have by now become stock images, commonplace in advertising, film and video.

The extent of the visual rebellion was no less than the literary one and the artists had to create venues and galleries for themselves to exhibit their work, as they were largely ignored by mainstream art critics and institutions. Based for the most part on the West Coast, most of them have come to be known under the rubric of the Assemblage Movement, assembling their art, as they did, from various media.

The collage ethic that underlies much of Beat spirit (Burroughs's cut-ups, for example) fully inhabits the visual art of the Beats. This collage ethic, relying as it does upon the often jarring juxtaposition of unrelated materials and images, can be seen today in the rapid cuts and splices of network news and MTV. What was disorienting to an older, more literate and linear culture is comforting and familiar to generations since raised on electronic information and rapid segues of emotion and knowledge.

The Beats were the great watershed prefiguring this seismic shift in actual perception wrought by the flood of technological innovation as our nervous systems began to leak from our bodies, inhabiting TV and cyber and media space. Those of us reading this book actually perceive differently from older generations. The gulf in perception and interpretation is as wide as that between the Native cultures and the European explorers they encountered. We indeed have set foot on a new world, mapped only by our ability to assimilate information in often jarring and disconnected ways.

Many of the original Beat writers attempted art themselves, most notably William Burroughs, who, in his later years, has turned almost exclusively to art. Allen Ginsberg, known to sketch and illustrate his own poems occasionally, had in recent years received acknowledgment for his photographic work. Jack Kerouac fooled around with art as well, leaving behind paintings of Buddhist and Catholic themes.

What we discover as we explore the Beat spirit is the democracy of spiritual technology available to us as tools for transgression, transcendence and transformation. That most of these tools—writing, art, drugs and sex—spring from the right brain or more intuitive "spiritual" side of our biology is little surprise. In a world where reason and logic (primarily left-brain activities) have largely led to ecological devastation, poverty and war, it is now the right brain that seeks to have its day, first reappearing in modern times under the guise of the Beats.

The left brain views these activities as, at best, economically marginal, and at worst, a threat to be brutally suppressed. We, however, in the spirit of our right brains, can also view them simply as *fun.* So have fun with these art exercises as you create a new world for yourself, crawling out of the salty ocean of the limited self and standing upright on the shore of who you really are and who you might become, supported by the Beat spirit.

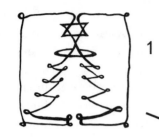

1 / **New** Traditions

Jay DeFeo was one of the most original of the Beat visual artists. Her masterpiece, *The Rose,* took seven dedicated years to complete and was so heavy that it had to be removed through a bay window with the help of a crane company. The move itself was documented by filmmaker and artist Bruce Conner. DeFeo died in 1989, some say in part to lead poisoning received as a result of the paint she used in creating *The Rose.*

Talented in a variety of visual media, she would pose nude in front of her works, documenting not only her output, but herself as well. This tradition of documentation among all the Beat principals has left us with the most complete record of a modern culture of resistance, in photographic, filmed and written form. Natural archivists, the Beat writers and artists all seemed keenly aware of their eventual place in history and of the importance of their actions.

A couple of DeFeo's noted activities have relevance for us as we seek to act out the Beat spirit in our own lives. Two traditions of hers that revolved around Christmas continually crop up in memories of her. The first is that she never threw away a Christmas tree, instead piling them in the corner until they resembled skeletons of holidays past. The second was her habit of suspending presents from the ceiling, almost like a Calder mobile or Mexican piñata.

Implicit in both these "traditions" is her own unique way of doing things, of finding different avenues of approach to living, which is really all the Beat spirit is about.

Can you think of any new ways to celebrate holidays, however eccentric they may seem to others? (If you can't come up with something, then hang some presents from the ceiling this year at Christmas or Hanukkah. Be sure to hang a rose for Jay DeFeo.)

Create your own traditions appropriate to your personal culture of resistance; traditions that serve to wake you up from the relentless consumerism that taints community celebration. Can you think of any different traditions you, family or friends already practice? If not, borrow one from other religions or cultures.

Another way to do this: at your next holiday, bring this subject up with friends and family. It'll make for a very different discussion and I'll bet you'll all arrive at some new traditions together, or one resurrected from your family's past.

In my house, we dye eggs red at Eastertime, something I learned from my Greek mother-in-law. After dinner, we try to crack each other's eggs by banging them together until there's a victor with an uncracked egg.

Another new tradition I've participated in is to get together with friends, Jewish and non-Jewish, around the holidays for a very American take on Hanukkah and Christmas. It's a weird enough time alone. Sharing holiday foods such as latkes and fruitcake makes it much more meaningful.

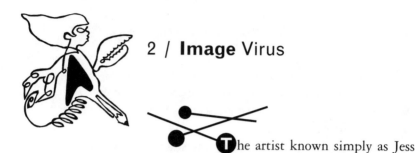

2 / **Image** Virus

The artist known simply as Jess was the lifelong companion of San Francisco poet and scholar Robert Duncan. In his "previous" life, Jess had worked as a chemist on the Manhattan Project, which resulted in the creation of the atomic bombs dropped on Japan.

Dreams of instant annihilation were commonplace throughout the early Cold War and The Bomb's specter hung over every heart, giving lie to the outward myth of tranquility and prosperity. The ever-underlying current of existential dread associated with The Bomb informed much of the Beat spirit, investing it with a "be here now" attitude. Jess himself says he had a dream in which he realized that the world had only twenty-five years before atomic incineration. He immediately dropped out and moved to San Francisco to become a painter.

His early (and later) works display a mastery of the collage method, utilizing pictures and words cut from magazines, comics, old books and newspapers. Collage, of course, has a long and honorable history, being first utilized to great effect by surrealist Max Ernst, who composed entire wordless novels out of pictures cut from old books. The collages of Jess comment on American consumer culture and parody its worst aspects.

Collect a pile of old magazines and books. Cut out images that either appeal to or repel you or both. You'll need scissors, a glue stick or rubber cement, maybe an X-Acto knife. Words and phrases, too. Paste them together on a page of your Journal or a separate sheet of paper. Use your collage to subvert some ubiquitous message such as "Cleanliness equals Godliness" by using advertising images concerning cleaning products by linking them with images of war. The cover of this book, designed by artist Susan Shankin, is an excellent example of Beat-style collage.

Abandon any ideas of "quality" or artistic content. Instead just make a mess and have some fun, rearranging the image in the same spirit that we rearranged the words in the Burroughs exercises. In a culture literally hemorrhaging visual images on TV, print, billboards and computer, your scissors and glue are your best line of defense against the manipulation of the image virus. Inoculate yourself by cutting them up. Burroughs says that he has "images, millions of images." So do you. Create a new one by using a few from your treasure trove.

1 / **Mail** Art

allace Berman's hand-produced *Semina* was an extremely limited magazine. Each issue was produced by hand with things glued precariously inside. Sometimes the enclosures were loose or tucked inside pockets. Things such as photos, seeds and little poems found their way into each issue, which went out to a very small and select mailing list. Created to be ephemeral and intensely personal, Berman's *Semina* featured the work of many early founders of the Beat movement, both literary and visual.

Each issue would have a loose theme that was not always readily apparent from its contents, but present nonetheless. This sort of art production was resolutely noncommercial and personal in a way that subverted mass art and production by its very precarious existence. Quite often, most of the recipients were the contributors as well.

Many of us have gotten out of the habit of writing letters or even of using the post office, having become meat extensions of technology, E-mailing, faxing and voice-mailing each other from the cold electronic glare of our computers and phone lines. The feeling of paper, the ambience of color and the tactile sensuous element have fled our correspondence.

Pick someone you haven't written to in a while; someone you'd like to surprise and who would be open to anything. Fill a small manila mailing envelope with objects, clippings, photos and things that sort of go together, things they might enjoy.

Perhaps your friend likes Chinese food. Throw in some fortunes from fortune cookies; a new pair of chopsticks. Cut out a picture of China and stick it in the envelope. One of those straw finger trap novelties described as a Chinese finger torture. A pack of hot take-out mustard. A stick of incense.

The contents are limited only by your imagination. You don't have to include a letter of explanation. The medium is the message and the message is "I took the time to do this for you, choosing with care objects to delight, surprise, inform, outrage and tickle you."

Real things. Real effort. Real friends. That's really the message of Berman's *Semina.*

4 / **Picture** This

Photographer Robert Frank's *The Americans* drew wide acclaim in the fifties for its realistic portrayal of everyday people and objects across the country. What attracted the Beats to his work was its element of absolute beatness, in the word's original sense of being beat, as in "dragged out, beaten down, and just plain old tired."

Jack Kerouac, in his introduction to *The Americans,* says that "after seeing these pictures you end up finally not knowing anymore whether a jukebox is sadder than a coffin." Frank went on to become closely associated with the Beats, directing the prototypical "underground" film *Pull My Daisy,* based on a script by Kerouac and featuring Corso and Ginsberg. Active until the present day and the subject of a Smithsonian retrospective in 1995, Frank's work has always provided the photographic analog of the Beats' words and art.

At your next party or family gathering, buy a few of these disposable cameras and distribute them with the instructions that there are to be no posed shots, only candids. Have people trade off using them, taking pictures of things one ordinarily wouldn't, say the sad chip bowl, the overflowing ashtray, someone knocking on the bathroom door, the pizza delivery guy. When the film is developed, make a scrapbook of these shots; an art piece constructed by its participants and seen from a number of different vantage points.

As Frank's work has demonstrated, art and poetry are to be found in the everyday and "mundane," waiting only for our imagination and consent to be released onto film or paper. Kerouac said that Frank "sucked a sad poem right out of America onto film, taking rank with the tragic poets of the world."

Can your camera suck any poems out of your world? Snap! Paste some of these photos in your Beat Journal.

A Selected Prophetsography

The Writers

The works listed below are all either important representative selections or the most recent collections by the authors.

Baraka, Amiri (LeRoi Jones). *Transbluesency: Selected Poems.* New York: Marsilio, 1995.

Brautigan, Richard. *Trout Fishing in America, The Pill versus the Springhill Mine Disaster,* and *In Watermelon Sugar.* Boston: Houghton Mifflin, 1989.

Bruce, Lenny. *How to Talk Dirty and Influence People.* New York: Fireside, 1992.

Corso, Gregory. *Mindfield: New and Selected Poems.* New York: Thunder's Mouth, 1989.

DiPrima, Diane. *Memoirs of a Beatnik.* San Francisco: Last Gasp, 1988.

———. *Pieces of a Song: Selected Poems.* San Francisco: City Lights, 1990.

Ferlinghetti, Lawrence. *These Are My Rivers: Selected Poems.* New York: New Directions, 1993.

Kandel, Lenore. *Word Alchemy.* New York: Grove, 1967.

Kaufman, Bob. *Cranial Guitar: Selected Poems.* Minneapolis: Coffee House Press, 1996.

Leary, Timothy. *The Politics of Ecstasy.* Berkeley: Ronin, 1991. Classic and essential collection from the sixties.

—————. *Chaos and Cyberculture.* Berkeley: Ronin, 1994. Leary for the millennium.

—————. *You Can Be Anyone This Time Around* (CD, Ryko). Late sixties; musicians include Jimi Hendrix, Stephen Stills.

—————. *Right to Fly* (PsychoRelic). Leary's last CD; death songs, even rap and heavy metal.

Rothenberg, Jerome. *Poland/1931.* New York: New Directions, 1974.

Waldman, Anne. *Helping the Dreamer: Selected Poems.* Minneapolis: Coffee House Press, 1989.

In addition to their own publications, examples of their work can be found in the anthologies recommended at the beginning of *Beat Spirit.* Several of the "prophets" also can be heard on the CD sets listed in the same place.

The Artists

Frank, Robert. *The Americans.* New York: Grove Press, 1959.

—————. *Moving Out.* Washington, D.C.: Scalo, 1994. Catalog of 1994 retrospective show at National Gallery of Art.

Other **artists:**

To date, there are no major studies of the individual artists discussed. The best source for both histories and reproductions of images is by Rebecca Solnit: *Secret Exhibition: Six California Artists of the Cold War Era.* San Francisco: City Lights, 1990.

Also valuable, lavish and exhaustive is *Beat Culture and the New America.* Paris and New York: Flammarion, 1995, a book/catalog published in conjunction with the historic 1995 show at the Whitney Museum of American Art.

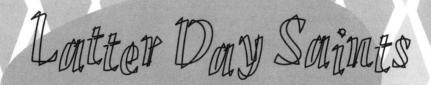

Latter Day Saints and Heirs

The **Way** of Spiritual **Anarchy**

(*"Outside of society..."*
Patti Smith)

_T_he force of the initial Beat spirit resounded through subsequent generations, being reshaped and adapted to meet the need of the new eras. In the mid-sixties, a new form of beatnik appeared, the hippie, to much media and national outcry. The children of the postwar generation, they had grown up not only on TV, but on the writings of the Beats as well.

In the fifties, Gary Snyder foresaw a rucksack revolution for the coming decade, millions of young people taking to the roads of America in search of visions and a better way of life, dharma bums. At that time, a new band called the Beatles exploded worldwide, bringing not only the beat but the Beat as well to millions. Lawrence Ferlinghetti pointed out that "the Beatles were spelled B-E-A-T. That wasn't a coincidence." John Lennon himself went on to assume saintlike status as he fulfilled his role as a Beat messiah, maintaining ties with Ginsberg and other Beat authors.

Kerouac's friend Neal Cassady became Ken Kesey's driver of the fabled bus "Furthur" as it spread the Beat/hippie message across the country with its entourage of Merry Pranksters. Kesey himself became a new "Kerouac," the psychedelic spokesman for at least part of his generation. The Grateful Dead were the house band for Kesey and his group, who also were allied with Allen Ginsberg, who, by the sixties, had become an internationally renowned countercultural leader spreading the gospel of meditation, gay liberation and psychedelics.

The Human Be-in in San Francisco's Golden Gate Park in 1967 marked an acknowledgment of the older generation. One of the first mass gatherings of the new tribes, it was presided over by Beat godfathers Timothy Leary, Richard Alpert (more commonly known now as Ram Dass), Michael McClure, Lawrence Ferlinghetti, Alan Watts and Gary Snyder, who spoke and read between performances by the new voices, bands such as the Dead and the Jefferson Airplane; for this generation would find its voice in music rather than on paper.

Bob Dylan has often credited his discovery of the Beats as the main influence on his work, particularly his college-age readings of *Howl* and *Mexico City Blues*. Janis Joplin regarded herself as a beatnik when she attended college in the early sixties and credited the Beats with inspiring her awakening. Jim Morrison of the Doors collaborated with Michael McClure in the writing of his lyrics, and Doors keyboardist Ray Manzarek tours today with McClure, backing up his poetry on keyboards.

The human potential movement that arose in the sixties and continues to this day, centered at such retreat centers as Esalen in Big Sur, was deeply influenced by many of the Beat writers and their friends, such as Watts and Leary. The movement's belief in the transformation of self and society through a variety of physical, psychological and spiritual techniques influenced in turn the nascent New Age movement.

As the hippie movement waned with the ending of the Vietnam War, something new began to appear. The punks of the late seventies derided the hippies for their softness and wide-eyed innocence, as well as for their selling out, as many former hippies became yuppies, pursuing the almighty dollar as ferociously as their parents ever did. At the same time, larger forces had begun moving to clamp down on the Beat spirit that was loose in the land.

The imprisonment of many of the "leaders," such as Leary and Abbie Hoffman, the discrediting and marginalizing of others through media ridicule, and the onset of a hypocritical war on drugs all contributed to a closing down of pregnant possibilities, and instead delivered a stillborn future to the kids who would become punks.

"No future" was the attitude and atmosphere. Diminishing expectations for either Beat utopia or even a minimum-wage job in Moloch fueled the punk anger, as did the seemingly immovable and aging hippie hierarchy that ruled the musical and countercultural world.

Punk was a return to the roots of rebellion, where anybody could play music or make one's own culture. As the new punk culture began to gain a sense of itself, it instinctively turned to forefather William Burroughs, whose novels are full of descriptions that are beginning to eerily resemble the real world.

Burroughs's no-bullshit attitude and acerbic refusal to cooperate with the forces of Control made him a new icon for a new generation, and he began a career as a spoken-word performer, seen today on Nike ads and heard on a CD backed up by the late Kurt Cobain of Nirvana, who for many of his generation represented the Beat spirit incarnate.

The Beat influence today has permeated nearly every aspect of modern culture. It can be found in every town and city, and in the resurgence of coffee houses and poetry readings. Performers such as Tom Waits, Lou Reed and Bill Laswell and his CD label Axiom, and bands such as Soul Coughing, Drunken Boat, Material, Genesis P-Orridge and Psychic TV, and R.E.M. all represent an outspoken commitment to the continuation of the Beat spirit in terms that continue to confront us with the possibility of magic and the sometimes gritty face of reality.

Writer and National Public Radio commentator Andrei Codrescu, another prominent Beat heir, was influenced early on by the Beats in his native Romania and has since continued the Beat spirit with books such as *Road Scholar,* a modern tribute to the *On the Road* experience, and his magazine *Exquisite Corpse.*

What follows is a selection of some heirs to the Beat tradition, some well known, some not. When you're finished with this book, start looking for the Beat spirit in other modern writers and musicians. Better yet, look for its traces in yourself. We are all heirs and descendants of our big Daddy-O's, the Beats.

1 / **Sacred** Drift

ntological anarchist Hakim Bey, a contemporary heir to much of the Beat ethic, a friend of Ginsberg, Burroughs and Waldman, as well as a teacher at the Beat-founded Jack Kerouac School of Disembodied Poetics in Boulder, draws much of his inspiration from heretical aspects of mystical Islam, or Sufism.

One facet of Sufism that particularly attracts his attention is the practice of "drifting," or the journey without goal, almost a physical analog of the meditative state of mind.

In Islam, the pilgrimage to sacred places such as Mecca is of paramount importance. However, the Sufi practice of pilgrimage removed the goal or firm destination and instead took its road map from coincidence, synchronicity and whim. You might already have done this exercise without having a name for it, such as driving around with no particular goal, just to see where you ended up. What Bey calls the "Sacred Drift" is nearly the same thing.

You can do this in a car, but if you walk, the drift is much more immediate. I've done it using unfamiliar subway systems in major cities.

The Situationists of sixties France did something similar as well in the streets of Paris.

Just begin walking at a time when you have nothing else scheduled or pressing. Set aside a time for this exercise and commit yourself to it. As you walk, just be attentive. If something catches your senses, drift to it, be it a street, sound or smell. Be completely spontaneous. Let the environment determine your route. Just drift with the interactions of your awareness and its surroundings like a leaf on rippling water. You'll see things you've never noticed before. You might actually end up at some very significant places or experiences, or run into someone known or about to be known, rendering your drift sacred indeed.

Sacred drifting involves a certain amount of what is glibly called "letting go" in psycho-babble. This is how you begin to let go of robotic, mapped behavior and begin to reclaim a sense of the mysterious, sacred and spontaneous. Kerouac's *On the Road* is in many ways an account of a Sacred Drift undertaken in a car in the fifties. Your drift can be a periodic and cleansing pilgrimage for your soul. No agendas, no destination, no expectations.

Once you've "drifted," you'll realize that, contrary to our beliefs, much of our lives are determined by unconscious drifting and influenced by subtler and more significant maps than we dreamed possible. Or in the immortal words of Chuck Berry, "No particular place to go!"

After you've done your first Sacred Drift, draw a map of it below, to the best of your memory. This is the reverse of most travels, in that you usually refer to the map first. In this case, the map becomes the souvenir. Post-mapping also might reveal aspects of your drift you were unaware of. Do not map while you drift, however: do not carry pencil and paper, do not be consciously storing memories for your actual map.

This map, as semantics reminds us, is most emphatically not the territory, just as Watts reminds us that the menu is not the meal. This map is another exercise in drifting inspired by the first. Write on it, draw on it. Paste pictures on it in your Journal. Include smells, people, music heard, emotions felt, scraps stuffed in your pockets as you drifted. This map is not a literal picture of your drift. Drift as you construct it. This is what your drift *felt* like.

Date of Drift: Locale: Duration:

Beginning &
ending here

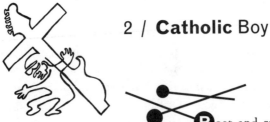

2 / **Catholic** Boy

Poet and rock singer Jim Carroll is noted for his famous *Basketball Diaries,* which chronicles his growing up in New York. Also appreciated for his early-eighties punk-style music, he continues to give readings and publish poetry nationwide, often sharing a platform with his Beat forefathers and -mothers.

A former junkie, inspired in large part by the early Beats, Carroll came of age in the late sixties, and his career has taken him through his influential role as a punk ambassador in the eighties, and on into the nineties as an influential and literate voice of resistance.

Closely allied with Patti Smith during his musical years, Carroll has had unique perceptions forming an unbroken Beat thread, containing in microcosm an entire history that the Beat spirit has taken as it has transmuted and changed through successive generations. Heir to a lot of the Beat spirit, the early punk rockers exemplified the DIY (do-it-yourself) attitude and community building of the Beat fore-runners, especially in their unflinching look at the so-called darker sides of life.

The title song of Carroll's first album, *Catholic Boy,* surely resonates uncomfortably with many of his listeners, themselves self-defined "re-covering" Catholics, with its refrain of "I was redeemed through pain, not through joy." We've looked at many religious issues in *Beat Spirit,* mainly in positive ways, such as exploring unfamiliar traditions. But now, through Carroll's eyes, we look at the damage done to us by our ancestral religions.

"Catholic Boy" is a musical mini-autobiography with a litany of (to the devout) blasphemous images, such as "I put my tongue to the rail whenever I can" (meaning the communion rail), "I made allies in heaven, I made comrades in hell" and "I make angels dance and fall to their knees, when I enter a church the feet of statues bleed."

Along with being accused of being pornographers and subversives, the Beats also were held guilty of blasphemy, or at the very least, dis-respect for traditional religion. As we've seen, the attitudes of Kerouac, Snyder and Ginsberg in particular give lie to the accusations. The Beats were indeed, as Kerouac said, "beatific," that is, saintlike in their extreme expression and their devout search for meaning, Ginsberg, in *Howl,* calling them "angelheaded hipsters."

Part of reclaiming your own version of spirituality is to recover from the religious damage done to you. Like Carroll, come up with a statement about your native religion that to you seems shocking and blasphemous. Do this in your Beat Journal or below. Like Carroll's friend Patti Smith, who in her first song chanted, "Jesus died for somebody's sins, but not mine," you too can refute or reverse dogma that has caused you guilt and pain.

Last time I looked, there was not *yet* an Inquisition, but you might be wise to share this exercise only with sympathetic friends. Create one "blasphemous" statement. Or even a joke. Like this one about my own tradition of Zen Buddhism, which I have formally left:

Q: *How many Zen masters does it take to screw in a lightbulb?*
A: *They don't screw in lightbulbs. They screw in hot tubs.*

(The joke alludes to the sex scandals that have tarnished Zen as much as Christianity.)

A blasphemous statement or joke:

_____

_____

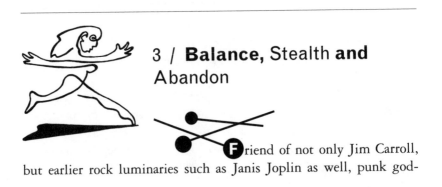

3 / **Balance,** Stealth **and** Abandon

riend of not only Jim Carroll, but earlier rock luminaries such as Janis Joplin as well, punk godmother Patti Smith consciously places herself in a tradition stretching back to Rimbaud. Also claiming as her role models Jim Morrison, Jimi Hendrix, Lou Reed and the Beats, Smith's emergence on the moribund music scene of the mid-seventies influenced the culture forever, nudging it in a direction prophesied decades earlier by the Beats.

Her 1975 album *Horses,* with its disturbing imagery and propulsive beat, revolutionized music and eventually spawned what we know today as punk music. Her lyrical images, inspired by Burroughs, are filled with sex, death and drugs; of walking the razor's edge of experience.

Immediately embraced and recognized by her heroes, Patti posed for photos with Burroughs and Ginsberg, and has collaborated with Bob Dylan. Transcending and even ignoring gender, Smith represented an androgynous and classic artist figure, who took the Beats at their word and pushed the limits of what was both possible and permissible.

That a woman should become one of the most visible and anointed heirs to the often misogynist Beat heritage was breathtaking in its implications for the future of the counterculture. Found among the mourning crowd that had gathered outside Ginsberg's apartment the day of his death, Smith has always acknowledged her Beat roots.

Women rockers and poets were at best tolerated twenty years ago. Today, women represent the cutting edge of avant-garde thought and performance, thanks in large part to the trailblazing work of Smith. Like Carroll, for whom rock was an afterthought, Smith is primarily a poet and spoken-word performer with roots in New York's Village scene. Author of various books and veteran of countless readings, Smith retired from rock in the early eighties to raise a family with husband Fred "Sonic" Smith of the revolutionary Detroit band MC5. After her husband's tragic death in 1994, Smith has reemerged with new writings, concerts and performances.

A new generation of Bohemia, writers and musicians, continue to acknowledge her as a prime influence. Appearing in an R.E.M. video and on countless magazine covers, Smith has returned to claim her counterculture crown. For many of her generation, she represents a valuable role model for growing up and older in a culture that equates submission and surrender with age. Smith's immense dignity and courage continue to inspire Bohemians young, old and elderly.

Smith's work is always filled with a full-face look at mortality, spirit and potential, giving lie to Nietzsche's adage that if one looks into the abyss long enough, one becomes the abyss. Smith's gaze into the abyss redeems us, and the darkness she brings forth is a comforting and reassuring darkness.

Smith's throwing down of the poetic and musical gauntlet set the tone for a generation that followed, a generation raised on broken dreams, shattered promises and a diminishing future. The old -isms were dead and no new ones were sought. We stand alone on the edge of history, she seems to say in her work, terribly freed of beliefs and even the promise of salvation. Smith's songs seem the sound track for apocalypse: personal and planetary.

Smith's experiences with the death of loved ones, raising her children, and surviving as an artist have eminently qualified her to offer us advice on living the Beat or Bohemian life. In the foreword to her *Early Work,* she offers this following bit of sage wisdom, perhaps the most important bit of advice in all of *Beat Spirit* as well, with its exercises and examinations of extremes in sex, drugs, politics and revolt. Smith advises:

> In art and dream may you proceed with abandon.
> In life may you proceed with balance and stealth.

The pages of countercultural history are littered with the names of those who have died as a result of their lack of "balance and stealth," with those who took "abandon" as the only rule, and not as a temporary technique to freedom. Your own experience, I'm sure, can provide examples of the results of reckless "abandon": overdoses, suicides, accidents, lost opportunities.

If you choose the Beat path, the way of one who courts experience instead of settling for descriptions of it, then plan on being in it for the long haul. The long haul is what Smith's prescription is all about, a hip version of Socrates' "moderation in all things" and Buddha's "middle path" between extremes of denial and indulgence.

a) Can you name any behaviors that you used to indulge in that you have moderated, in which you have attained "balance and stealth"?
b) Do you at present have any behaviors (or attitudes) that could use some balance, things that are potentially self-destructive?

My answers:

a) I've managed to live long enough to write this book by (1) quitting drinking, (2) moderating my anger and (3) learning patience, with people, with the rate of change and mostly with myself.
b) I would like to quit smoking.

Try to seek balance in the behavior you've identified in the last question. For example: I switched to a pipe instead of cigarettes. Did I quit smoking entirely? Not yet. But at least I'm edging toward moderation, and smoking a lot less.

Ask close friends this question as well, if you feel emotionally secure enough for some honesty. What do they see as your most unbalanced behavior?

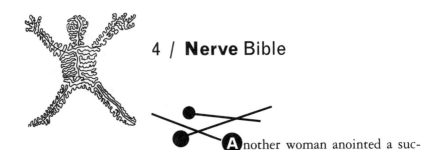

4 / **Nerve** Bible

Another woman anointed a successor by the Beats is performance artist Laurie Anderson. Anderson virtually defined and invented the term *performance artist* with her emergence on the scene in the seventies. Her albums and performances, filled with postmodern irony and oblique cultural references, represent the full flowering of Beat culture.

Much of her work is, like Burroughs's, an examination of the means for our control. Using a device known as a vocoder, Anderson electronically alters her voice to assume the pitch and timbre of what she calls "authority" in her assault, through words, music and image, on the dominant culture of consumption and hypnosis. Some of the voices she mimics in her performances are those ubiquitous and anonymous voices of authority we've become deaf to, such as the disembodied voice of an airline pilot or the recorded voices announcing rules and schedules in malls or the intrusive pitches on your telephone.

For the next week, note any of these ghostly voices you hear as you go about your business. Record any voices you hear here or in the Journal. The voices must be heard over an electronic system, either live or prerecorded. Try to identify at least three of these voices. "Attention, shoppers," "Please hold for an important message," "Sorry. All our lines are busy . . . ," "Doors opening . . ." List place and message in your

Journal. In the old days, if you heard a voice giving you instructions without seeing a body, they'd call you crazy. Nowadays, if you obey these voices, they just call you a good citizen.

Location of instruction _____ **Message** _____

_____

_____

Anderson is widely considered an expert on language, media and alternative culture. Through the use of state-of-the-art electronic equipment, she uses the tools of the techno-elite to attack their methods of indoctrination and control, in the spirit of the old Communist joke that the capitalists would sell you the rope to hang them with.

Anderson has collaborated with many of the original Beats, most notably William S. Burroughs, in both recorded and filmed performances. Her film *Home of the Brave* features her song "Language Is a Virus," a concept she obviously credits to Burroughs. In the film, Burroughs emerges to dance onstage with Anderson, a poignant and surreal handing of the torch from the male Beat literary culture to the female proto-punk electronic one in the making.

One of her latest CDs is composed of readings from her book *The Nerve Bible.* The Nerve Bible is her metaphor for the human body, again another mark of Beat philosophy: that all salvation and necessary knowledge for liberation lies locked within our meat and that spirit is in no way separate from our muscles and bone.

The Nerve Bible (the book, not your body!) is a collection of stories, memories and anecdotes drawn from Anderson's own experience. Stories about travel, her grandmother, camping, airplane flights and apartments she's had flesh out *The Nerve Bible.* Anderson says that she recorded the stories because she believes that "language is alive" and has an entirely different meaning when spoken aloud than when you see it printed on the page.

Write out a short memory or experience from your life in your Journal or on a separate piece of paper. Again and again in this book, we've seen the importance the Beat spirit places upon the redemptive power and dignity of our own experience. Telling our own stories brings our own nerve bible, our bodies, to life, and what can be read there will seem revelatory and redemptive. We, after all, die for our own sins.

Limit yourself to the space allowed. Take no more than five minutes to do this, writing perhaps about a swing ride you took as a child, the sky so impossibly blue and the motion of the swing so comforting and eternal, or perhaps write about an accident you passed on the highway. Whatever.

Have a friend do this exercise as well. Read to each other the stories from your nerve bibles as dramatically as possible. As we share our living language, our nerves touch and we become one Bible, one flesh, freed of dead meanings, cold print, and Control.

5 / **Graffiti**
Hieroglyphics

While the Beat spirit continued to inspire many, if not most, modern visual artists, the one most closely identified with the Beats was Keith Haring. Attending art school in New York in the seventies, he began to do anonymous art, tagging subway stations and walls around the city with his idiosyncratic form of graffiti. In short order, he was discovered and became an icon of the art world, his images adorning T-shirts, books and other products. Heir as well to the pop art aesthetic of Warhol, Haring was inspired early on by writings of the Beats, eventually collaborating on a major project, *Apocalypse,* with text by William S. Burroughs, whose cut-up experiments had deeply influenced Haring.

Friends as well with Timothy Leary, Haring developed his art into a complex and cartoony symbolic language, nearly hieroglyphic in its impact. Repetition of particular motifs, such as rays of light, wings and flying saucers, gave the work a nearly literary flavor. Most people, if not familiar with Haring's name, have seen his barking dog and "radiant" crawling baby, or his cartoonlike angels.

Termed a "future primeval" by Leary, Haring pioneered what Leary calls an "iconic language." Just as people are expected to read and write, Leary says that in the future one will be expected, as well, to "graphicize," that is, to rapidly "read" graphic symbols.

We already do this with traffic signs and such, knowing immediately, for instance, that a stick figure in a dress means a women's rest room is nearby. Haring's work incorporated not only this intent of "signing," but that of computers as well, based as they are on small, compact, universally understood graphic icons alerting the user to its uses, such as the "trash" barrel on screen. Leary says he showed Haring's art to Australian Aborigines, who nodded and grinned. They understood. Haring was dealing in "global icons," transcending language and provincial literacy. Called a "prophet" by Burroughs, Haring died of AIDS-related illnesses in 1990.

Do you find graffiti annoying, assaultive or intrusive as you view it on walls and subways? Try to study a piece of graffiti more closely some-time, trying to figure out the iconic content of the "tag." While much of it borders on simpleminded vandalism, a good percentage represents powerful statements of personality and social critique. Indeed, some of it begs to be framed and hung on your wall, don't you think?

At the beginning of this exercise is an iconic graffiti-style image of my own creation, my "tag," in the tradition of Keith Haring, representing myself. In your Journal or the margin of this book, create your own highly compact icon "word" or "sign." Think of Haring's images, keeping in mind signs that you are familiar with, graffiti you've seen. Proceed to use this icon on letters, paint it on your clothes in lieu of a little alligator or polo player; paint it on your house or mailbox. Use it to sign guest books.

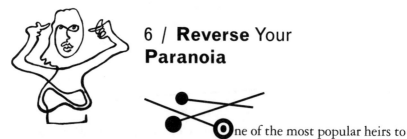

6 / **Reverse** Your Paranoia

One of the most popular heirs to the Beat tradition is novelist Tom Robbins, author of *Another Roadside Attraction, Jitterbug Perfume* and other books. He credits both Jack Ker-ouac and Henry Miller as influences on his style and has appeared at conferences with members of the original Beat nucleus.

His books, filled with playful revolt, surreal humor and insightful looks at art and religion, have influenced a generation of writers and readers. Robbins's books are far from the "boys' club" mentality of many Beat texts. Just as many of the Beat heirs are women, so too are the main characters of nearly all of Robbins's books: strong women, spiritual women, transgressive and transcendent women, even women as potential messiahs. The themes of his novels examine the hidden and often suppressed undercurrent of female spirituality and knowledge.

Like all the Beats, Robbins sees his work as transformative and liberating, as actual tools as much as mere books: "I view my books as cakes with files in them. You can eat the cake and lick the frosting, but inside there is a file that you can chop through the bars with, if you are so moved. I really believe we do not have to be weighed down by the past."

Some very Beat advice from Tom Robbins's *Even Cowgirls Get the Blues* that you can turn into exercises:

> . . . *all a person can do with his life is to gather about him his integrity, his imagination and his individuality—and with these ever with him, out front and in sharp focus, leap into the dance of experience.*
>
> *Be your own master. Be your own Jesus! Be your own flying saucer! Rescue yourself. Be your own valentine! Free the heart.*

My favorite Robbins exercise, from *Another Roadside Attraction:* "Those people who are following you? Pretend they're talent scouts."

This is not only good advice for paranoia, but for all our usual fears as well. For example, if you think someone's looking at you, judging you negatively because of your appearance, clothes, whatever it is that pushes your secret buttons, if you're feeling uncomfortable and not fitting in because you're so concerned about what other people are thinking, then just shift your thoughts ever so slightly to: They're not judging me, THEY'RE ADMIRING ME!

Believe me, I've really done this exercise a lot, and after a while it has become second nature, relieving me and my brain of a lot of ridiculous, ungrounded fears. The exercise is this: the next time you become aware that you're uncomfortable around unfamiliar people, even a cashier in a store, think to yourself: "They could be a talent scout in disguise."

Act accordingly, as though that Hollywood role depends upon it. Next time you catch people looking at you, instead of the usual self-doubts, catch yourself and realize that they just might be admiring your good looks. This isn't just your brain's wishful thinking. This is your brain on Tom Robbins.

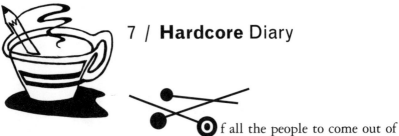

7 / **Hardcore** Diary

Of all the people to come out of the punk and hardcore scenes of the late seventies and eighties, Henry Rollins has become the foremost practitioner of the modern Beat ethic, having become a prolific poet and writer, even to the point of founding his own small press, 2.13.61, to publish not only his own work but that of others as well.

His writing and spoken-word performances resemble his early work with his influential hardcore band, Black Flag, in their unrelenting and abrasive take on culture and current mores. Often cynical to the point of nihilism and skeptical to the point of complete rejection of society, Rollins fully embodies the farthest reaching point of the Beat spirit as we enter the next century. His synthesis of punk anger and Beat literary traditions provide a valuable rallying point for young (and not so young) people searching for role models of commitment and talent.

Rollins has many techniques and methods in his writing. Two of these that recur are his use of dream recording and keeping a diary. Earlier in this book, we've seen the importance of dreams to the Beat spirit. This time, we'll examine the significance of recording observations of everyday life à la Rollins.

For the next week (seven days), make a diary entry just before going to sleep. Keep it short, no more than two or three paragraphs, recording not so much literal events, as your take on them. At the end of the week, see if you can discern an emotional or spiritual pattern to your awareness as traced out by your mini-diary.

In Rollins's book, *Black Coffee Blues,* he uses the motif of coffee as his daily taking-off point and poetic anchor in his diary, describing the cup of coffee and the emotions and day surrounding it. In your Journal, start by describing the clothes you wore that day or some other event, such as coffee, that recurs daily.

The entry could start like this; say you picked clothes as the theme: "3/27/97: Pulled on the old jeans, holes in knees. Black T-shirt. Black T-shirts remind me of bikers, of Jerry Garcia. The Dead. Dead. Remembering people who died. People I should really call. I called up X and . . ."

Here's an example from Rollins: "3.6.86, Linz, Austria: Staring at cup #3, not so hot. Not half as hot as the waitresses in this place . . ." He goes on to describe the restaurant.

Even if the connection isn't immediately obvious, still work a mention of your motif into the entry. Try to do this with paragraph-length entries in your Journal for the next week.

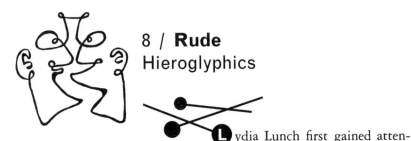

8 / **Rude**
Hieroglyphics

ydia Lunch first gained attention in the late seventies for her work in punk and new wave bands, such as Teenage Jesus and No Trend. Since that time, she's gone on to become a well-known cultural commentator and spoken-word performer of the most extreme sort, attacking technology, patriarchy, sexual repression and consumerism. With her longtime collaborator Exene Cervenka, she tours nationally and releases CDs of her work such as *Virtual Unreality* and *Rude Hieroglyphics,* sonic and over-the-top assaults on late-twentieth-century culture.

Exene Cervenka, former lead singer and lyricist, along with John Doe, for the seminal Los Angeles punk band X, has linked her work with Lunch's since the early eighties, as well as pursuing a solo musical career, providing a strong female voice strongly rooted in the Beat tradition of poetry, confrontation and mystical visions.

It is a curious fact that the Beat movement, notorious for being a nearly exclusive "boys' club" and even misogynist, finds its strongest heirs in the form of women, such as Cervenka, Lunch, Anderson, Smith, and even influences such performance artists and writers as Kathy Acker and Karen Finley.

In their 1982 collection of poetry, *Adulterers Anonymous,* Lunch and Cervenka write by trading off lines or sections. Each is identified by her own typeface within the poem. This spirit of collaboration and merging of personalities is also founded on the Beat spirit of mutual influence and a united front.

With a friend, write a collaborative poem or prose piece in your Journal or a shared sheet of paper. Choose a topic you both can agree upon, a political or spiritual one, say perhaps incidents of sexism one encountered in the workplace. One of you will print your lines. The other will use cursive to distinguish the voices. Try to be influenced by the line you read before you write your own. Hopefully, when you finish, the piece, although written by two different people, will assume the voice of the third that you create together, a sheet of "rude hieroglyphics."

Here's an example of poetic collaboration by me and the intrepid editor of *Beat Spirit,* Alan Rinzler, on the author/editor process. The bold type is mine and the other is Alan's:

Beat Spirit is nearly done,
but what has really been done?

Two guys on opposite coasts;
one an artist, another the coach;
one creative, one critical, cajoling . . .
Has this conspiracy borne fruit?
Is it deep? Is it fun?

Always incomplete,
even off to the printers, the bindery, the store,
nagging doubts, regrets.
The book no longer mine alone,
but the editor's as well,
his voice invisible ink between black lines,
his face a mirror,
mine only white acid-free paper.

A warning to writers:
Editor is sometimes a kindly surgeon
with scalpel here to save the ailing book,
deliver a healthy baby,
other times a thug with bloody switchblade
in the back alley of my literary mind,
gleefully carving me up.

    Advice to writers: Trust the alley.
                         Flee the operating room.
    Advice to readers:

Trust the Doctor.
Flee the alley.
Everybody needs an editor, a literary soul-mate,
cheerleader, stern father, nurturing mother,
to frame and focus,
to help the unconscious become conscious.

These words are scars.
These paragraphs purple hearts.
This book given a spank on its bottom,
gasping for air.

Yes, the book cries, it laughs, it sings
and reminds us of the cosmic giggle.
Don't worry, Mel,
it has a life of its own now.

Proud, grateful author/parent.
Kindly editor/doctor.
(The hired gun waits in the hall, pacing nervously,
passing out cigars like a proud uncle.)

A Selected **Heirsography**

Laurie Anderson

Books
Stories from the Nerve Bible. New York: HarperCollins, 1995.

CDs
Big Science (Warner Bros.)
Home of the Brave (Warner Bros.) CD and film; guest-stars Burroughs.
The Ugly One with the Jewels. Readings from *The Nerve Bible.* (Warner)
You're the Guy I Want to Share My Money With (Giorno Poetry Systems), with Burroughs and John Giorno.

Hakim Bey

Books
Immediatism. San Francisco: AK Press, 1994.
T.A.Z.: The Temporary Autonomous Zone, Ontological Anarchy, Poetic Terrorism. New York: Autonomedia,1991.

CD
T.A.Z. (Axiom)

Jim Carroll

Books
The Basketball Diaries. New York: Penguin, 1987. Made into a major motion picture.

Fear of Dreaming. New York: Penguin, 1993 (selected poetry and prose).

CD
Best of the Jim Carroll Band (Rhino).

Keith Haring

Future Primeval. Normal, Illinois: University of Illinois Press, 1990. Includes appreciations by Burroughs and Leary.

Keith Haring: The Authorized Biography, by John Gruen. New York: Prentice-Hall, 1991.

Lydia Lunch and Exene Cervenka

Books
Adulterers Anonymous. New York: Grove Press, 1982.

CDs
Rude Hieroglyphics (Ryko Voices). Rants and roars.

Tom Robbins

Another Roadside Attraction. New York: Ballantine, 1972.
Even Cowgirls Get the Blues. Boston: Houghton Mifflin, 1976.
Jitterbug Perfume. New York: Bantam, 1984.
Skinny Legs and All. New York: Bantam, 1990.

Henry Rollins

Books (all published by 2.13.61, Los Angeles)
Art to Choke Hearts & Pissing in the Gene Pool
Black Coffee Blues
Eye Scream

CDs
Many with Rollins Band and Black Flag. Listen loud.

Patti Smith

Books
Babel. New York: G. P. Putnam's Sons, 1978.
Early Work. New York: W. W. Norton, 1994.
Woolgathering. New York and Madras: Hanuman, 1992.

CDs
Horses (Arista).
Radio Ethiopia (Arista).
Easter (Arista).
Wave (Arista).
Dream of Life (Arista).
Gone Again (Arista).

Other Material of Interest

Offbeat: A Red Hot Sound Trip (Wax Trax/TVT); CD of modern musicians inspired by Beat aesthetics, containing samples of Beat authors; released in conjunction with Whitney "Beat Culture" show, also as benefit for AIDS.

f you've stuck with me this far and avoided arrest, madness and social ostracization as a result of our activities together, then I extend a hearty congratulations! Chances are, you've experienced some personal transformation and gained some reassuring and even alarming insights into your true nature. I trust you've had a lot of fun as well.

But the book really isn't ended and your work isn't really done. The Beat goes on and you must go with it. The work that we have started stretches out into the next century and beyond, the work of realizing our full potentials as potentially godlike creatures, and of preserving the planet from those who would seek its ruin. The Beat spirit, once invited into your soul, is a very hard guest to kick out. Get used to it. Add to it.

Continue adding to it in your own Beat Journal, making up your own exercises, answering your own questions and recording your own experiences. The Journal will become one of your most treasured possessions, something to return to again and again when you want to remember how you got from this book to where you are now. Make keeping a creative journal a lifelong habit, filling a shelf with sequel after sequel, a constantly evolving documentation of your continually changing life.

The spirit of the people we've hung out with in the course of this book will be with you as you continue to discover who you really are. They'll always be there to return to for encouragement and advice in the pages of their books.

As you create your own alternative paradigm for your life and begin to inhabit the future that is now, transgressing, transforming and transcending, have courage, have faith and, above all, have patience with yourself and others. We're not here long enough to take ourselves too seriously. In the words of William Burroughs, "We're here to go."

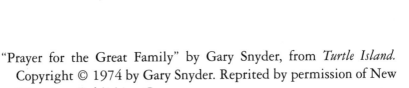

Permissions

el Ash is a writer, artist, and teacher/performer with a lifelong experience of Beat and Bohemian culture and spirituality, having been involved in both the hippie and punk movements as a result of his early readings of the Beats.

A former Zen teacher, he teaches workshops nationally and is also the author of *The Zen of Recovery* and *Shaving the Inside of Your Skull,* both published by Jeremy P. Tarcher/Putnam. He is currently working on his first novel, *Zaddik.* Married to radio personality Sarah Owens-Ash, he has two sons and lives in Providence, Rhode Island. Available for workshops, he may be contacted through the publisher.